D0082773

Myth or Reality:
Adaptive Strategies of
Asian Americans in California

DEDICATION

We dedicate this book
to Ardeth, Laura and Phillip
to Koun-Ping and Philip Si-Wei
and
to Leslie, Mariko, Marinosuke and Wally

This book belongs first and foremost to the new Asian Americans
of California whose lives are studied herein.

Myth or Reality:
Adaptive Strategies of Asian Americans in California

Henry T. Trueba
Lilly Cheng
Kenji Ima

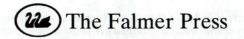 The Falmer Press

(A member of Taylor & Francis Group)
Washington, DC • London

UK   The Falmer Press, 4 John Street, London WC1N 2ET
USA   The Falmer Press, Taylor & Francis Inc., 1900 Frost Road, Suite 101, Bristol, PA 19007

© H.T. Trueba, L. Cheng and K. Ima 1993

First published in 1993

A catalogue record for this book is available from the British Library

Library of Congress Cataloging-in-Publication Data are available on request

ISBN 0 75070 072 6 Cased
ISBN 0 75070 073 4 Paper back

Jacket design by Caroline Archer

Typeset in 10/12pt Times
Graphicraft Typesetters Ltd., Hong Kong.

Printed in Great Britain by Burgess Science Press, Basingstoke on paper which has a specified pH value on final paper manufacture of not less than 7.5 and is therefore 'acid free'.

Acknowledgments

The authors are deeply grateful to the Asian American communities, especially those in Southern California, who shared with us their life accounts and their aspirations for a better life, one in which there is freedom, economic security, peace, quality education and the opportunity to excel. As immigrants, we ourselves share with these communities the democratic ideals that brought us to America.

Many scholars and writers have influenced our intellectual development and guided us in our efforts to make sense of our experiences as immigrants and as members of ethnic minority groups in the United States. We want to thank all our professors and mentors. A special debt of gratitude is owed to anthropologists, sociologists and psychologists whose work is cited here. Their insights and theoretical contributions made this book possible. Indeed much of the conceptual infrastructure presented here was inspired by the work of scholars such as George and Louise Spindler, George DeVos, Fred Erickson, John Ogbu, and Marcelo Suárez-Orozco; as well as by unique contributions of Lev Semenovich Vygotsky and his followers. We are also thankful to Huynh Dinh Te, Edmund Lee, Ruben Rumbaut, Jean Nidorf and Rosita Galang, and others who offered valuable comments and suggestions to improve this manuscript at its various stages of development.

The production of this volume required the assistance of many persons to whom we express our sincere gratitude. We have a special debt of gratitude to Joy Pace who devoted many hours to reading and editing the manuscript, as well as to Paul Borowsky who was highly instrumental in the reorganization and last revisions of the manuscript. We are also grateful to Kathleen Akong, Patrice Koffman, Julie Chase and Jill Reed for their support services.

In the last few years of work with Falmer Press we have found in Carol Saumarez an intelligent, competent and extremely knowledgeable editor who provides systematic, consistent and most valuable advice. We have indeed a special debt of gratitude to Carol; without her clear and forceful direction this manuscript either would have never seen the light or would have been of lower quality. It has been a genuine privilege working with such a wonderful teacher, who with enormous patience and tact made our tasks most pleasurable and instructive.

Last but not least, we want to thank our families for tolerating our absences, our late hours at work, and even our lack of sensitivity to their needs for our time and presence. Their moral support and assistance are deeply appreciated. We want to thank our spouses, Ardeth, Koun-Ping and Leslie. This book is as much theirs as it is ours.

Contents

Contents

Tables and Maps

Tables

Maps

Preface

A non-Asian faculty member, observing how quiet his Asian students were in the classroom, told me that they seemed to have no problems with the course material since they never asked any questions. When asked about the teacher's perception, an Asian student in the class clarified that he had a lot of problems in the course, and explained that he had three reasons for not asking questions in class. First, he felt self-conscious and embarrassed about his accent. Second, he did not want to hold up the progress of everyone else in the class. Third, he did not want to embarrass the teacher by suggesting that the lecture was not clear enough the first time.

Variations of this situation at my university occur daily in every grade level at schools throughout the country where rapid demographic growth of Asian Pacific Islander students has created conditions of culture shock, not only for the immigrant students and their parents, but for teachers, administrators, and policy-makers. In the above situation, my colleague had not recognized threats to the cultural validity of his assessment. Talking to the students revealed alternative explanations for the classroom dynamic, and more importantly, showed that the students were not learning to their full potential. What can be done?

In this volume, Professors Trueba, Cheng and Ima serve multiple audiences — teachers and researchers, parents and communities — who confront these challenges of changing demographics. With Asian Pacific Islanders already constituting close to 10 per cent of California's work force and over 10 per cent of its K-12 student population, this pathbreaking work addresses the critical need for serious research on Asian Pacific Islander students' and communities' relationships to schooling.

Chapter One places this study in the context of macro- and micro-ethnographic research paradigms, particularly within the ongoing debates of educational anthropologists and cultural ecologists regarding immigrant and minority educational achievement. Setting the stage for what follows, the chapter concludes: 'the theoretical argument here is that historical and ethnographic research helps teachers to build a comprehensive and rich picture of the culture of minority children.'

Chapter Two compiles demographic data and background profiles of each major Asian Pacific Islander group in California, demonstrating the complexity and diversity within and between the various nationalities who comprise the country's fastest-growing minority. Though focused on California where nearly 30 per cent of the country's Asian Pacific Islanders reside, the profiles in Chapter Two, as well as the case studies, recommendations and theoretical perspectives in later chapters are relevant to researchers and practitioners nationally.

Chapters Three, Four and Five examine critical educational issues in relation to the ethno-historical and socio-cultural contexts of Asian Pacific Islanders. Each chapter integrates theoretical perspectives with illustrative case studies, and provides rich descriptions of issues ranging from academic achievement and language proficiency to cultural conflict and adaptation involving the home, school, and community and concerns about the unrecognized needs of Asian Pacific Islander at-risk youth. Chapter Six outlines thoughtful and realistic recommendations with which teachers and parents can strengthen the overall participation of Asian Pacific Islander students in their educational process.

Finally, Chapter Seven returns to some of the theoretical perspectives introduced in Chapter One, showing how the case of Asian Pacific Islanders illuminates the importance of ethnohistorical and ethnographic approaches. Drawing from neo-Vygotskian theories of socially-based cognitive development, Freire's concept of *conscientization* and the Spindlers' practice of cultural therapy, the authors argue for an ethnography of empowerment which enables teachers, students, parents and communities to develop individually and collectively to achieve their full potential. It is a powerful vision rooted in the practice of what works.

The authors challenge us to move beyond the stereotypic notions of Asian American academic success by recognizing, first of all, that the diverse Asian Pacific Islander communities include large numbers of at-risk students, and secondly, that even with academic achievement, if there is not comparable social development, then the promise of equality remains unfulfilled. They argue persuasively that we need to crack the glass ceiling and transform both the myth and the reality.

This original collaboration between Professors Trueba, Cheng and Ima will be one of our most valuable guides into the 21st Century. For their shared commitment and contribution to educational equity as well as for their generous invitation to write this Preface, I am deeply grateful.

Peter Nien-chu Kiang
University of Massachusetts-Boston

Chapter 1

Theoretical Perspectives: America's most Recent Immigrants

The recent arrival of Asian immigrants and the emergence of their adaptive strategies in the 1990s is a phenomenon without precedent. The sheer number of Asian newcomers, their cultural similarities and differences, the paths for adjustment and the coping mechanisms chosen as a means to resolve cultural conflicts are most instructive; but also their socioeconomic mobility, their educational attainment, and most of all, the folk stereotypic explanations of their success are characteristics which distinguish Asian immigrants in the last two decades of this century and mark important trends for the twenty-first century. The circumstances of these historical phenomena are intriguing and their theoretical implications are significant.

Adjustment to Mainstream Culture

Scholars in the social sciences have been debating since the 1920s, and more passionately since the 1970s, the reasons why some refugee, immigrant and minority families successfully adapt to the American mainstream way of life, and move upwardly in our society, while other families choose adaptive strategies that slow their integration into mainstream society. George and Louise Spindler have argued (Spindler and Spindler, 1971, 1990) that the adaptive strategies exemplified by the Menominee Indians, who are variably acculturated into the American mainstream are often found in other groups in our society. These stages shown in response to cultural conflict are the following:

1 *Reaffirmation*: characterized by a nativistic orientation and efforts to revive native cultural traditions, accompanied by rejection of the mainstream culture.
2 *Synthesis*: a selective combination of various cultural aspects of one group with those of the other in certain domains of life, especially with respect to religious rituals and beliefs.

3 *Withdrawal*: a position of rejection of both conflicting cultures, and a choice of a transitional stage with no commitment to any specific set of cultural values.

4 *Biculturalism*: full involvement with two cultures requiring a position of effective code-switching (cultural and linguistic) and permitting individuals to function effectively with members of both the mainstream and the home culture.

5 *Constructive Marginality*: a position of tentative and superficial acceptance of two conflicting cultural value systems in which one keeps a conscious distance from both cultural systems. This position is characterized by selective choice of one or another value system (code-switching) as required by the circumstances that permit the marginal person maintenance of personal equilibrium through moderate participation in both cultures.

6 *Compensatory Adaptation*: individuals become thoroughly mainstreamed and may reject, or at least avoid, any identification with, or display of, their native culture.

While in their earlier writings (1971) the Spindlers viewed some of these stages or adaptive strategies as intermediate and temporary linkages in the acculturation chain, more recently they have regarded these adaptive strategies as reflecting quasi-permanent responses to conflict on the part of some individuals. That does not preclude, however, that some individuals fluctuate from one stage to another, or that some move progressively to full acculturation (personal communication, November 1, 1990). The choice of adaptation strategies is contingent upon the cultural background of the individuals, the opportunity they have to interact with members of mainstream culture, and their ability to function in that culture.

What is common to all individuals attempting to resolve cultural conflicts, regardless of their choice of adaptive strategies, is that all of them experience cultural discontinuities (Spindler, G., 1968 and 1974). However, not all discontinuities are destructive. What are the individual or collective cultural factors in the home culture that determine the response of an individual to these discontinuities? Research conducted among Mexican American, Asian American (especially Indochinese populations) and others suggests that the responses to cultural conflict within the same mainstream culture are better understood in the historical, sociological and political contexts of the immigrant communities. (Trueba, 1988a, 1989, 1990; Trueba, Spindler and Spindler, 1989; Suárez-Orozco, 1989; Trueba, Jacobs and Kirton, 1990; Delgado-Gaitan and Trueba, 1991; and many others).

The present volume, which is a clear example of the diversity of adaptive strategies selected by Asian and Pacific Island immigrants from various linguistic and cultural groups, goes into the linguistic, anthropological, sociological and political contexts of many Asians. By implication, the data presented here argues for the need to better understand intragroup differences within each of the subcategories of Asian immigrants who have recently arrived in America. Beyond the linguistic and cultural differences, and beyond the differences in socioeconomic class, there are pre-arrival experiences and backgrounds that best explain the choice of adaptive strategies as well as the pace of adaptation.

We suspect that no single theory in the social sciences can do justice to the complex phenomena of immigration and adaptation of any group. At the same time, current data suggest that some of the ongoing theories can be modified in specific directions, insofar as those theories are used to explain the adaptive strategies of immigrant children to mainstream schools, and the resulting differentiation of immigrant children in schools. In turn, the study of immigrant children must take into account their communities in their broader sociological, cultural and political contexts. By studying the community context we will be able to understand the psychosocial mechanisms that lead to higher achievement motivation and performance of minority children. Issues related to children's superior interactional skills, inquiry strategies, inferencing powers, creative discovery of knowledge, and overall language mastery for academic achievement are clearly related to learning environments at home and in the community.

Some scholars have argued strongly against a myopic or microscopic approach to minority achievement and have advocated studies which are ethnohistorically broad, with substantial data on the economic, political and social characteristics of the ethnic communities. Equally strong has been the suppport for long-term studies which focus on issues related to the ethnography of communication, such as interactional analysis of specific events, cross-cultural comparisons of behaviors in certain settings, detailed documentation of instructional processes and student participation, analysis of adaptive behaviors at home and in school, teachers' communicative strategies, or other specific dimensions of academic activities that can enlighten our understanding of the social and cognitive processes associated with higher or lower learning outcomes.

The debate over the legitimacy of either broadly conceived studies (macro-ethnographic) in contrast with narrowly conceived studies (micro-ethnographic) has been going on for almost a decade, and is addressed in recent writings (Ogbu, 1987; 1989; Trueba, 1988a, 1988b; Erickson, 1987; Suárez-Orozco, 1987; Gibson, 1987; Moll and Diaz, 1987; and Foley, 1991). Perhaps it would be appropriate to provide a wider context for this debate in order to understand its implications for this volume.

Pioneers in Educational Anthropology

After World War II, the field of educational anthropology was founded by George Spindler and other scholars. The publication by Spindler of *Education and Anthropology* in 1955 (Stanford University Press) collected some of the most powerful statements from Dorothy Lee, Margaret Mead, Jules Henry, Solon Kimball, Bernard Siegel, Alfred Kroeber, and George Spindler. Their insights and commitment to pursue educational anthropology raised the enthusiasm for a new field that is now one of the strongest in the American Anthropological Association and has remarkable consistency in ideology and methodological pursuits. Dorothy Lee at the Carmel Conference of which *Education and Anthropology* is a faithful report, states:

> He [George Spindler] describes what he's doing at Stanford, and we know what Sol Kimball, for example, is doing at Columbia. But a number of anthropologists are terrified at the thought of teaching anthropology to people who will not be anthropologists. . .George [Spindler] and Mr. Quillen suggest that the teacher who is passing on culture not only consciously and deliberately but unconsciously and with every gesture that [he or] she makes will be helped if [he or] she can be aware of what [he or] she is passing on (Spindler, G., 1955a:30).

At that time various anthropologists argued that, in addition to the teaching of a few courses in anthropology, teachers also needed guidance in order to diagnose or interpret children's behavior, and to select ways of teaching using appropriate cultural patterns in order to improve teaching. Jules Henry adds, 'I would like to give an example out of my own experience in working in a school system. I used to have lunch with the teacher and chat with her, and our conversation was geared to what had happened in the classroom ten minutes ago' (Spindler, G., 1955a:31). J. Henry, recognizing that it would impossible to have enough anthropologists to eat lunch with teachers, suggests the need to have an anthropologist present a case in the school:

> This person [the anthropologist] would attempt to show, in terms of social science frames of reference, how the case related to social and cultural situations and points of view. . .I think that. . .would help to make the school staff aware of the significance of their own problems with the children in terms of social science perspectives (Spindler, G., 1955a:31).

The discussion concludes with the idea that anthropology should be an integral part of teacher preparation, and that the anthropologist has a role as a teacher of teachers. Dorothy Lee adds the following statement:

> [It] should be possible to structure a course where teachers will go through an experience of another culture, perhaps where certain values, concepts, ways of doing things, approaches, attitudes, will become pointed up but will remain at the same time concrete and

embedded in a whole way of life, and will serve as a springboard for discussion to help the teacher to awareness of her own way of life (Spindler, G., 1955a:31).

Margaret Mead describes her experiences at Columbia Teachers College for many years with a course entitled 'Anthropology and Educational Methods' in which students were asked to conduct a project emphasizing comparisons:

> In my course no one was allowed to do a project that didn't compare something with something — either two periods in the same culture, or two cultures. . . . And they analyzed all sorts of things: television shows and radio shows; they compared. . .French and American textbooks in elementary education, in a very wide range of materials which were accessible to them, where they had to identify the cultural differences, identify and document. . . . I taught them about 50 per cent of the time by having people who were wrestling with comparable problems come in and give interim reports (G. Spindler, 1955a:33).

George Spindler finds three effective methodological approaches to working with teachers:

> 1) The culture case study. . .You provide the student with a vicarious kind of experience and usually that seems to come best from one's own field work. . . . It can be left at an intellectual level and it can be rationalized in or out of any particular problem situation as the student wishes. 2) The type of case treatment where an educator, an anthropologist, and, in our particular case at Stanford, a psychiatrist, go into a school system, take a classroom, a teacher, a whole school, and study the role of the teacher, the culture context that the teacher is working from, the cultural position of the children, the selective perception by the teacher of the differential cultural positions of the children, and so on. 3) The formal course approach — at Stanford we have a psychological foundations course and one in social foundations. I have taught both and found that in the psychological foundations course. . .I was after *self*-awareness; I found that in the other course it was *cultural* awareness (G. Spindler, 1955a:32).

Much of what happened in the following years can be viewed as an unfolding of the original conception described above. It was not coincidental that in 1955 George Spindler would also publish his psychocultural study entitled 'Sociocultural and psychological processes in Menomini acculturation', (1955b). One of the most important theoretical foundations of educational anthropology has been borrowed from cultural and psychological anthropology. The numerous publications during the 1960s and 70s increased the significance of the field and provided us with a rich theoretical framework. Part of this framework dealt with cultural continuities and discontinuities in a cross-cultural setting.

Castelike Minorities in School

In cultural anthropology the discussion of caste and differential treatment of caste groups was taken to a psychoanalytic level by the work of George DeVos. He applied this term to the Burakumin, a disenfranchised group of immigrants in Japan who were characterized by persistent marginalization, school underachievement, lower income, higher crime rates and other dysfunctional attributes. DeVos' work on the Burakumin (since 1970) resulted in term *castelike* and the discussion of cultural characteristics leading to adaptive strategies of this group in Japan resulting in the social isolation and underachievement of the Burakumin. Later on, DeVos and his associates wrote extensively on ethnic adaptation and minority status, and on caste, culture and personality (DeVos and Wagatsuma, 1966; DeVos, 1980). The fundamental thesis in the writings of DeVos was that social class or other social structural elements did not explain fully the adaptation responses of certain ethnic groups, and that it was necessary to resort to cultural and psychological factors rooted in the socialization of these groups, and, therefore, ultimately representing a collective cultural response to conflict. The implication was that castelike groups shared cultural values that did not emphasize achievement in the host countries, but rather a nativistic response (or the *reaffirmative* response, to use the Spindlers' terminology). The wealth of psychological materials (especially projective techniques) used by DeVos, and the substantial sociocultural, political, and economic information he presented, made a very strong case in Japanese society.

In an effort to explain minority school performance, John Ogbu, combining a number of theoretical approaches from anthropology, sociology and psychological anthropology (especially concepts such as castelike used by DeVos and the *discontinuities* by G. Spindler), developed the cultural ecological position (Ogbu, 1974, 1978, 1987, 1989). This position was clearly a reaction against pseudo-theories of cultural deprivation and of genetic or biological determinism that was fundamentally biased and undocumented. Ogbu's initial contribution based on his Stockton study (1974) was to note:

> the importance of minority community's experiences in the post-school opportunity structure and how minority community members' perceptions of dismal future opportunities influence their perceptions of and responses to schooling (Ogbu, 1987:313).

Ogbu, along the lines pointed out by Mead, Spindler and others, conducted a cross-cultural comparative analysis on the basis of existing studies of differential performance of minority students (summarized in his article of 1987:315–16). The crucial question Ogbu was asking himself was:

Why are some minorities successful in school even though they face barriers in culture, language, and postschool opportunities faced by the minorities that are not successful? It is one thing to conduct research to discover cultural solutions or other remedies for the school failure of some minorities; it is quite another thing to conduct research in order to account for the variability in the school performance (Ogbu 1987:316–17).

According to Ogbu, the main problem in the academic performance of minority children 'does not lie in the mere fact that children possess a different language,' or a unique learning style or communicative or interactional patterns; 'it is not even that the children face barriers in future adult opportunity structure' (1987:317). The explanation of differential performance is in the 'variability in school adjustment and performance'. Given the societal forces and conflicts faced by minorities, different groups respond in different ways. To continue his explanation, Ogbu distinguishes minorities in three different groups: autonomous, immigrant (or voluntary), and castelike (or involuntary) minorities. Although autonomous minorities may suffer prejudicial treatment, 'they are not socially, economically, and politically subordinated' nor do they 'experience disproportionate and persistent problems in learning to read and to compute,' due in part to their home culture that 'demonstrates and encourages school success' (Ogbu, 1987:320). Immigrant minorities, like the autonomous, voluntarily come to the United States in search of 'greater economic well-being, better opportunities, and/or greater political freedom'. They face problems due to language and cultural barriers, but 'they do not experience disproportionate school failure' (Ogbu, 1987: 321). Finally, the castelike (or involuntary) minorities are 'people who were *originally brought into United States society involuntarily* through slavery, conquest, or colonization. Thereafter, these minorities were relegated to menial positions and denied true assimilation into mainstream society' (Ogbu, 1987:321).

The examples used by Ogbu are native Americans, black Americans, native Hawaiians, Mexicans, and others. 'It is castelike or involuntary minorities that usually experience more difficulties with social adjustment and school performance' (Ogbu, 1987:321). More recently, Ogbu has modified his typology (1989:181–204); he has dropped the use of castelike and simplified all three types of minorities into two: voluntary and involuntary. He has retained fundamentally the same essential characteristics of the groups: immigrants come voluntarily, in search of freedom and economic opportunities; in contrast, involuntary minorities are brought as a result of slavery, conquest or colonization. Then he adds:

They [involuntary minorities] resent the loss of their former freedom; they perceive the social, political, and economic barriers against them as part of their undeserved oppression. American Indians, black Americans, Mexican Americans in the Southwest, and native Hawaiians are United States examples. Similar minorities exist in Japan, namely, the Buraku and Japan's Koreans, and in New Zealand, namely, the Maoris (Ogbu, 1989–187).

Furthermore, Ogbu suggests that voluntary minorities exhibit, in their adjustment to the mainstream culture, primary cultural discontinuities. Primary here means discontinuities resulting from differences that existed prior to their cultural contact with the host or mainstream society. Involuntary minorities, in contrast, exhibit secondary cultural discontinuities, that is, discontinuities resulting from the contact with the host or mainstream population (Ogbu, 1987:321–22). One question is why contact with the host society causes some discontinuities in involuntary populations and not in voluntary populations? Another question is whether or not we can ascertain collectivities or individuals regarding their willingness to come to America. What is the difference between populations who were annexed to this country as a result of colonization, in contrast with those who we presume came voluntarily? In some ethnic groups (Indochinese, for example) decisions to immigrate are made collectively, while in others, individuals are quite independent in making their decisions to immigrate or to stay in their countries of residence. But even in those groups of immigrants who presumably come voluntarily there are individuals who have no choice. Is this criterion of voluntary arrival an empirically or historically discernible one? Why, for example, are Mexican Americans in the Southwest an example of involuntary immigrants, but not those residing elsewhere in the country? What is the basis for assuming their unwillingness to come to the US, or once they are here, to stay? Each day Immigration and Naturalization officers send back to Tijuana between 3000 and 4000 undocumented workers who illegally cross the border between Tijuana and San Diego. According to some economists, if there were no borders, it is possible that ten to twelve million Mexican people would cross willingly in search of economic opportunities.

In Ogbu's theoretical framework, the ultimate reason that involuntary minorities experience difficulties in adjusting and succeeding is that they are the object of *cultural inversion*, which is defined as follows:

Cultural inversion is the tendency for some members of one population, in this case involuntary minorities, to regard certain forms of behavior, certain events, symbols, and meanings as inappropriate for them because they are characteristic of members of another population (e.g., white Americans); at the same time, the minorities claim other (often the opposite) forms of behaviors, events, symbols, and meanings as appropriate for them because these are not characteristic of white Americans. . .Cultural inversion usually results in the *coexistence of two opposing cultural frames of reference* or ideal ways of orienting behavior, one considered by the minorities as appropriate for themselves and the other as appropriate for white Americans (Ogbu, 1987:323).

This principle of cultural inversion leads involuntary minorities, in Ogbu's opinion, to develop a social identity in opposition to the identity of the mainstream population, but only after these minorities have internalized their subordination. Ogbu states that the cultural models of involuntary minorities are different from voluntary minorities in several important ways: '[T]he cultural frame of reference for comparing present status, the folk theory of getting ahead, the collective identity, the cultural frame of reference for judging appropriate behavior, and the extent to which one might trust white people and the institutions they control' (Ogbu, 1989:191). This nonoppositional cultural frame of reference is the fundamental reason why voluntary immigrants have the 'ability to cross cultural and language boundaries in the school context', and why they 'interpret the language and cultural features necessary for school success. . .as *barriers to be overcome* in order to achieve their long-range goals of future employment, economic well-being, and other benefits' (Ogbu, 1989:192). This reasoning seems to make good sense. Yet, one can ask the question: Why would only involuntary minorities be unable to see the need to succeed economically, or the need to succeed in school in order to succeed economically? To pursue the issue of ambiguous definitions further, why should the slavery status of three previous generations affect some black children and not others? Why don't some of the blacks, Chicanos, native Americans, Hawaiians, develop oppositional social identities while others do, if all these individuals share the same historical background? There must be additional factors affecting intragroup differences of such magnitude. It must be more than the sheer willingness or unwillingness to succeed in school, the experience of success, or the early academic socialization for success. The experience of actually learning and becoming a competent participant is perhaps far more important for many children than a historical past so far removed from them.

The most crucial issue in the discussion of the academic failure of many castelike (or involuntary) minorities is whether or not we want to accept that as a result of a historical past (slavery, conquest, oppression) these minorities are permanently and irreparably disempowered, or that their state of disempowerment (their inability to function well in school) is linked to the organization of schools, of instruction, and to the lack of preparation of these individuals as they enter school. In other words, that their state of disempowerment is repairable and can be remedied by preparing them academically and emotionally, as well as by enabling teachers, principals, and superintendents to reform schools. Is there anything that can be done after having discovered that certain individuals (called here castelike) are at risk, predictably potential school failures, disempowered, disenfranchised, alienated and unwilling or unable to achieve academically?

A subtle point in the entire discussion of castelike minorities is whether or not a definition of castelike (or involuntary) is primarily the result of their academic failure and our attempt to find an acceptable rationale to explain such failure, or if, indeed, there are essential attributes that castelike collectivities and/or individuals share in common. The oppositional social self-identity described by Ogbu could be the result of school failure, and not the other way around. Early failure in school, and early socialization for failure (vicarious experiences of failure or internalized failure of other persons closely related within the family) can explain much of this oppositional social identity without having to rely on far-removed historical experiences.

Another difficult point associated with the castelike concept is that of imputed willingness to achieve certain goals perceived as being in contradiction with one's own cultural principles. The Spindlers have described in great detail the enormous intragroup differences they found among the Menominee. Collectivities do not move in blocks. They recognize different responses from groups of individuals to the mainstream culture. Not all of them perceived American mainstream culture as being in opposition to their Indian culture. While some groups were eager to assimilate and some became bicultural, others remained transitional or even nativistic in their reaffirmation of their traditional cultural patterns (Spindler and Spindler, 1971; 1990).

Similar studies of intragroup differences among Chicanos would show that the Spindlers' model is far more applicable than a single castelike blanket category for all Chicanos, or blacks, or Hawaiians or other groups. The theoretical model is too rigid, extremely difficult to verify either historically or empirically in terms of voluntary or involuntary immigration, and in terms of a cause-effect relationship between perceived oppositional social identity and academic success or failure. While George and Louise Spindler focus on a number of social and cultural elements explaining the choice of different adaptation strategies to cope with cultural conflict (1990), DeVos and Suarez-Orozco examine the relationship between the early socialization stages of children in which literacy and other academic values are embedded in the home culture, with success in school, or the lack of socialization for academic success due to a peer socialization in which cultural and social conflicts are resolved through different mechanisms, including those suggested by the Spindlers, of withdrawal, opposition, synthesis and biculturalism. (Spindler and Spindler, 1990:79–84).

Foley (1991), in his critique of Ogbu's theories, has assumed that Ogbu is using castelike in the sense of caste, and has compared Ogbu's cultural ecological perspectives to the culture of poverty as defined by Oscar Lewis (1968). While the parallel is very tempting, especially if we conceive the castification process as being primarily related to the experience of poverty (associated with social abuse and alienation), there are also clear differences. Oscar Lewis compared behaviors of poor people in various parts of the world and somewhat stereotyped the poor as being unable to participate effectively in social institutions, and as being psychologically handicapped beyond repair. Lewis did not point out the social structural elements affecting the behavior of the poor, while Ogbu clearly pointed to the job opportunity structure associated with upward mobility of blacks, or lack of such mobility regardless of educational level achieved. Lewis did not develop a sophisticated theory of cultural involution or the development of an oppositional social identity to explain collective rejection of mainstream values as Ogbu did.

Ultimately, Ogbu has successfully built a very strong theoretical apparatus, and a clean-cut typology of minorities. Ogbu's contributions to sensitize scholars to the psychodynamics of academic achievement and the problems faced by certain minority groups are indeed admirable and unmatched during the last three decades. There is a need, however, for reform and further clarification in both the application of his typology and the conceptual clarity of his definitions. In order to clarify definitions it will be essential to discuss intragroup individual differences in such a way that the attribution of psychological characteristics of a group will render each individual unable to make his/her own decisions. Indeed, oversimplification in the researcher's interpretation of psychosocial factors affecting decisions must be more flexible and allow for empirical verification of theories.

The work of the Spindlers, deeply rooted in systematic ethnographic fieldwork, shows that the origin of intragroup differences is precisely the rich and multiple strategies for adaptation taken by individuals sharing the same culture and same social pressures from mainstream cultural institutions. A large body of psychological literature has also emphasized the importance of early socialization at home, in school, on the street, everywhere. Schools play an important, and often decisive, role, but children come to schools with differential academic preparation and commitment to achievement. Furthermore, the school environment often persuades certain children that they do not belong there. The 'hidden curriculum' literature in sociology and anthropology, some of which is alluded to in this volume, can shed some light on the discussion of differential early socialization patterns in school affecting children's motivation to achieve.

If we are going to take seriously the literature on empowerment that has made a significant impact in teacher education, curriculum reform, and in the definition of research priorities and examination of equity issues in a number of fields (health sciences, education, etc.), we must also examine the ultimate consequences of explanations based on theories such as the *cultural ecological theory* presented by Ogbu. This theory assumes that entire ethnic groups, or a significant number of members in these groups, behave as castelike. This means that they are essentially unable to achieve because they define their culture in opposition to the mainstream culture. Consequently, their self-identities reject mainstream definitions of success. These individuals are trapped in the dilemma of either rejecting their own self-identity or failing; there is no way out of this dilemma. Most people tend to retain their self-identity and their culture as a mechanism of collective and individual preservation. If they are forced to abandon their culture in order to succeed academically, they are destroyed psychologically even if they succeed by mainstream standards. What is the solution for the 'castelikes'? Is it simply to reject their own culture the way Richard Rodriguez did in his account of *Hunger of Memory* (1982) in order to become mainstream? Or is it possible for them to become bicultural thereby accepting certain values from mainstream culture which are compatible with the home culture? Apparently, ethnographic accounts show that some individuals and entire groups have become bicultural. Under what conditions is it possible for a castelike person or group of persons to become a noncastelike? How do we ascertain the change from castelike to noncastelike — by checking his/her grade point average? There are a number of alienated students from minority groups who had high grades and yet dropped out of school because they felt they did not belong, or that there were less painful avenues for economic success than schooling.

The presence of minority populations in California antedated that of Europeans, as well as that of most refugee and immigrant minorities by many centuries and has never ceased to exist. In a very real sense, minority populations, native Americans and other minorities, have always made their presence felt. As in most other regions of America, the immigrants were the Europeans. In the course of the last century the flow of Asian and Hispanic immigrant groups created the strong agricultural economy of California. The role of immigrant and refugee families in the state economy is recognized by all. What is less recognized, however, are the numerous contributions these families made to our cultural and intellectual life, to the sciences and many other academic fields. These contributions were possible only after these families were successfully settled and adjusted to the new cultural environment.

The adjustment of immigrant and refugee families depends much on their ability to recognize their worth and overcome the conflicts associated with drastic cultural changes: the new beliefs, the codes of behavior, the miscommunication, the stress, and often the prejudice they face because of their differences. It is precisely in this context that the work of educators takes special significance (Trueba, 1983, 1987a, 1987b, 1988a, 1988b, 1988c, 1989). Teachers must not only be the key persons responsible for transmitting objective academic knowledge to all students, but also must be able to interpret history to students, or more accurately, genuine ethnohistory that allows minorities to see their contribution in American society. Teachers are the role models of American democracy, in charge of helping all children internalize cultural knowledge and values that are congruent with our social institutions.

Because refugee and immigrant children cannot succeed in our society without a high level of literacy in English, the acquisition of the English language is crucial for them. Equally important is the acquisition of self-worth and pride in one's own culture. The overall adjustment of minorities to the new values and their participation in academic activities depends on how well they understand their role in this country. Even the acquisition of English is contingent upon their feeling of belonging in this country. Therefore, the question is: How can one expedite the smooth adjustment to American values and the acquisition of English? What instructional and language policies, what educational philosophy and classroom organization can maximize the learning of English by newcomers? This question has been addressed by recent researchers (Trueba, 1987a, 1987b; Goldman and Trueba, 1987; Trueba and Delgado-Gaitan, 1988; Trueba, 1988a, 1988b, 1989; and by many others). This study intends to show that knowledge of the role of minorities in American history is an important step in the adaptation of minorities and their achievement in schools.

Persistent low literacy levels in English cannot be explained by linguistic deficiencies or cultural incongruities only. The overall participation of minority communities in the life of American cities, particularly in the schools, seems to be linked to both social and structural elements beyond the control of these communities, as well as to social and cultural factors peculiar to each group. These two types of elements are clearly linked to the sense of alienation and distance exhibited by minority students in mainstream schools. What is the nature of American society and American institutions and why do minorities feel alienated? Is there a rejection of minority populations? If so, does this rejection contribute to the underachievement of minorities, especially in schools with a rapid influx of minority children without a tangible increase in financial resources? Does English literacy play a key role in the active participation of immigrant, refugee and other minority families associated with mainstream schools?

In order to answer those questions one needs to develop a method of inquiry that explores systematically and over a period of time the complex issues of minority adjustment in American society. School administrators, teachers, and researchers consider literacy a key element in the acculturation of minorities and their empowerment as active members of American society (Spindler, G., 1974, 1982; Spindler and Spindler, 1983, 1987a, 1987b; Giroux and McLaren, 1986; Shulman, 1987a, 1987b; and Sockett, 1987; Delgado-Gaitan, 1990; Spindler and Spindler, 1990; Delgado-Gaitan and Trueba, 1991).

An understanding of the relationship between the sociocultural framework within which schools exist and the role of schools in the socialization of students to become productive members of society has been examined recently (Trueba, Spindler and Spindler, 1989). George and Louise Spindler (1989) argue that in other cultures individuals are all geared to belong, to succeed and to take a functional place in society, while in American society many minorities are socialized to become marginal and to dropout. Indeed, they feel that the culture of resistance is 'formed out of the long experience of these minorities in an essentially racist society' (1989:13).

It has been shown that the rate of acculturation of some immigrant children is slowed down by the trauma associated with their sudden uprooting and the home values and skills which do not necessarily enhance the literacy and other academic values stressed in this country (Trueba, 1989; Jacobs and Kirton, 1990; Spindler and Spindler, 1990). However, we know that the pace of acculturation is different for both collectivities (special ethnic groups) as well as individuals within each group. What are the historical factors and social structural arrangements that facilitate the acculturation of some and hinder the acculturation of others? And what are the social and cultural factors unique to each collectivity that determine the pace of acculturation?

The present study focuses on the historical context of the newest Asian and Pacific Island minority population's arrival and acculturation in California. Since the last century, different ethnic groups have arrived in California and have made their homes in our cities. The increasingly active role of these minorities, especially of Asians and Hispanics, is another study in itself. The historical context presented here is intended to provide an adequate framework for other studies of minority acculturation and active participation in the various cultural, educational and social institutions of cities in California. The recognition of immigrant and minority communities as an integral part of California communities, not just as temporary hand labor, has been dramatized by the active role of Asian Americans in public education.

Intelligence and Acculturation

Following earlier psychologists, teachers and administrators often see intelligence as the IQ score of children, rather than their ability to pursue individual and group cultural goals through activities viewed as effective means of enhancing the home cultural values. Intelligence is definitely not the ability to score high in tests constructed by individuals from a foreign culture, based on narrowly defined literacy and problem-solving settings. Cultural anthropologists (DeVos, 1983; DeVos and Wagatsuma, 1966; Wagatsuma and DeVos, 1984; Ogbu, 1974, 1978, 1987, and others) have documented the differential performance of the same ethnic group immigrating to diverse countries, who are collectively low achieving in one country, but high achieving in another. The Koreans, for example, are considered outcasts in Japan, yet they get recognition as outstanding students in the continental US, Hawaii and Europe.

The fact that many immigrant and refugee children live in poverty, and that their parents are isolated in rural areas and discriminated against, forced to live in crowded dwellings where they lack privacy, toilet and shower facilities, comfort, and basic medical attention, is not irrelevant to these children's school achievement and their acculturation to American society. When the economic conditions improve for minority families and discrimination is kept in check, minority school children achieve at the normal level. Child abuse, malnutrition, poor health and ignorance are not a reflection of their intrinsic qualities or values, but rather a measure of societal neglect. There is also cultural and linguistic isolation that results in cognitive underdevelopment, educational neglect, late exposure to literacy, and low school achievement often resulting in stereotypic classification into learning disability groups.

Anthropological studies show that the lack of appreciation for one's own culture and lack of self-esteem are intimately related to social structural factors extrinsic to the ethnic group, as well as to cultural and psychological factors intrinsic and peculiar to the group. Low aspirations and social and economic dependence on low-paying jobs, alienation, underachievement, marginality and overall maladjustments to mainstream society are complex phenomena constituted by the relationships between the mainstream values and culture and the values and culture of the ethnic group (Spindler and Spindler, 1990).

Added to the complexity of the adjustment process is the painful experience of shock and incompetence felt by some individuals coming from rural and isolated settings. Their dealings with representatives of the mainstream culture, such as clerks and officers in social institutions (schools, banks, hospitals, stores, recreation facilities, churches, businesses, and service agencies) become traumatic. Consequently, adults who often face serious difficulties in written and oral English communication with mainstream persons depend on their children who are partially bilingual and can interpret for them. These children may be forced into a position of adult responsibility relative to making economic, social, medical and other difficult personal decisions.

The above can help us understand the deep frustration of some Asian American parents dealing with teachers and other people in day-to-day interactions, and their suspicion of unfair treatment or even racism. It is tragic that these parents' feelings and views create in children vicarious hostility towards mainstream values and people, thus perpetuating the alienation of ethnic people from one generation to the next.

Acculturation phases do not affect equally all members of the minority families. Older immigrant, refugee and other minority children have burdens and responsibilities that their younger siblings rarely face (Delgado-Gaitan, 1990; Trueba, Jacobs and Kirton, 1990; Delgado-Gaitan and Trueba, 1991). There is a great deal of diversity among the cultures of immigrants and refugees living in America. Trueba (1988a, 1988b, 1988c) describes the reaction of some Indochinese children in the California schools. For example, a third grade Hmong child, Chou, and a Mexican fourth-grader, Rosita, are described as keeping their heads down on the desk the entire class period, just sitting quietly, daydreaming as if they had completely given up attempting to cope with the world around them. Their decreasing attempts to participate in school activities were signs of the emotional turmoil hidden by a seemingly expressionless face, or by physical restlessness, changing gaze, or uncontrolled movements of feet and hand.

School as a Mirror of Society

To what extent does the school environment reflect the social environment? How do the school and social environments affect the acculturation phases of children, their ability to integrate the values of the host culture with their home values? Finally, to what extent is the successful adjustment and ac-culturation of minority children a precondition for successful schooling? In other words, how do we account for the differential performance of minority students in school? This is the central question raised by the work of recent scholars (DeVos, 1973, 1980; DeVos and Wagatsuma, 1966; Spindler and Spindler, 1987a, 1987b, 1987c; Ogbu, 1974, 1978, 1987, 1989; McDermott, 1987a; Trueba, 1983). I believe that an answer must be grounded in deep historical knowledge of the process of acculturation and adjustment of minority groups to specific settings.

While oral proficiency in English seems to persuade teachers that these language minority children are making normal progress in school, the opposite, children's inability to rapidly acquire English literacy skills, may lead to the classification (or misclassification) of children as learning disabled and ultimately may result in the dropout phenomena (Rueda, 1987). Studies have consistently shown that linguistic minority children's learning problems are manifested in three forms: 1) Lack of overall participation in whole class activities, 2) lack of academic productivity in school and at home, and 3) the presence of vague and pervasive stress, fear, confusion and other signs of ongoing emotional turmoil. Consequently, we must face two important issues: the role of language in instruction (first- and/or second-language *vis-a-vis* the purpose and nature of instruction), and the role of language and culture in the acquisition of English literacy skills:

1   What is the most effective use of language in the classroom if the primary goal of instruction is to foster cognitive growth in children?
2   If some of the literacy problems faced by Limited English Pro-ficiency (LEP) children are related to their different experiences, cultural knowledge, values and overall background, could the use of the native language facilitate the cultural adjustment of children to school?

The English-Only movement reflects the political clouds that have obscured the discussion of fundamental pedagogical principles applicable to all children. These principles suggest that cultural differences may often interfere with children's learning, if the instruction ignores such differences. We all must go through cognitive processes such as automatization, encoding, cognitive construction strategies, internalization of mental procedures and others which require a culturally congruent learning environment. In order to understand contextual clues and the nature of a cognitive task, children from other cultural and linguistic backgrounds must be given the opportunity to capitalize on what they know.

These principles must be stated and applied, even if political pressure and racial prejudice become obstacles. One is prompted to ask: What has been historically behind such strong political movements which attempt to curtail the use of non-English languages in educational and other public institutions? From the early 1880s when Connecticut, Massachusetts, Rhode Island, New York, Wisconsin and other states declared English as the mandatory school language, to the late 1960s when the Bilingual Education Act was approved, there have been important changes. Yet the memory of jailing and subsequent trials for speaking other languages is still fresh in the memory of some older minority persons.

The education of linguistic minorities is primarily intended to help students acquire high levels of literacy so they can process information and develop their cognitive skills. Cognitive skills (the ability to structure learning tasks and knowledge itself effectively) can be best acquired through the native language and then easily transferred to a second language. Use of native language, to the extent that it is possible in the school setting, facilitates children's ability to develop critical thinking skills. The reason is that cognitive structuring is conditioned by linguistic and cultural knowledge and experiences that children usually obtain in the home and bring with them to school (Cummins, 1986; Goldman and Trueba, 1987; Trueba and Delgado-Gaitan, 1988; Delgado-Gaitan and Trueba, 1991). Unfortunately, schools do not always have the resources to instruct children in their own language; but the use of tutors and peers can help significantly.

Reflections on Theory and Practice

The nature of the literacy problems faced by linguistic minorities is deeply related to their lack of the cultural knowledge that is presumed by the instructors and writers of textbook materials. Additional knowledge of children's culture and genuine respect for their home life-style can help school personnel and textbook writers to make lesson content more accessible and meaningful for minorities, prevent negative stereotypes and raise awareness of children's learning potential.

We need to pursue a systematic socialization of students and school personnel whose main purpose is to construct a positive learning environment, to facilitate the cultural adjustment of children and resolve the cultural conflicts arising in school. To develop such a learning environment teachers and children need to learn a great deal more about each other, to understand each other's actual home cultural background and previous experiences, and to engage in cooperative activities which guarantee academic success.

People need extra time and flexibility to place themselves in a new cultural environment in which behavior can have different interpretations and the experiences faced by them daily in the home, school and community have different meanings and values. The value of ethnohistorical research consists precisely in offering an inside view of the process of acculturation to a new cultural environment, an interpretation of new linguistic and cultural codes, and integration of codes.

Children and their teachers may come to realize that their own intra-psychological processes are linked to their home interpretations of events and behaviors not shared with other persons in school. Thus, in order to help children make the transition, reduce stress to tolerable levels, and participate actively in school learning activities, teachers themselves need a guarantee of academic success. Because children's adjustment to school is often impacted profoundly by the pre-arrival experiences they face, the loss and separation from relatives, the feeling of guilt associated with this loss and separation, as well as the many degrading and traumatic incidents (DeVos, 1984) experienced by many refugees and low-status immigrants, teachers should not blame themselves for the slow progress shown by some children. Pleasant school encounters may easily lead to the healing and may result in feelings of self-worth, personal safety, and happiness so that children are enabled to learn effectively.

Teachers must maintain a great deal of faith in children's potential and a positive outlook on their incremental accomplishments. But in order to do this, teachers need an appreciation of the historical role played by children's ethnic community. To permit teachers to acquire and use a rich historical perspective and cultural appreciation of their students' families, they should be given a great deal more latitude in parcelling the curriculum tasks over a period of time, and in searching for strategies to maximize community participation and children's engagement in meaningful learning activities (meaningful from the perspective of the ethnic community). The theoretical argument here is that historical and ethnographic research helps teachers build a comprehensive and rich picture of the culture of minority children. Consequently, *both* are complementary tools in the hands of teachers seeking to become effective instructors in culturally diverse schools. The meaningful participation of minority students in the learning process requires that teachers understand children's home culture and use it in the organization of instruction.

Chapter 2

Asian Diversity and the Challenges Faced by Newcomers

The main purpose of this chapter is to provide some basic information on the most salient groups of Asian and Asian Pacific Americans who came to this country as immigrants and refugees. Because most of them live on the West coast and share in common certain cultural elements, they are often stereotyped and their differences are not appreciated. Asian and Asian Pacific Islanders' within-group and intergroup diversity is a key issue in order to understand their differential academic achievement and educational needs. In providing the reader with some of the social and cultural contexts of these groups we attempt to emphasize the notion that the cultural diversity and uniqueness are linked to the different origin, ecological adaptations and histories of these groups, regardless of their racial similarities. We also try to present some descriptive cross-cultural comparisons for the major groups. The major groups of Asian Americans are East Asian, i.e. Chinese, Japanese, Korean, Filipino; Pacific Islanders, i.e. Fijian, Guamanian, Hawaiian, Marshall Islander, Melanesian, Palauan, Samoan, Tahitian, Tongan, Trukese, Yapese; Southeast Asian, such as Hmong, Indonesian, Khmer, Lao, Malayan, Mien, Singaporean, Thai, Vietnamese; and South Asians, such as Bangladeshi, Bhuanese, Burmese, Indian, Nepali, Pakistani, Sri Lankan, Sikimese.

This chapter is divided into three sections and a brief conclusion. The first section deals with the Pacific Islanders, the second with the Southeast and East Asians. The third section offers some data and reflections on culture and academic achievement of Asian and Asian Pacific Islanders. Finally, the conclusion attempts to bring together the various ideas presented in the chapter and discusses the challenges facing schools.

Pacific Islander

Hundreds of islands are spread across the Pacific Ocean, a body of water covering 64 million square miles of the earth, that is, one third of the earth's

Map 2.1   Pacific Culture Areas

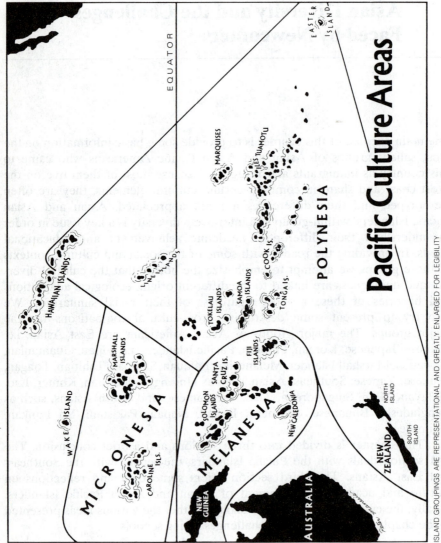

ISLAND GROUPINGS ARE REPRESENTATIONAL AND GREATLY ENLARGED FOR LEGIBILITY

Pacific Culture Areas

EQUATOR

EASTER ISLAND

MARQUISES

LES TUAMOTU

POLYNESIA

HAWAIIAN ISLANDS

LINE ISLANDS

COOK IS.

SAMOA ISLANDS

TOKELAU ISLANDS

TONGA IS.

WAKE ISLAND

MARSHALL ISLANDS

SANTA CRUZ IS.

FIJI ISLANDS

MICRONESIA

CAROLINE ISLS.

SOLOMON ISLANDS

MELANESIA

NEW CALEDONIA

NORTH ISLAND

NEW GUINEA

NEW ZEALAND

SOUTH ISLAND

AUSTRALIA

Source: Peter Manesis

Table 2.1   Pacific Islander population in the United States, 1990

Hawaiian	211,014
Samoan	62,964
Guamanian	49,345
Tongan	17,606
Fijian	7,063
Palauan	1,439
Northern Marianas	960
Tahitian	944
Others	13,716
Total	365,051

Source: US Bureau of Census, 1990.

surface. The Pacific Islands are grouped into three clusters: Polynesia, Melanesia, and Micronesia. The total Pacific Islander population in the US, as reported in the 1990 Census report, is 365,051 (see Table 2.1), a 40.6 percent increase from the 1980 Census. The three most numerous groups among the Islanders are the Hawaiians, Samoans and Chamorros. The Pacific Islands are a very massive region, not only in terms of the area they cover, but also in terms of the number of land areas they connect. Distances between the islands can be enormous; for example, there are 5000 miles between Hawaii and Guam; and 3000 miles between Fiji and Guam. Many of the islands are small and some are uninhabited; others are atolls with small populations (Cheng and Ima, 1989). In the western Pacific, there is an Association of Southeast Asian Nations (ASEAN) representing countries such as Thailand, Singapore, Malaysia, Indonesia, Brunei, and the Philippines, which share some common interests with the Pacific Islands. Unlike other countries in the Pacific Basin Islands, the Southeast Asian Nations are situated in close proximity.

Although Polynesia, Melanesia and Micronesia are groupings of islands primarily composed of a variety of indigenous peoples, European colonization left its mark on the local cultures. The Pacific Basin includes three main groups: the Samoans, the Hawaiians and the Chamorros. Many of the islands became territories of France, Spain, Portugal, Germany, Great Britain, Japan and the United States, and were, therefore, influenced by the cultures of those countries. American Samoa, for example, follows the US educational system, while British Samoa follows the British system. The Chamorro people from Saipan and Guam have been heavily influenced by the Spanish culture.

The largest group of Pacific islanders in California is the Hawaiians. The Hawaiian Islands have been heavily influenced by many cultures, including the Chinese, Japanese, Korean, Filipino and Portuguese. Japanese words such as bento (boxed lunch), soyo (soy sauce), ajinomoto (accent), and zori (slipper) have been incorporated into the everyday vocabulary of the

Islanders who also share many values and beliefs. Some authors include in their descriptions of the Hawaiian values the 'aloha' concept of generous hospitality, humility, spirituality, graciousness, loyalty, intelligence, cleanliness, helpfulness, forgiveness, self-reliance, industriousness, cooperation, excellence, courage, obedience, playfulness, and competitiveness (Kanahele, 1980). Others (for example, Ashby, 1983) discuss issues of self-determination.

Each group of Pacific Islanders possesses a rich history, one that underlines the struggle for cultural maintenance in spite of colonial oppression and economic exploitation. The Samoans are a very special group. They come to the United States from islands 2300 miles southwest of Honolulu in the South Pacific. At the beginning of the nineteenth century, Samoa's isolation was broken by missionaries and traders from Germany, Great Britain and the United States. The islands are divided into two parts: American Samoa and Western Samoa. American Samoa is approximately twenty-five miles long by five miles wide in area, and it lies thirty miles from Western Samoa. In 1899, Western Samoa became a German colony, and the United States acquired American Samoa for a naval station. After Germany's defeat in World War I, Western Samoa was transferred to New Zealand under a League of Nations mandate. In 1962 Western Samoa became an independent nation, while American Samoa continued to be a territory of the United States. Although American Samoans are considered US nationals, they are not viewed as American citizens. During the 1920s, some Samoans left their homeland in order to build a Mormon temple in Hawaii. It was not until the 1950s that large groups of Samoans left for Hawaii and the continental US. There are approximately 60,000 Samoans living in mainland United States and in Hawaii. Only 30,000 Samoans remain in American Samoa. Among the many reasons Samoans give for leaving their homeland are to search for a better life, access to health care, better education, and an escape from the traditionally authoritarian system (Cheng, 1989).

Indigenous Samoa is organized in clans, and emphasizes the extended family. The patrilineal clans function as economic, social and political units, and supervise the observance of rules determining descent, marriage, kinship relations, and property rights. The chief of the clan (Matai), is elected by the patrilineal clan members, and becomes responsible for locating and managing clan resources (for example, fish, food, land, and housing). In the Samoan language there is no word for person, because in their culture a person is only a part of the whole group. The social system is based on tracing ancestry through the paternal lines, in contrast with the Trukese and Chamorro which have matrilineal descent systems, whose women are heads of the families and clans, and become responsible for managing common resources, including land property titles. The Samoan clan chief holds authority to decide disputes on titles, and the appropriate inheritance of such titles. The chief uses ceremonial forms of the language, a high form of Samoan, whereas the rest of the people speak common Samoan.

The schools in Samoa are bilingual and teach both Samoan and English,

which are the two official languages. The Samoan English has unique seman-
tic, syntactic and phonetic characteristics which are perceived in the United
States as non-standard. For this reason, many students from American
Samoa have encountered academic problems in school, and are classified as
Limited English Proficient (LEP). Rumbaut and Ima (1988) reported that in
San Diego County, Samoan students have the lowest grade point averages of
all groups. Similar reports can be found in Hawaii, where there are large
groups of Samoans.

A second group of Pacific Islanders in the American Southwest is the
Hawaiians. Hawaii is composed of five main islands: Hawaii, Oahu, Maui,
Kauai, Molokai, and Lanai. These islands form a 1500-mile archipelago. The
first Hawaiians arrived from other Polynesian islands about 400 AD, and in
the following nine centuries have maintained continued contacts with people
from other Polynesian groups such as the Tahitians. Since those early days,
the Hawaiians have developed their own distinctive culture, different from
those of other Polynesian peoples. Nevertheless, they share similar racial
characteristics and a similar binding norms or strict laws set down by their
ancestors. The Englishman James Cook arrived in Hawaii in 1778, and established close contact with the Hawaiians. The following forty years saw an
influx of Europeans and Americans who changed the religion, language and
the Hawaiian ways of life. As it happened in many colonies of the new
world, it is estimated that less than a quarter of the native population
survived the onslaught of disease brought by the Europeans and Americans
to Hawaii.

By the late nineteenth century indigenous rulers had lost political
control to the Europeans and Americans, and in 1898 Hawaii was annexed
by the United States. With the influx of Chinese, Filipino, Japanese, Korean,
Portuguese and numerous other peoples, the islands became multiethnic and
multicultural. The main ethnic groups today are the American, European,
Japanese, Filipino, Chinese, and Korean. In addition to English, many other
languages are spoken in Hawaii, including Cantonese, Mandarin, Hawaiian,
Ilocano, Tagalog, Korean, Japanese, and Samoan. The vast majority of
indigenous Hawaiians intermarried with other ethnic groups, and many have
lost fluency in their original language. Many who are still identified as
Hawaiians have found themselves at the bottom of the socio-economic hierarchy, receive lower education, have higher rates of incarceration, are in the
lower income brackets, and take low-paying jobs. These factors affect the
academic performances of students of Hawaiian extraction. For more information about the Hawaiians, see Cheng and Ima, (1990) and Kanahele
(1980).

The third largest group of Pacific Islanders in the United States
(especially in California) are the Chamorros. Guam, a territory of the United
States, lies at the Southern end of the Mariana Islands in the Western Pacific,
and along with the Marshall, Caroline and Gilbert and other islands make up
Micronesia. Guam is the largest island in the Pacific Ocean between Hawaii

and the Philippines, extending nearly thirty miles long and four to nine miles wide. As many others, Guam is a volcanic island in origin and covers an area of approximately 212 square miles. The official languages of Guam are English and Chamorro, although the use of Japanese is increasing due to the investments made by Japanese in the hotel business. Both Chamorro and English are languages taught in the public and private schools, as well as used in official documents. The population of Guam in 1990 was estimated to be approximately 116,000. Chamorros make up the largest ethnic group, representing approximately 42 per cent of the total population. Europeans and Americans account for approximately 24 per cent; Filipinos, approximately 21 per cent; other ethnic groups include the Japanese, Koreans, Chinese, and natives of other Pacific islands.

The Chamorros are believed to have migrated to Guam as early as 2000 BC. Linguistic and archaeological evidence suggest that they probably came from Indonesia and the Philippines. Magellan sailed into Umatac Bay in 1521, and Spanish missionaries, soldiers, and government officials followed in the 1600s; Guam became a colony of Spain. The Spaniards left an enduring legacy in the religion, culture, architecture, family names and language of the Chamorros. Spain christianized many of the islands where the merchant galleons stopped to and from New Spain. Clear evidence of the Spanish legacy is found in the architecture of official buildings and older homes, the vocabulary introduced in the home language, and the Spanish names of many Chamorros, such as Martinez, Gutierrez, Rodriguez, and many others. In 1898, when the United States defeated Spain in the Spanish-American War, Guam was placed under the administration of the US Department of the Navy. During World War II, the Japanese occupied Guam for two-and-half years, but the United States regained control immediately after the war.

Although some islands, located thousands of miles apart from each other in the Western Pacific, maintain unique social, political and linguistic characteristics, Micronesians seem to share many customs, beliefs, traditions and proverbs. The sea permeates their legends, folktales, idioms and religious practices. This folklore is part of their rich oral tradition. In these legends, magic and myth are very important. Their narratives focus on important aspects of Micronesian ethnohistory and culture which are central to the socialization of children and the transmission of values. Proverbs are used widely to provide children and young adults with vivid lessons in life and appropriate norms of conduct. There is a great deal of respect for the power of the natural elements, the sea, the wind and the earth, and widespread popular knowledge regarding the best means to survive in the land, to sail and to orient oneself by looking at the stars and following marine currents.

Relatively few Micronesians practice polygamy, and all Micronesians are exogamous (marry outside of their residential group, or their village — which is mostly composed of persons belonging to one's own kindred). The society is matriarchal, and descent is tracked down matrilineally, thus it focuses on the role of the mother in the family. Some marriages are still arranged by heads of matrilineal clans, without the consent of the future spouses, although this practice is disappearing rapidly. Wedding ceremonies generally take place at a Catholic or Protestant church, and are followed by a conspicuously expensive family celebration with abundant food and drinks. In recent years, there has been an increase in the number of marriages between Micronesians and non-Micronesians.

Chamorro students are often told before they come to the United States that their academic level is one or two grades behind that of US students. This assessment often becomes a self-fulfilling prophecy of failure. Chamorro students often perform lower in their elementary and secondary education years, and many of them do not expect to continue to college. Relatively few Chamorros have obtained advanced degrees, and consequently there are not enough Chamorro university professors. Chamorros, however, seek and obtain political and administrative positions.

Chamorros seem to have a rather relaxed attitude toward life. Time-lines for getting things done are not as important as making people happy and comfortable. Consequently, their philosophy of life is to enjoy it and to help others enjoy it too. Emphasis on discipline and hard intellectual work is a Western concept that is gradually becoming accepted by school personnel and students. Chamorro teachers in primary and secondary schools have a high rates of absenteeism, even to the point that some schools have been closed for a period of time because there are not enough teachers. In the American schools, Chamorro students seem to suffer from low self-esteem. Some have mentioned the lack of role models, and the lack of intellectual support in the home.

Southeast and East Asians

Indochina is geographically situated to the south of China and to the east of India. It is comprised of Vietnam, Thailand, Cambodia, Laos and Burma. These countries have similar foods, geography and climate, but diverse languages, customs and cultures. There are very few immigrants from Thailand and Burma in the United States; most of the Indochinese that live in America are refugees from Vietnam, Cambodia and Laos.

Southeast Asians, in particular Indochinese refugees, have grown significantly in California and the Southwest during the last two decades: Hmong, Khmer, Laotian, and Vietnamese families number several hundred thousands in the Southwest. Other Southeast Asian groups, such as the Filipinos, have established migration patterns for a much longer period of time, dating to World War II. The East Asians, especially the Japanese and Chinese, have an even longer history of immigration into the United States, dating back to the search for opportunities in America since the 1840s. There are vast, important social and cultural differences between Southeast and East Asian immigrants, yet they share a similar view of Western culture and

Map 2.2   *Indochina*

Source: Peter Manesis

respond to culture shock and acculturation forces with similar cultural resources, although in different degrees. These issues include respect for authority, commitment to family traditions and hierarchical organization, intensive work, choice of home cultures to assess own's success in the host country, and strong ethnic affiliation.

Terms such as Indochinese or Southeast Asian refugees are often used in their restricted sense referring only to people from Cambodia, Laos and Vietnam who escaped in fear of persecution from the communists and in search of political asylum in 1975. The first influx of refugees began in April–May 1975, when the US government evacuated about 120,000 refugees to the US. After the communist takeover, people continued to escape from Southeast Asia. It has been estimated that more than half of the 'boat people', who escaped by small often homemade boats, died during their flight because of starvation, hardship, shipwreck and the atrocities committed by pirates in the Gulf of Thailand. Before 1975, there were very few Cambodians, Laotians or Vietnamese in the United States. The Indochinese are traditionally deeply rooted in their native countries and villages, thus reluctant to resettle in distant lands, especially those with Western cultures. The Hmong were no exception to this rule, although in a historical sense they have a long-term experience of migration starting in China over the last hundred and fifty years, and extending throughout Indochina prior to their massive 1975–1985 migrations to western societies. The Hmong are originally from Mongolia, and descend from the *Miao* or *Meo*, which are ethnic minority groups — some eight million people living in the mountains of South and Southwestern China in the provinces of Guizhow, Hunan, Yunnan, Sichuan, Hubei, Guangxi and Guangton.

The Hmong began to move from China to the mountainous area of Indochina at least two centuries ago. It is calculated that close to 1.5 million of them left China, and are now scattered throughout Laos, Thailand, Burma and Vietnam. The Hmong have a rich oral history, but their written language only developed in recent years (Cheng, 1991, p. 49). For a more detailed account consult Trueba, Jacobs and Kirton (1990). While among the Hmong there are a number of subgroups with substantial linguistic and cultural differences, there are also persistent unique characteristics common to all groups. Often their languages have similarities and even are mutually intelligible; they share a similar beliefs in animism and ancestor worship, a distribution of labor within the family according to age and sex, a social structure (patrilineal clans and patrilocal residence) based on kinship descent through male line and the construction of dwellings grouped around male siblings. Most of all, Hmong peoples share a long tradition of statelessness and migration from southern China to Indochina, and from there to the United States and other western countries; within the host western societies, Hmong people experience a secondary and even tertiary migration (Trueba *et al.*, 1990:21–25). It is estimated that approximately five million Hmong (in contrast with the larger Miao groups which include peoples with more diverse linguistic and cultural differences) live today in China, Burma, Vietnam, Laos and Thailand. Approximately 190,000 of them have become refugees in the United States, and they live mainly in the West coast (60,000) and in the Midwest (especially Minnesota, and Wisconsin); half the Californian Hmong live in the San Joaquin Valley, more specifically in the Fresno area (Trueba, *et al.*, 1990:x–xii).

Because many of the Hmong were rural prior to their arrival in the United States, the tradition of schooling beyond the early years of elementary school did not exist in the families, thus the expectations that adults have for younger Hmong often contradicts the ambitions and desires of younger and academically competent Hmong persons, especially women. (Ima and Cheng, 1990). Some of the most influential adults believe in maintaining their traditional practice of early marriages. This practice often places in jeopardy the college education of many Hmong, especially women. The significance of gender — and often the dominance of males — is an important factor in the life of the teenage Hmong. However, the impact of American education is gradually building a stronger literacy and schooling tradition among the younger generations, based on the value of a good education as a means to obtain better employment. Naturally, all young Hmong persons raised in America, in spite their struggles with their ethnic identity, want the American dream of becoming affluent, and many of them realize that education is essential to fulfill this dream; yet, many are still reluctant to upset their parents by refusing parental demands to comply with traditions. They feel obliged to honor their parents' wishes regarding early marriage and manual labor, thus making it difficult for themselves to gain upward mobility and perpetuating their own social underclass.

The hectic years of war in Indochina, and the hurried escape of many families forced villagers to seek unions that best enhanced their survival from brutal violence and starvation. Therefore, it is not unusual that some Hmong, Khmer and Laotian pursued intermarriages. Many Indochinese families, during the years of waiting in the Thai camps associated across ethnic lines and even obtained names and identification documents incongruent with their family's ethnic names. Laos was the main theater of cycles of poverty, meager agricultural activities and war supported by either the United States or the Communists. Laos is situated east of Thailand and west of Vietnam. It is a country with tropical forests in two-thirds of its territory. There is a dry season from November to April, and a wet season from May to October. Rice and fish are the main sources of food (Cheng, 1991:43).

Traditionally, for the Cambodians and Lao of late nineteenth century and first half of the twentieth century, school was associated with religious activities in the Pagoda intended to teach students to chant and interpret the sacred Buddhist texts. Though this type of literacy has remained as the main focus of the education of selected youngsters, in the decade prior to 1975 there was a concerted effort to modernize schools along the western fashion, using first the French and later the American school models. Hence, education for most of the Lao and Cambodian families was a relatively late and limited phenomenon, in contrast for example, with mainland Chinese who had a longer and greater preoccupation with formal schooling. Thus the concerns with text, historical documentation, philosophy and other characteristics of educated Chinese persons are not likely to be found with the same force and intensity among Lao and Cambodian families.

Some researchers and other observers have the perception that Cambodian and Lao immigrants in the United States, especially those seen in the West coast, lack the motivation and initiative to achieve academically, or to pursue graduate degrees, partially because few families have the experience of adults with college education. Learning is not necessarily seen in the community as an inherently desirable end in itself, in contrast, for example, with some educated Vietnamese families who attended Western schools for second or third generation.

The Vietnamese, who lived under Chinese rule for a thousand years, assimilated many of the Chinese values, including the value of literacy, art and philosophy. Like many Chinese American parents in the United States, Vietnamese immigrant parents hire tutors to teach their children. These tutors are hired based on similarities of religion, regional origin, and profession, which reflect similar practices used by the Chinese. Like the Chinese, many Vietnamese parents send their children to language schools.

For Chinese, Koreans, Japanese, and to some extent Vietnamese, the Confucian philosophy is very much alive and becomes a powerful force in their daily behaviors, attitudes and practices demanding reflection, moderation, persistence, humility, obedience to superiors, and stoic resistance to pain. However many Southeast and East Asian immigrants are increasingly questioning the wisdom of putting much emphasis on the Confucian cultural principles, which often seem to conflict with the values stressed in modern, competitive industrial and technological societies. Many of the values of the Confucian tradition are still very functional in modern societies, in so far as they stress the wisdom of hard work, literacy and learning. Confucian philosophy supports the belief that education is not only important for upward mobility, but also a way to achieve self-actualization, to fully develop one's own talents. Many of the adaptive strategies adopted by Asian Americans seem to mirror the strengths and weaknesses of their prearrival experiences, and their ability to understand technological societies. Some groups, for example the Vietnamese, appear to be more active participants in the political arena than others. Indeed Vietnamese teachers and scholars have taken leadership roles in organizations such as the National Association for Bilingual Education, and the California Association for Bilingual Education. The Filipinos, Japanese, Chinese Americans and other Asian American have also participated in the political process.

The Filipinos constitute a nation that is highly diversified ethnically and racially. Many of them are direct descendant of the Spaniards who conquered the Philippines and christianized most inhabitants; others are black-Africans who represent several racial types (including the highland Negritos, small black tribes people and people from Malay origin). The Philippines is an archipelago of more than 7200 islands, with a land mass of the size of the State of Arizona. It is a tropical country with unpredictable and at times violent typhoons — especially in the summer. Ninety-five per cent of the population are of Malay origin, although Spanish, Chinese, Amerasian and Japanese are also found. There are a number of aborigines living in preliterate and pre-industrial villages. (For more information see Kitano and Daniels, 1988, and Cheng, 1991).

Filipino immigrants have been coming to the United States in larger numbers since the mid-twentieth century. According to Kitano and Daniels, (1988), by the end of the century, the Filipino population in the US will reach two million, including both first generation and US-born Filipinos. Most of the Filipinos live in urban areas, and their educational needs have often been ignored because of their fluency in English and their apparent middle-class status. Consequently, some scholars (such as Monzon, 1984) urge us to take a closer look at the education of Filipino American students, especially at the K-12 levels.

Although public education at the elementary level is compulsory in the Philippines, it is often not enforced. Filipino immigrants bring with them very diverse linguistic skills in English and diverse educational backgrounds. Most Filipinos, however, view education as essential to secure a good job. Many Filipinos in the United States have continued their education and obtained excellent jobs, such as skilled lab technicians, nurses, sales clerks and managers, accountants, teachers, computer experts, and data analysts. In comparison with the Filipino, however, other Asian immigrants (especially Japanese and Chinese) seem to reach a higher level of technological expertise and to obtain a larger share of graduate technical degrees.

Japanese Americans have recently become the target of racist attacks related to the economic competition that Japanese products are creating for American goods and services. As happened during World War II, Japanese immigrants are viewed with suspicion and even anger, in spite of the fact that most of them have nothing to do with the competition between the United States and Japan. Japan, a country with a total land mass smaller than the State of California, is comprised of four main islands, Hokkaido, Honshu, Shikoko and Kyushu. The total population of Japan is over 110 million, which is approximately half of the US population and reflects one of the highest densities of urban inhabitants in the world. The first group of Japanese immigrants came to America between 1891 and 1907. The US Bureau of the Census of 1890 reported the number of Japanese residents was 2039. We also have a record indicating that in 1907 there were 10,000 Japanese immigrants entering the country. In the early 1900s, a Gentleman's Agreement between America and Japan was signed restricting the number of Japanese persons allowed to emigrate to the US.

During the Second World War, many Japanese living on the West coast were, without a clear justification, forced to sell or abandon their properties and confined to various detainment camps. It was not until the mid 1980s that the American Government agreed to recognize the wrongdoing and make a token compensation for the losses of the Japanese families. This decision was and is still highly controversial and has divided public opinion at all levels. After the World War II abruptly ended with the atomic bombs dropped on Hiroshima and Nagasaki in 1945, very few Japanese immigrants came to the US. As time went by, and especially in the last fifteen years, there has been a steady increase of Japanese immigrants, including major investors, entrepreneurs and manufacturers who set up numerous businesses throughout the US. The new immigrants, in contrast with those that came the previous century until the 1920s — farmers and unskilled laborers for the most part — are generally highly trained (Cheng, 1991:71).

The Japanese are no longer one of the largest Asian group of immigrants; they now have been superseded in numbers by the Filipinos and Chinese. Waggoner estimates (1988:69–108) that the 1980 US Bureau of the Census recorded 542,000 Japanese Americans (English and non-English speaking), following Greeks (548,000), Filipino (713,000) and Chinese (769,000), but preceding native Americans and Alaskans (512,000), Portuguese (480,000) Yiddish (430,000), and others, including Korean (384,000), Vietnamese (250,000) and Thai (127,000).

The Japanese Americans constitute a unique group comprised primarily of US-born, second, third, fourth, and fifth generations. There is within the Japanese community a small number of recent immigrants and an even smaller number of Kaisha, or children of Japanese businessmen, who are on temporary assignment in the US. Two factors explain the smaller growth of the Japanese American population: 1) over three-quarters of them are US-born in small families with very few children, and 2) immigration from Japan that had a quota (set up by immigration laws in 1965) of 20,000 per year has never been met; indeed fewer than 4000 Japanese emigrate to the US every year. Japanese in Japan have an average annual income which is several thousand dollars above that of the average income of Japanese Americans, thus the economic incentive for potential immigrants to leave Japan is not there. In contrast, the quotas of other Asian countries seeking immigrant status in America, such as those of Korea, Hong Kong and Vietnam, are always filled. Obviously the political and economic situation provides them with a clear motivation to go to the United States.

There is another characteristic of Japanese in Japan and Japanese Americans. They are very careful to provide the very best education they can for their children. For a Japanese family, the most fundamental value it cherishes, and consequently one of the most critical decision it faces, is to make a choice of educational institution for the children's higher education. The Japanese see clearly that higher education as the main instrument of upward mobility. Consequently, parents' most important obligation is to start early in life preparing children for higher education, to locate the very best elementary and secondary schools that can prepare their children to pass entrance examination in the top universities. Education is a common topic of family discussion and a serious preoccupation.

This concern is a family affair, and it begins to characterize other Asian and Asian American families, such as the Chinese and Korean families who send their children to America for a good education. The larger picture of upward mobility among Asian and Asian Americans is clearly more complicated than just family values and commitment to education. The economic trends and recent successes of the Koreans, almost replicating the technological and economic development of Japan, have naturally opened a rapid channel of upward mobility for many Koreans and emphasized the need for university training. The Korean population deserves a special mention because of its increase in immigration to the United States and the role of a possibly united Korea in the future industrial development of all Asian countries.

Koreans share a common racial and cultural origins with many other peoples from North Asia (their language belongs to the Altaic family of that region), but they also share cultural values that form the main patrimony of Japanese culture. The Koreans were in constant conflict with the Chinese and were a Chinese colony until 668 AD. The cultural similarities and agricultural traditions have linked these two countries for centuries. By the end of the nineteenth century, however, Western cultures and industrial development began to attract East Asia after Japan opened the doors to the West. (For additional valuable information see *The New Encyclopaedia Britannica*, 1984 edition, Volume 10, pp. 507–534). Korea tried to cope with Western technology, but was soon the prey of Japanese imperialism. Japanese rule started in 1905, and the Korean army was dispersed. In 1910 Korea was annexed to Japan, and many Koreans emigrated to Manchuria, Shanghai and Hawaii. Freedom of speech, of assembly, and a free press were denied. The Japanese built an economic and transportation infrastructure and a new monetary system. The Japanese rule eventually ended as a result of the massive peace protests of 1919 in which over 2 million people took part, and which was met with brutal repression on the part of the Japanese who arrested close to 50,000 and killed or wounded nearly 23,000. The relations between Japan and Korea became more stable, and democratic and patriotic anti-Japanese manifestations continued even in the late 1920s. In 1931 Japan imposed obligatory military service on Korea once more and drafted thousands of Koreans to fight for Japan and meet the economic needs of Japan in the mines, factories and military bases (Ibid., pp. 511–12). The surrender of the Japanese in 1945 ended thirty-six years of Japanese rule in Korea, which was followed by a complex set of international political currents and the division of Korea. At the Yalta Conference of February 1945, President Franklin D. Roosevelt proposed a trusteeship (never agreed upon) for Korea to be divided between the US, England, the USSR and China. Soon after the July 1945 Potsdam Conference in which the US was attempting to bring the Soviets to join the war against Japan, while at the same time reaffirming Korean independence (along the terms of the previous Cairo Conference of December, 1943), the Soviet troops went into Manchuria and took the northern tip of Korea. Japan agreed in 1945 with the provision that Japanese forces north of the 38th parallel had to surrender to the Soviet commanders, while those south of that parallel would surrender to the US commanders. This first military expedience resulted in the division of Korea and the serious internal conflicts between two republics. Attempts at reuniting failed in the later 1940s and then soon after the Korean War broke out. A series of Chinese interventions in the early 1950s (with over a million soldiers) forced United Nations troops to abandon the 38th parallel.

North Korea has about 55 per cent of the peninsular lands, and 80 per cent of all mineral deposits, and it has a population of over 20 million people. It maintains a close alliance with China and the former USSR, and like other communist countries, it pursues an economic emphasis on capital goods rather than consumer services. It has farm cooperatives, larger railroad transportation, and keeps a strong central political control. In contrast, South Korea is strategically located between China, Japan and the Soviet Far East. The Republic of Korea (South) is rapidly becoming urbanized, especially in the areas of Seoul and Pusan. South Korea has twice the population of North Korea. The rapid Christianization of South Koreans has impacted the pace of modernization and the increase in immigration trends to Western countries. South Korea has also adopted a fast increasing manufacturing and exporting economy, but the country has meager natural resources (coal, iron ore, graphite, zinc, lead, etc.), and consequently it has to import these materials from Japan or the United States. Culturally, South Korea remains strongly Asian, especially Chinese, in its Shamanism, Buddhism, and the prevalence of its Confucian philosophy, and it retains the major responsibility of reconciling the demands of modern industrialization and the political differences with the north, as well as retaining the support from the United States and Japan.

There has been a steady influx of South Korean immigrants to the United States since the 1960s. Korean children are socialized into an environment in which going to the best schools is highly valued, and they are accustomed to working extremely hard to obtain high scores in college entrance exams. Immediate success in business or other fields is not the primary focus of college students, but to obtain the best education. This orientation helps children to set up their major goals in life and to maintain a strong ethnic cohesiveness and self-identity, but it does not necessarily open for them all the possible opportunities which tend to develop from a more socially active and business oriented training in college. From their early schools years, they are directed by their families and friends into specific fields of science, medicine, or engineering, and few find social encouragement to go into the humanities, such as literature or fine arts. In general,

Korean Americans are early on-track and highly disciplined, thus, they rarely create delinquency problems.

Discussion of almost any Southeast or East Asian immigrants in the United States invites reflection on the Chinese immigrants themselves. Chinese Americans and Chinese returning to the mainland or to Taiwan, exhibit characteristics that are similar to those of other Asian Americans, but also exhibit unique characteristics and contrasts that deserve attention. First, we will discuss the Chinese from Taiwan who are a unique group and have finally been discovered because of the recognition and praise for their achievements in business and science.

Taiwan, off the southeast coast of the China mainland, was the seat of Nationalist China since 1949, and comprises fifteen islands forming the Taiwan archipelago and sixty-four of the Pescadores Archipelago, with a total extension of almost 14,000 square miles and a rapidly increasing population. Most of the population is originally from the Chinese provinces of Fukien and Kwantung (from the Han dynasty, speakers of Mandarin), but there were several groups of aborigines from Indonesian origin who cultivated shifting agriculture in the foothills and highlands. From 1970 when the total population of Taiwan was about 15 million (Taipei alone had 1.8 million) it has in the last two decades grown to around 22 million people. Some 1.8 million Chinese mainlanders moved to the island from 1949 to 1970. Taipei is one of the most modern and hectic cities in Asia, and has developed an international trade center. The natural resources of Taiwan are rich: coal, copper, gold, iron, sulfur-pyrite minerals, petroleum, marble, natural gas, and many other resources abound. But the basis for the economy is agricultural production, manufacturing and foreign trade. Because it has abundant rainfall (mean annual precipitation is 102 inches, but in a single summer they may get 200 inches some years), vegetation, forestry and animal life are rich.

Taiwan is multicultural. Beside the religion of the aborigines, many other religions have been introduced to Taiwan in the last three centuries. Chinese immigrants brought Buddhism and Taoism, but Protestantism and other Christian religions date back to the seventeenth century when Dutch and Spaniards visited the island. There are numerous Taoist Buddhist temples throughout the island, and a few mosques for the small population of Moslems, but the Christian population has also increased rapidly along with the Western cultural influence. Taiwan has developed into a strong, self-supporting country, which is now exporting technical skills to a number of Asian countries. Indeed, American business, science and entertainment have opened up the frequent and friendly relationships between the United States and Taiwan. These relationships have facilitated the travel between the two countries and the increase in immigrants coming to live in America.

The Chinese immigrants from Taiwan are one of the largest group of recent Asian immigrants to California. Prior to the 1960s, there were not many Chinese from Taiwan living in the United States. Between 1960 and

1975, more US-Chinese encouraged Chinese immigrants to pursue higher education in American universities. In the late 1970s, due to increased Taiwanese affluence and trade, more business connections developed between the US and Taiwan in the southwest and the east, and more businessmen moved to the US and formed large enclaves of Chinese communities — often called the new China Towns — in California's cities of Monterey Park, Flushing and South San Francisco. In the 1980s, a larger wave of high school students have come to the US with the purpose of learning English and gaining admission to American colleges. Many Chinese immigrants have recently immigrated from Taiwan and Hong Kong to La Mar, a large Chinese community in Southern California. In La Mar Elementary School, 20 per cent of the students in the lower grades belong to Chinese families from Taiwan. Parents of these children tend to help each other.

The existence of community groups empowers parents, especially those who come from different areas, to help each other. Churches, languages, businesses and even neighborhoods are ties that these parents share. There are approximately eleven such social groups. Information derived from social activities in these groups is helpful to parents who are trying to adjust to America and provide their children with a number of services. Some of the mothers in this community play Mah-jong together and often exchange information about advanced school programs, summer swimming classes, piano teachers, soccer games, reading programs, and summer camp information. Most of these parents send their children to the weekend Chinese School, and develop support groups to exchange further information about community resources available for their children. They are well informed about American standardized tests, for example the SAT, CTBS, and Stanford-Binet. Those who have older children learn about college entrance information and prepare their children for college applications. They want their children to go to the top American universities: Stanford, Harvard, Berkeley, Yale, Cornell, Brown, University of Michigan, or University of Pennsylvania. With the relaxation of the US Government's foreign students policies, it is likely that the influx of youngsters from Taiwan will increase significantly in the next decade.

There is another group, the so-called junior foreign students, not to be confused with the foreign students, who come to the United States in pursuit of advanced degrees MAs and PhDs. Junior foreign students are high school age students, typically ages 12 to 13, who come from affluent business parents who must travel often. These children may live with relatives or friends of the family under little or no supervision. Many of them have access to large amounts of money often used at the whim of these youngsters. Because of their abundant financial resources, these children can rent an apartment or a house to live there unsupervised. The development of their Chinese language skill as well as the acquisition of English as a Second Language tend to be lower in comparison with those of children who come at later stages of their life or seem to be better prepared academically. Schools find it difficult to work with these junior foreign students. Some of them go through years of educational programs before they finally begin to integrate, but some of them never make a successful transition into the American school system. These students may present behavioral problems in schools and outside the schools, often becoming involved with drugs or developing delinquent behavior. The junior foreign student problem reflects family problems, and is a challenge to parents who are trying to find solutions. This group is seldom discussed, but now that their problems are somewhat acute, the Taiwanese government has begun paying more attention to them.

The influence of Chinese cultures and peoples around the world, despite the isolation of mainland China, has been undeniable since 1949, and it has systematically increased in the last three decades of contact between Chinese and Western European and American institutions. Obviously a country with the largest population in the world, which additionally possesses yet fully undisclosed rich natural resources, is the focus of much international attention. The struggles of the last few years between the traditional government and the liberation attempts by the younger generations of university students seeking democracy, poses for China an unprecedented challenge. Beside the chronic economic problems of China, the political international infrastructure has changed drastically in the last two years, especially with the disassembly of the Soviet Union and the revival of many national enclaves, each with its own ethnic cultural and linguistic resources as well as its conflicts.

The Peoples' Republic of China has a total population of at least 1.2 billion persons, according to Yuan Tien (1989). From this population (and these figures are probably outdated by a decade) about 93 per cent (some 937 million) are Han and speak a form of Mandarin, the Chinese *lingua franca*. There are however, ten to fifteen other major ethnolinguistic groups among the Han people, groups which have considerable cultural differences. The Han people settled in the North of China where the lower Yellow and Wei Rivers spread over a large area and where the Han Dynasty and Chinese ancient civilization developed. Other population groupings, which constitute some 167 million persons, form ethnic nations. Scholars estimate that there are over fifty ethnic nations comprising collectively over 100 million minority groups. It is calculated that at least fifteen of those groups have populations of over 1 million, such as the Zhuang with 13.4 million, the Hui with 7.2 million, the Uygurs with 6 million, the Yi with 5.5 million, the Miao, ancestors of the Hmong, with 5 million, the Manchus 4.3, the Tibetans 3.9 million, the Mongols with 3.4 million, the Tujia with 2.8 closely related to the Tong with 1.4, the Buyi with 2.1 million, Koreans with 1.8 million, Yao with 1.4 million, Bai with 1.1 million, and Hani with 1.1 million (Yuan Tien, 1989:501–503).

More immigrants from Hong Kong have arrived in North America in the last five years than from other parts of Mainland China. In fact, many people from Hong Kong have emigrated to Australia and the United Kingdom, as well as Canada and the US. Many of these individuals are fearful of the Peoples' Republic of China's takeover of Hong Kong in 1997.

Some of the regions have been profoundly affected by Western cultural values because of the colonial influence from England and the United States. Hong Kong is a classic example of the blending of Eastern and Western economic traditions. Hong Kong's population increased from 1.5 to 5.2 million between 1945 and 1981. Given the total land of 410 square miles and the shortage of flat land, its fast population increase is putting enormous pressure on urban development in Hong Kong. This British colony, placed in the Kwangtung Province, acquired by England on a 99-year lease from China, is supposed to return to China in 1997. Hong Kong has served important purposes for both China (who uses it as a means to get imports from the outside world) and western societies who need information about the events inside of China.

About 99 per cent of the population in Hong Kong is ethnically Chinese, many originally from the southern Chinese provinces of Kwangtung and Fukien, but about half of the population consists of Chinese born in Hong Kong. There are a number of language groups, but the most numerous are Cantonese speaking. There are also Hakka speakers, mainly rural people, and Hoklo and Tanka speakers most of whom had been living in boats until recently. Overall, about 87 per cent of the population lives in urban areas. Hong Kong has become an industrial area, and has moved from an import-export region to a more aggressive entrepreneurial society. Its relations with China and North Korea made this possible after the economic embargo imposed in 1952 on those countries as a result of the Korean War. Education is compulsory in elementary and secondary levels, and about half of the elementary schools are private. The University of Hong Kong, founded in 1911, receives public subsidies. The Chinese University of Hong Kong, founded in 1963, and the Hong Kong Polytechnic established in 1972, are modelled on the British system and offer limited and competitive enrollment. Consequently, many students seek higher education in the United States, Japan or England. (For more information see *The New Encyclopaedia Britannica*, 1984 edition, Volume 8, pp. 1060–1065).

The Chinese society of Hong Kong has multiple social strata, and has established traditions of contact and education in Western countries. The wealthiest people have been educated in England or in America, and they may also possess degrees from Chinese universities as well. Graduates from Cambridge, Oxford, Stanford or Wisconsin universities are found at all levels of business and government. Foreign students and other immigrants from the upper strata Chinese families tend to form their own associations in the United States. There is a second group of immigrants in search of economic opportunities who in their home land are low-wage laborers and arrive in the China Towns of the west as low-paid workers in restaurants, clerks and unskilled laborers, but who often stay long enough to have their children born in America and eager to share in the American dream. There is still a third group of Chinese who were unable to find refuge in Hong Kong, escaping originally from mainland China or Indochinese countries, and have neither the literacy tradition of the rich, nor the connections of the low-income immigrants. This third group often suffers from the scars of political persecution. These groups respond to American society in different ways, and present three very different behavioral profiles. More recently, there have been waves of Indochinese immigrants, many of whom have been deported against their will.

In the last ten years, Chinese from the People's Republic of China have been emigrating to the United States. Some Chinese have petitioned for permanent residence status after the June 4, 1989, Tienanmen Square incident. The majority of these individuals have come as students or exchange scholars, and some have come sponsored by their families. This group of Chinese has experienced the Cultural Revolution, and many have not had the opportunity to receive uninterrupted education. Many of them coming to America with outstanding educational records (they were teachers, doctors or other professionals) are now working in restaurants and factories. They experience a serious loss of status and face very difficult adjustment.

From the previous pages one can immediately detect the significant cultural differences among Asians and Asian Americans, as well as their different adjustment patterns to a Western society. Adjustment is often conditioned by the level of literacy and exposure to Western cultural values. The next section raises issues about the impact of cultural differences among Asian Americans in their schooling.

Culture and Academic Achievement

It is not enough to recognize cultural similarities and differences, ethnic backgrounds and experiences in immigration and refugee groups. The central question is how to deal with the different needs of children with such differences. What can parents and school do together in order to assist children to adjust to a new country and enhance their academic achievement? First of all, there is fast growing evidence that the 'model minority' has serious flaws; that is, not all Asian and Asian American students do well in school. Indeed some of the Asian American children are having serious academic problems. Perhaps, more than anything, adjustment and academic achievement reflect differences in family support and values, as well as different preparation of children to engage in competitive school activities — especially if they are not fluent in standard English, or at least the English of the school they attend. Take, for example, Pacific Islanders from Asian background. To what extent do they share the Chinese values of education? If they do, how well are they prepared to attack academic tasks given their preparation in their home school.

Some school personnel may argue that the Pacific Islanders have views and life styles (based on their home culture and personal experiences) that does not favor academic achievement. The Hawaiian, Tongan, Samoan, Fijian, and other groups may share some commonalties with other Asians, but perhaps not other Asians' Confucian tradition. Some teachers and academicians think that the Pacific Islanders did not regard formal education as a part of their cultural tradition until the Europeans came in contact with them. Much of their education was conducted through oral tradition; the knowledge they needed for their survival skills to navigate, fish, and their cultural history were effectively transferred by word of mouth. Literacy traditions entered with European and American influence and occupation. Schooling in America represents for these children a drastic departure from the home environment and an intensive and demanding set of academic activities. Schooling is not easy for any Asian children, including Chinese children who come from families with high levels of literacy and intellectually stimulating environments. But for other Asian children, the challenge can be overwhelming. Not only does American schooling contradict their own cultural system, but it also basically undermines their sense of well-being and self-confidence. Their ethnic identity is tied to the group and the life-style they had in their home countries. In contrast, American schooling emphasizes independence and individualism, self-confidence and hard competitive efforts to excel and achieve. Perhaps American schooling could use less competitive and more cooperative strategies in teaching and learning, and thus allow for a less traumatic experiences of immigrant children from other lands.

Many groups in the Pacific Islands develop cooperative working strategies and depend on each other for subsistence and emotional support. Isolation from the nuclear or extended family, or from other voluntary associations is perceived by children as a deprivation of their support system. The Tongans, for example, have a tradition of working in groups as they make a fabric of mulberry barks, and while doing so, they sing and pound together in unison. Preparation for important religious or social celebrations, rehearsing for a dance or a ritual and many other group activities, always include an element of togetherness, cooperative efforts, consumption of food and enjoyment. Some teachers feel that the abundance of food, mild temperatures, the collective nature of local traditions, and the emphasis on ritual group behavior, all make it essential that schooling be less individualistic than it is in the United States or other Western countries. Individual competition and individual work does not make much sense to many other peoples. Mother washes the fish, children collect the banana leaves and break the coconuts and father grinds them. All help to prepare for a Sunday meal before they go to church. This commitment to the collectivity, community orientation, and the significance of group traditions makes it most difficult for a child to stand out and say, 'I know how to do this, but you don't.' He is more likely to state, 'Let's all work on it together. I'll show you, and you show me. The Pacific Islanders treasure and value collective reliance and trust, that is, the total confidence that the existence and effectiveness of the group cannot and should not be opposed to the efforts of the individual. Therefore, their first encounters with other school children confuse them and discourage them. For a Pacific Islander to go into a school environment and find children not reading in unison, not depending on each other, but rather working alone or in competition with each other is shocking, and at first glance, unacceptable. Why would they not read in unison? In the US we may have five reading groups in one small class. Both the organization of academic activities and teachers' expectations violate Pacific Islanders' basic work principles of cooperation and their notion of best modes for transmission of knowledge. This certainly separates the Pacific Islander from mainstream American children.

Those Chinese children, on the other hand, who come from families whose cultural tradition views education as one of the most important values, may be better prepared to face the challenge of American schools and, in spite of their initial cultural shock, will achieve at the level expected by teachers. Naturally, Chinese children who are not fluent in English and have been uprooted from friends and their extended family suffer a serious shock. Their initial reaction is to make consistent efforts in the new language, while continuing to achieve in their home language. Even though there are some serious cultural conflicts they must face everyday in school, the learning objectives and the subject matter are similar to those they knew in China, and, for example, in mathematics, the Chinese child may feel better prepared than his American peers. There are conflicts and also barriers, but the Chinese know that persistent work will remove them. Often a Chinese child from highly educated parents will see at home the intensity of intellectual work and will aspire to high degrees. This may occur with less frequency in the case of children coming from the Pacific Islands, whose families never discussed the possibility of earning a higher degree in a major university, and who never used text or had a limited experience with books at home.

Despite linguistic and cultural differences, most children with parental support do succeed. Parents can help their children achieve through community networks, resources and information gathered by the cumulative efforts of parents involved in the schools who have empowered themselves. These parents mentor other parents and motivate them to do the same. There are many success stories that illustrate the collective power of parents. What follows is some information on the differential academic achievement of New Asian Americans, starting with the achievement of Asian Pacific Islanders.

Statistics on the Asian and Pacific Islanders show support for a general picture of well being. There are, however, important differences in achievement levels within and between various ethnic groups. In general, Asian and Pacific Islanders have an above-average profile of well-being as reflected in above-average income, low levels of poverty, family stability, and low levels

Table 2.2   1979 Median family incomes

Groupings	Income $
All Families	19,900
White Families	20,800
All Asian American Families	23,600
Japanese	27,350
Asian Indians	24,990
Filipinos	23,690
Chinese	22,560
Koreans	20,640
Vietnamese	12,840

Source: Bureau of the Census (1988), *We, the Asian and Pacific Islander Americans*, Washington, DC: US Department of Commerce.

of welfare dependency. Table 2.2 displays their median family income and reveals above-average family incomes for all groups except the Vietnamese. The 1987 income estimates for the first wave of Vietnamese families exceed those of mainstream families; whether or not these estimates predict higher income for subsequent Vietnamese refugees is difficult to say, given their lower levels of education and meager resources of recent arrivals.

Higher median incomes for Asian families may also reflect a greater number of workers per family. In 1980, 63 per cent of Asian families had two or more workers, and 17 per cent had three or more. In contrast, comparable figures for white families were 55 per cent and 12 per cent. Disaggregated scores of specific Asian American groups reveal important pockets of at-risk students. For example, among Filipinos, it is common to hear of both parents working not only one but several jobs, often having to leave their children unattended. These children may experience cultural conflicts in school and the lack of parental supervision; both of these factors may explain lower academic scores, in spite of the higher family income. There are problems in interpreting the income figures without attending to the details of the lives of these families.

Table 2.3 identifies the percentages of each group which live below the poverty level. Except for Japanese, Filipino and Asian Indians, more Asian than white families live below the poverty income levels. In 1976, the Chinese poverty level was 1.7 times the white population, but in 1979 it had risen to 1.5 times the white level. The figures for the Chinese mask the wide diversity of economic well-being of the Chinese population. The more recent arrivals have a significantly lower income levels than those of long-time residents. Furthermore, the distribution of poverty is clouded by the variable of residence. The Chinese Taiwanese seem to have a higher social status if compared with the Chinese Vietnamese, as measured by the years of formal education and other indices of well-being; indeed the Chinese Vietnamese are more likely to fall below the poverty level if compared with the Chinese

Table 2.3   1979 worker incomes and family poverty levels

Population	Per cent of families below poverty level
White	7.0
Black	26.5
Hispanic	21.3
Asian Groups	
Japanese	4.2
Chinese	10.5
Filipino	6.2
Korean	13.1
Asian Indian	7.4
Vietnamese	35.1

Source: Gardner, R.W., Robey, B. and Smith, P.C. (1985), 'Asian Americans: Growth, change and diversity', *Population Bulletin* **40** (4).

Table 2.4   Per cent of selected Asian American Groups living below poverty levels

Group:	Chinese	Japanese	Korean	Filipino	Asian Indian	Vietnamese
Arrival Date						
US Born	5.7	2.7	3.6	11.0	21.6*	NA
Bef. '65	7.2	9.6	4.5	5.2	5.0	NA
1965–74	11.3	6.2	8.0	3.9	4.8	30.3
1975–80	38.8	9.4	19.5	11.6	23.2	43.9

* The Asian Indian figures are inflated due to the inclusion of Native Americans.
Source: Gardner, R.W., Robey, B. and Smith, P.C. (1985), 'Asian Americans: Growth, change and diversity', *Population Bulletin* **40** (4).

Taiwanese. Figures for other Southeast Asian refugee groups indicate poverty rates higher than those for blacks. For example, 90 per cent of the Hmong families have incomes below the poverty level (Rumbaut and Ima, 1988). To obtain a more accurate assessment of poverty levels among Asian Americans, it is necessary to take into consideration factors other than ethnicity, such as recency of arrival, country of origin and socioeconomic status in the home country.

The relationship between recency of arrival and poverty is displayed in Table 2.4; it documents the percentage living below poverty level by the time of their arrival in the US. Two factors appear to account for this relationship: 1) the time it takes new arrivals to adjust to a new society, as well as their loss of both occupational position and income, and 2) the selectivity of migration that reveals that later arrivals are less likely to have the socio-economic resources of the earlier arrivals. In general, US-born Asians are unlikely to live below the poverty level, while recent immigrants and refugees are frequently below poverty level. It is precisely in the latter group where we find language minority students.

Table 2.5 Reliance on public assistance in 1979

	Per cent of households with	
	No income from earnings	Public assistance
White	18.4	5.9
Black	23.4	22.3
Hispanic	15.7	15.9
Japanese	9.5	4.2
Chinese	10.2	6.6
Filipino	7.0	10.0
Korean	8.1	6.2
Asian Indian	16.3	4.5
Vietnamese	20.1	28.1

Source: Gardner, R.W., Robey, B. and Smith, P.C. (1985), 'Asian Americans: Growth, change and diversity', *Population Bulletin* **40** (4).

Table 2.5 shows statistics on public assistance by ethnic group. Compared with blacks and Hispanics, Asians are less likely to be on public assistance. Specifically, Japanese and Asian Indian are less likely to be on public assistance than mainstream whites. Vietnamese, however, are the one group most likely to receive public assistance, according to the 1980 Census. However, the figures do not separate out other refugee groups, nor do they reflect the patterns of public assistance dependency since 1980. The pattern of dependency varies by group and their length of residence in the US. The Vietnamese people who arrived in 1975 have decreased their welfare dependency to levels below those of blacks. Although the image of Asians as welfare-free prevails, recent migrants and refugees suffer from serious poverty and have high levels of welfare dependency, especially Southeast Asian refugees.

Although we have not been able to obtain more recent sources, the data on which Tables 2.4 and 2.5 are based (Garner, Robey and Smith, 1985), indicate that several of the Asian American groups have a considerable proportion of their populations living below poverty levels upon arrival to the US, and consequently, many of them have required public assistance. Table 2.4 shows that US-born Chinese, Japanese and Korean have lower percentages of persons living below poverty levels than members of the same groups born outside the US, and that members of the same groups who arrived after 1975 tend to be of lower income than their predecessors. In contrast, US-born Filipinos and those who arrived between 1975 and 1980 have about the same proportion of members living under the poverty level. The Vietnamese population (which did not arrive in significant numbers to the US until after 1975) shows a trend toward an increase in low-income population.

Table 2.5 shows an overall distribution of both mainstream white and ethnic populations needing public assistance. There is an striking contrast

Table 2.6 *Ethnicity and per cent of school-aged children living below the poverty level in 1979*

Ethnicity	Below poverty (per cent)
White	10.0
Black	35.6
Chinese	15.7
Japanese	4.2
Korean	12.0
Filipino	6.2
Vietnamese	43.4

Source: Gardner, R.W., Robey, B. and Smith, P.C. (1985), 'Asian Americans: Growth, change and diversity', *Population Bulletin* **40** (4).

between two groupings; while mainstream whites, Japanese, Chinese, Asian Indians, and, to a lesser extent, Koreans tend to rely on private resources in order to solve their economic problems in times of insufficient or no earnings, black, Hispanic and Vietnamese resort to public assistance. Again, this information is outdated, and does not include more recent arrivals, especially the Hmong, Khmer and Cambodian, but no recent information was available to the authors. Is there a net decrease in the use of public assistance on the part of the Chinese, Japanese and Koreans? From data in the previous table, this seems to be the case.

While the previous information on the proportion of various populations below poverty level is important, it is also important to examine the relative impact of poverty on school-age children. Table 2.6 gives us a general picture of the comparison between white and Asian American populations. Poverty seems to have the least impact on two groups, the Japanese and Filipinos, who have relatively small groups of school-age children living in poverty. All other groups, Vietnamese, Blacks, Chinese and Korean have higher percentages of children living in poverty than whites.

The condition of poverty has an overwhelming impact on school-age children. Although we do not have recent figures on Asian American populations, especially on the more recent comers (Hmong, Khmer and Cambodians), we know that a good portion of these groups lives in very poor neighborhoods. It is estimated that 90 per cent of the Hmong live at or below the poverty level. We feel that the economic differences among Asian Americans predetermine their educational achievement.

Often the educational success of Asian Americans is explained in terms of the high expectations held by teachers and other adults. Along with this factor, the cultural values of the Asian families, the family cohesiveness as a source of emotional support and motivation for high achievement can be a critical factor in explaining the drive for success of many Asian American children. What are the characteristics of Asian American households in this country? Table 2.7 shows the household composition by various ethnic groups. A female-headed household is often seen as an indicator of being

Table 2.7   Household composition in 1980

	Per cent female-headed household	Household size	Per cent non-nuclear
White	10.1	2.7	5.9
Black	29.8	3.1	12.9
Hispanic	18.1	3.5	10.6
Japanese	10.1	2.7	8.4
Chinese	11.1	3.1	11.6
Filipino	12.3	3.6	15.2
Korean	11.2	3.4	8.4
Asian Indian	6.4	2.9	8.8
Vietnamese	14.2	4.4	20.3

Source: Gardner, R.W., Robey, B. and Smith, P.C. (1985), 'Asian Americans: Growth, change and diversity', *Population Bulletin* **40** (4).

at-risk. In general, Asian families are as likely or slightly more likely to have female-headed households than white families. At the same time, however, Asian families have a significantly lower percentage of female-headed households than blacks and Hispanics. Vietnamese Americans, whose refugee experience generated considerable family disruption (such as the death or separation of spouses) prove the exception. Other Southeast Asian groups are also likely to have high percentages of female-headed households due to disruptions caused by wars and their aftermaths. Approximately one out of every four adult Cambodian females is a widow and, in a sample of Cambodian students, approximately half live in single-parent households (Rumbaut and Ima, 1988)). Since most statistical surveys remain insensitive to the consequences of war and the traumas inflicted on refugee populations, these observations only hint at the problems affecting disrupted households.

Other variations reflect recency of arrival of Asian populations. Those who came more recently have larger household sizes, more children and members of the extended family. In general, Asian households are more likely to have more members of the extended family than other groups, thus indicating a greater reliance on extended kin networks. This characteristic is typical among Filipino, Chinese and Vietnamese households. These figures are conservative when compared with Asians who have entered the US more recently, especially Southeast Asian refugees such as the Hmong, where the average household size is approximately 8 persons.

Table 2.8 describes average household sizes of recent immigrants and the presence in the household of non-nuclear family individuals among various ethnic groups. Additionally, the table describes those characteristics of households of immigrants who entered the US between 1975 and 1980. On the average, Asian households are larger in size, especially those groups with a substantial proportion of recent immigrants. The more recent arrivals have a larger than average household size. Non-nuclear members refers to relatives outside of the nuclear family and to those not related to household

Table 2.8 Ethnicity, household size, per cent non-nuclear member

	Total		Immigrated 1975–80	
	Household size	Per cent non-nuclear	Household size	Per cent non-nuclear
White	2.7	6		
Black	3.1	13		
Hispanic	3.5	10		
Japanese	2.7	9	2.9	37
Chinese	3.1	12	3.9	53
Filipino	3.6	16	5.4	60
Korean	3.4	8	4.8	51
Asian Indian	2.9	9	3.5	45
Vietnamese	4.4	20	4.4	62

Source: Gardner, R.W., Robey, B. and Smith, P.C. (1985), 'Asian Americans: Growth, change and diversity', *Population Bulletin* **40** (4).

members. Ethnographic observations suggest that household composition varies with groups, with Cambodians more likely to have non-kin in the same household (Ima, Velasco, and Yip, 1983).

Members of the extended family and other household non-related members often bring additional monies to help boost the family income and cushion temporary unemployment of the adults. They also make it possible to share child care services and the cost of rents or mortgages. In all like-lihood, the extended family household will continue among Filipino and Vietnamese families into the next decade, but for Asians as a whole, there appears to be a tendency towards the American standard of nuclear family households with a residual temporary group of relatives or friends in the household.

What implications do these household characteristics have on the academic achievement of Asian American youngsters, especially those non-fluent in English? In general, households reflect both a support system and a drain on family finances. Among some groups, such as the Vietnamese, large households are positively associated with schooling since larger households pool resources and are better able to cover the needs of individuals (Rumbaut and Ima, 1988). On the other hand, other groups, such as the Samoan households, which are already large and have family traditions that rely on collectivity to obtain financial support for travelling and covering special expenses, seem to create conditions of lesser upward social mobility and to encourage youngsters to leave schooling before the completion of secondary or post-secondary credentials (Hsu, 1971). Among the Viet-namese, resources are shared to finance schooling, and hence the social mobility of youngsters is promoted. These observations suggest a complexity which combines both structural characteristics, such as household size, with cultural norms, thus generating different schooling outcomes.

In sum, the socio-economic data offered uncover a wide range of relative success and well-being, or even at risk characteristics of some Asian American populations which affect both school failures and successes. The Southeast Asian refugee groups are poorer and rely more on public assistance than even the traditionally at-risk ethnic minority groups (blacks and Hispanics). When compared with whites, the Chinese, Koreans and Vietnamese have larger percentages of children living below the poverty level. Additionally, these same groups (and the Filipinos) have higher percentages of female-headed households, a measure commonly associated with educational at-risk students.

Aside from these comparative figures, we have addressed the apparent paradox of how these conditions exist in the face of the overall statistics of success and well-being for Asians and Pacific Islanders, but we noted the significant differences in income and education for that population. At one end of the spectrum, we have well-educated and well-to-do Asian immigrants, and at the other end we have illiterate and poor Asian immigrants and refugees. According to a study conducted by Wing-Cheung Ng (1977), 25 per cent of the Chinese labor force were professionals (with 7.7 per cent in engineering), a situation continuing into the 1990s. Chinese immigrants also had 19.8 per cent of workers in service industries and 17.8 per cent in craft work. Ng reported that 19.6 per cent of all Chinese males were involved in food service occupations, and of the Chinese females 14.5 per cent were in sewing occupations and 8.3 per cent in food services. Ethnographic observations of the various Asian and Pacific Islander ghettoes in New York's lower Manhattan Chinatown confirm the existence of hidden poverty, crowded quarters and crime. The reality of these at-risk conditions is associated with recency of residency in the US, which in turn is associated with the large percentage of Asian and Pacific Islander youngsters who are among recent arrivals. The troubles borne by the more recent arrivals are also seen in the figures on the larger sizes of households and percentages of households with non-nuclear family members. In short, any characterization of the socio-economic well-being of the Asian and Pacific Islander populations masks significant pockets of poor families with children who are at risk of failing in school.

School success of Asian Americans has attracted much attention in the anthropological literature (Ogbu, 1974, 1978, 1981, 1987, and 1989; Ogbu and Matute-Bianchi, 1986). Under the auspices of the California State Department of Education several significant papers on the sociocultural factors of minority achievement were published (1986). In previous publications sponsored by that office the language factors and theories on first and second language learning had been emphasized. A comparison of the differential achievement of various minority groups led several theoreticians, such as Ogbu and associates to create the 'model minority' and to identify cultural characteristics of the Chinese students not shared by the Mexican American, native Americans, Hawaiians, blacks and others students. The Chinese, according to Ogbu (1987, for example) develop a non-oppositional definition of ethnic identity, and retain as a point of reference for their work in the host countries their home cultural environment; consequently, they become immune to racism and oppression. School success for the Chinese, in Ogbu's view, is conditioned by cultural principles determining achievement motivation. Recent studies begin to show that not all Chinese student populations are equally successful, and that other minorities are also successful. Some scholars have argued (Wong, S. 1987) that we should search for the sociocultural factors that are unique to each language minority group, and then design programs which capitalize on these factors and are culturally congruent. These factors, which form the social and cultural context of learning, or the 'interactive and contextual nature of learning' (Rogoff, 1990) have been discussed by a number of scholars alluded to earlier (see Chapter 1).

Some twenty years ago the relationship of language and culture and the distinct relationships of both language and culture to learning were presented by scholars who compared African-Americans, Hispanics, native Americans and Pacific Islanders (Cazden, John and Hymes, 1972). We learned about the revealing differences of those groups, but we did not begin to identify the relevant parameters to address the wide variety of students from Asian Pacific Island backgrounds. We have made little progress in our empirical understanding of these populations. According to S. Wong:

> If, ten years after the immigration reforms took full effect, in a large urban center away from regions with the highest concentrations of Asian immigrants, schools still found themselves overwhelmed, one wonders whether the presence of Asian immigrant students and their language needs have been adequately recognized by decision-makers in education (Wong, S., 1988:204).

One of the most frequent details observed throughout recent studies is that East Asians seem to do well no matter the quality of the teacher (Wong-Fillmore and Britsch, S., 1988), and yet this presumed immunity to the quality of the teacher masks unmet needs (Tsang, 1983). Cummins has addressed these needs repeatedly (Cummins, 1986, 1989). The *Handbook for Teaching Khmer Students* (Ouk, Huffman and Lewis, 1988) is an especially notable example, because of its attempt to incorporate Cummins' and Krashen's theoretical frameworks into a format appropriate for Khmer students. The *Handbook* even suggests that teachers seriously consider using the Khmer language for teaching Cambodian-limited English proficient students. The Asian handbook reflects an attempt of the Bilingual Education Office to address the specificity of needs and solutions for the variety of Asian Pacific Islander groups. Nevertheless, the information is largely anecdotal, for the most part remains truncated and is only suggestive of fully developed programs. Indeed, the booklets can't be viewed as fully developed materials for schools wishing to develop a model bilingual program of the various Asian and Pacific Islander languages.

While decrying that little research has been done on this population, S. Wong suggests areas based on Schuman's acculturation model of second language acquisition:

1　Experience of immigration (struggle for survival)
2　Asian ethnicity (racial relations)
3　Linguistic and cultural baggage (home country ways)
4　Adopting unproductive responses when acquiring English
5　Distinct language needs (unique linguistic differences) (S. Wong, 1987:206–210).

What we find in S. Wong's analysis is an attempt to specify the historical as well as cultural conditions realistically shaping the learning environment in which Asian and Pacific Islander students work. Unfortunately, she presents modest empirical evidence to document the relationship between the sociocultural factors in the learning environment and the resulting educational outcomes. If S. Wong is correct, then the quality of the school learning environment and instruction has implications for student achievement. Lesson plans, intergroup relations and assistance to students with language problems are matters that should concern teachers. Wong does not seem to support Ogbu's cultural ecological position (Ogbu, 1974, 1978, 1981, 1987, 1989), but rather she emphasizes the quality of the learning environment as having significant consequences for all students, including Asian students.

The impact of demographics in the California schools is intimately related to the population trends among immigrant and refugee groups. Recent trends mean a continued increase in the school enrollment of Asian and Pacific Islander population, which, along with native American, black, and Hispanic populations are the major ethnic minority groups identified in California public schools (Garcia and Espinosa, 1976, Foote, Espinosa and Garcia, 1970). Of these four groups, the Asians and Pacific Islanders are the fastest growing, having increased by 142 per cent between 1970 and 1980 (US Bureau of the Census, 1981). While Hispanics will continue to be the largest ethnic group, the Asian and Pacific Islanders have become the second largest ethnic group in California since 1985. Their growth is not uniform, and it concentrates in the larger metropolitan areas such as San Francisco, Los Angeles and San Diego. In the San Diego City Schools, Asian enrollment reached 18.6 per cent during the fall of 1988, and in the San Francisco Unified Schools, the Chinese enrollment alone exceeded 23 per cent. Thus, the impact of Asians is more intensive in some selected areas, but reaches areas which traditionally had few Asians, including rural areas, which may be even less equipped to provide appropriate instruction for language minority students. Overall, the estimates of Asian and Pacific Islander student growth is probably conservative, with a possible 12 per cent of all K-12 students by the year 2000. Another projected figure is 13.5 per cent, but regardless of the precise figure, we anticipate continued significant

Table 2.9   Population projection of California's ethnic school enrollment

	1980 per cent	1990 per cent	2000 per cent	2010 per cent	2020 per cent	2030 per cent
Anglo	59.8	51.5	44.9	39.2	35.0	32.6
Black	8.7	8.3	7.7	7.2	6.8	6.4
Hispanic	24.6	30.5	35.3	39.2	42.0	43.4
Asian	6.9	9.7	12.1	14.4	16.2	17.6
Total	100.0	100.0	100.0	100.0	100.0	100.0

Source: Bouvier, L.F. and Martin, P.L. (1987), *Population Change and California's Education System*, Washington, DC: Population Reference Bureau, Inc.

Table 2.10   API K-12 California public school students for 1988–89

API ethnic group	Number	Per cent of total enrollment
Asian	345,201	7.5
Filipino	100,334	2.2
Pacific Islanders	23,754	0.5
Total API	469,289	10.2

Source: California Department of Education (1989) *Language Census Report 1988*, Sacramento, CA: California Department of Education.

Table 2.11   Projected percentages of ethnic group in California's work force 1980–2030

	1980 per cent	1990 per cent	2000 per cent	2010 per cent	2020 per cent	2030 per cent
Anglo	70	62	55	48	43	38
Black	7	7	7	7	7	7
Hispanic	17	22	27	31	35	38
Asian	6	9	11	14	15	17
Total	100	100	100	100	100	100

Source: Bouvier, L.F. and Martin, P.L. (1987), *Population Change and California's Education System*, Washington, DC: Population Reference Bureau, Inc.

growth. The projection shown in Table 2.9 has already proved to be over-ly conservative, as the actual enrollment for 1990 was 10.3 per cent, 0.6 per cent above the predicted 9.7. Table 2.10 provides the Asian and Pacific Islander K-12 California Public School Student Projection for 1988–1989.

What will happen to California's labor force composition as a result of these population changes? There will be an increase in the number of Asians and Pacific Islanders as well as Hispanic workers with a decline in the white labor force and a stationary black proportion of workers. Hence, the state's economy will rest more on Asian and Hispanic workers than the current levels as shown in Table 2.11. As a consequence, the education of these populations will become increasingly more important for both affirmative action goals and the sheer need for a trained labor force. Given the high rates of Asians and Pacific Islanders into the post-secondary educational system, California's investment in creating a skilled labor force will generate even higher rates of return among Asian youths because of their tendency to continue schooling. Hence, it would appear to be in the economic interests of California to carefully assess one of its main resources — people. The political ramifications of these changes are obvious with an increasing importance of Asians and Pacific Islanders as a constituency, but there remains a gap in the interim between today and the time when political influence of Asians and Pacific Islanders matches their numbers. The interim is a time for advocacy since the newer minority groups have less say in the political arena while needing, in many ways, more attention as they develop capacity for full participation in this society.

Hidden at-risk population, such as the English-monolingual Asian and Pacific Islander population, consists of those students whose families have been in this country for more than a generation, and of those who, having lived overseas, have a grasp of the English language sufficient to attend primary language programs. Though English-monolingual persons are not the central focus of this chapter, it has been noted that many Pacific Islanders and Filipinos from so-called English speaking homes manifest problems in the development of the English language for purposes of critical thinking necessary in academic assignments. Aside from those who are misclassified as deficient in English (due to phonetic differences), there are many whose English language is inadequate and non-standard, such as some Hawaiian children who speak pidgin English. These children need special attention and language development programs.

The use of standardized tests seems to reflect continued below-average performance in verbal tasks, especially for newcomers. While among older Asian communities student test scores have approached the levels of native US-born whites, controlling for educational background, a verbal gap still persists. Why? What does this suggest about the need to inquire into the verbal performance of Asian Americans? Do they need special attention in the development of oral and written forms of English? In short, little information is available on the monolingual English speaking Asian and Pacific Islander student population, whose language needs may indeed be diverse, and which includes individuals whose English language competency is below average. California State of Schools Superintendent Honig's advisory council for Asians and Pacific Islanders has suggested an investigation of this problem, now being pursued in a special study of 8th graders (Fong, Hom, Ima, and Yung, 1989).

Asians and Pacific Islanders as an aggregate are among the newest of the growing numbers of culturally and linguistically different school aged students in the US. Their numbers have grown and are expected to grow even further, resulting in increasing student diversity, especially in the large urban centers and also in smaller and more rural school districts. The public image of Asian Americans as high achievers, especially in light of the highly publicized studies of low academic performance of other students of color, has made them a center of attention by school administrators, and an incentive for finding alternative teaching strategies or for getting schools 'off the hook' by explaining outcomes as primarily a result of the children's cultural background. Although racial or ethnic origin as an explanation of differential achievement is clearly a parochial American view, it also raises important issues on a comparative basis for understanding the schooling of minorities in other societies as well as in our own society.

This past decade has seen a plethora of reports which document the inadequacies of American schools in meeting the needs of the changing school population. The *California Tomorrow*'s report (Olsen, 1988) and the *National Coalition of Advocates for Students*' report (First and Carrera, 1988) are only a few of the most recent statements to point out the inadequacy of current schooling practices in bringing quality education to Asian and Pacific Islander language minority students. The Advisory Council on Asian Pacific Affairs to the California State Superintendent of Public Instruction recommended measures directed towards the needs of students which have been neglected (Fong, Hom, Ima and Yung, 1989).

Governor George Deukmejian's *Commission on Educational Quality*, the *California Business Roundtable*, and other bodies reviewing the current state of California's educational system have added further commentaries on the need to upgrade educational services. These commentaries and the obvious demographic changes that have occurred and will continue to occur should make us understand that we are probably at a watershed point of critical changes in our schools (Gifford and Gillett, 1986).

During this past decade the support for bilingual education has diminished significantly all over the State of California and in the United States, as reflected in looser standards for requiring bilingual program services and training bilingual teachers, and the decisions of school boards and other bodies to abandon instruction in home languages. Bilingual education programs have slackened not only for Spanish language speakers but also for speakers of Asian and Pacific Island languages. Programs are facing reduced budgets, and primary languages are being replaced by 'sheltered English'. This turn of events does not create a disaster for all Asian American minority language students since the services provided under the auspices of bilingual laws are still in a rudimentary state. Nevertheless, if and when substantial bilingual legislation is passed, questions might be raised about the feasibility of new programmatic efforts to upgrade educational services for Asian and Pacific Islander students which approximate the quality of services being rendered to native English speaking students. Beyond the need for bilingual education, we need to look into the cultural and social conditions of Asian newcomers and the organization of school programs that are adequate to meet student needs.

Throughout the United States there has been a significant growth in the Asian and Pacific Islander population from less than one per cent in 1970 to one and a half per cent in 1980 and an expected 4 per cent in the year 2000, a projected growth of 300 percent in 30 years (Gardner, Robey and Smith, 1985). Asians are highly concentrated in a few states, especially California, Hawaii, New York, Illinois and Texas. Smaller, but historically significant numbers will emerge in other states as well. Their concentration occurs not only in particular states and cities, but in particular school districts such as Boston, Houston, San Jose, Santa Ana, and other districts generally located within large inner cities that provide low-cost housing and easy access to entry level jobs.

In California, Asians and Pacific Islanders currently constitute 7 per cent of the state's population with a projected growth to approximately 11 per cent in the year 2000. They have already affected school enrollments out of proportion to their numbers, since they are, on the average, a much younger population. At the K-12 level, their numbers exceeded the California's black enrollment in 1985; currently Asians and Pacific Islanders are 10.2 per cent of the K-12 population, whereas black students constitute 8.9 per cent of that population. Who could have predicted that this was to be a consequence of the 1965 immigration law, especially the growth of Filipino, Korean and other Pacific Islander populations? Who could have imagined the US defeat in Vietnam and the consequent flow of over 900,000 Southeast Asian refugees in the United States to date? Refugees now constitute over one million US residents (Rumbaut and Weeks, 1986). About 40 per cent of that refugee population resides in California. These two historic events, along with other more predictable ones, account for the rapid population growth. Additional circumstances, such as the transfer of power in Hong Kong to the mainland government, are likely to generate additional numbers of Asian Pacific Islander students in the American schools.

Prior to 1965, relatively few Asians migrated to this country due to immigration laws restricting the influx of individuals from Asian countries. The 1965 US immigration law opened the possibilities for Asian arrivals, resulting in the largest proportions in history coming from Asia rather than Europe. It should be noted that the motivation of migration stems not only from the openness of US policy but also from push factors which have been motivating Asians to leave their home countries. For example, the Philippines face an ongoing economic crisis resulting in the impoverishment of the average Filipino. Chinese from overseas countries are fleeing from persecution and economic instabilities in their countries of residence. On the other hand, individuals in countries which are prospering, such as most European countries and Japan, have little motivation to leave.

During the 1970s, the net immigration to the US numbered 6.6 million persons. Since 1960, the origins of immigrants were 34 per cent Asian, 34 per cent Latin American, 16 per cent European and 16 per cent other places. In 1979, 49 per cent were from Latin America, 41 per cent from Asia and 14 per cent from Europe. The earlier trend of shrinking proportions from Europe and increasing proportions from Asia and Latin America is strongly re-confirmed. In 1985, over 80 per cent of all immigrants came from Latin America and Asia. Secondary migrations from outside California and even secondary migrations within California have distributed Asian populations unevenly. The settlement locations have not been selected randomly, but rather chosen in urbanized sunbelt regions, where job opportunities are better.

In this country the median age for US-born persons is 32 years; for Cambodians 18 years; for Hmong 13 years; for Japanese 33 years; for Lao 19 years; for Mexican 22 years; and for Vietnamese 21 years (Rumbaut and Weeks, 1986). Another indication of the continued high rate of growth of the Asian populations is their fertility rate. Fertility rates of various groups are: Hmong, 11.9 per cent; Cambodian, 7.4 per cent; Lao, 4.6 per cent; Viet-namese, 3.4 per cent; Mexican, 2.9 per cent (Rumbaut and Weeks, 1986). As can be seen, the Southeast Asian groups have even higher fertility rates than those of Mexican origin, a group with a traditionally high fertility rate. These high levels of fertility among Asians and Pacific Islanders mean a continuing youthfulness of this population, and consequently continued growth of their school-aged populations.

Thus, while the flow of refugee and immigrant populations from Asia and the Pacific Islands continues, the main sources for over-representation in the school-age populations is the natural growth of the various Asian communities which are formed primarily by a large number of individuals in child-bearing age, and consequently with a potential for more rapid growth, in contrast with the mainstream communities in the US whose mean age is above that of all Asian immigrants except the Japanese. To this fact we must also add the cultural preference for larger families which are started at an earlier age. Although the average ages and fertility rates of Asian immigrant and refugee families will probably decline over time, at this point Asian Americans, like other minority groups (notably Hispanics) have a dispro-portionate share of the school-age student population.

It is very difficult to generalize the demographic characteristics of the Asian populations because of their intragroup and intergroup diversity. Some Asian families who have been in this country for several generations are more likely to have reduced their fertility rates and become part of main-stream middle or upper classes. However, the more recent arrivals, who are a very young population and have high fertility rates, will continue to grow more rapidly than both older groups and the general US population. It is precisely from these newer generations that the vast majority of Asian and Pacific Islander language minority students will come.

California's growth of the Asian and Pacific Islander populations ex-ceeds all other states, with the possible exception of Hawaii. California has the largest proportion of the growing Asian LEP population. California's projected population data indicates that by the year 2030, 50 per cent of

Hispanics and 75 per cent of Asians 3 to 24 years will be immigrants or children of immigrants who arrived after 1980. The bulk of the Asian population will consist of recently arrived individuals to the West coast, whose language and culture will be at variance with those of California's schools. However, the impact of Asian student populations will also affect other major urban centers and many previously untouched smaller cities in the Midwest, such as Des Moines, Iowa, in the heartland of America.

The consequences of growth for educational institutions are the increase of students with different languages, cultures and life experiences. In the face of these changes, are US schools prepared to meet the needs of their new students? What are the consequences for service providers? The Lau v. Nichols decision requires schools to take into account the student's home language, but because of the large numbers of Hispanic students, the impression in the public's mind is that bilingual programs serve primarily Hispanics. Therefore, it may surprise many to discover that half of all Asian and Pacific Islander youth comes from homes where a primary language other than English is spoken (Chan, K.S., 1983), and approximately a quarter of California's LEP students are Asians or Pacific Islanders. Wherever new Asian residents settle, whether in San Francisco or Syracuse (New York) the language issue will be of primary concern.

Although Asian and Pacific Islander language minority students form a significant portion of student enrollment in many school districts, they have not yet been fully incorporated into schooling programs such as special education, bilingual and other programs commensurate with their numbers. Nationally, even though there are some Chinese and Thai speech, language and hearing specialists in the United States, thus far, there is not a single registered specialist who is certificated to deal with any of the Southeast Asian groups (Cheng, 1991). The most advanced services have been extended only to Chinese speakers but not to Khmer, Hmong, Lao or Vietnamese language groups (Siegel and Halog, 1986). Teachers face the problem of ascertaining the source of a student's problems: is it linguistic or cultural, psychological and associated with trauma, neurological in origin, or perhaps a combination of the above? If a teacher observes heightened anxiety, confusion in the locus of control, withdrawal, or unresponsiveness of a linguistic minority child, can the teacher determine whether or not the child is suffering from cultural shock, or a handicapping condition or perhaps both? This small example alludes to the larger question of how well our schools have been prepared in general to deal with linguistically and culturally varied school-age populations.

One impetus for examining the education of Asians and Pacific Islanders is the uneasy feeling among educators that the needs of Asian and Pacific Islander language minority students are not being adequately served by bilingual programs throughout the country. Many schools appear to provide what amounts to a sink or swim language policy, contrary to the country's long standing policy of bilingual education. Thus, for example, in many schools Limited English Proficient Asian students are placed in English instruction classrooms without special linguistic services and the time needed to successfully integrate them into the regular classroom activities. Even where bilingual services are above minimum requirements, there is emphasis on English language-based methods in spite of repeated claims made by second language experts on the superiority of primary language-based programs. In the few Chinese bilingual programs which have had fully bilingual Chinese/English teachers, English is the main language of instruction, with supplementary use of the Chinese language. For example, Wong-Fillmore (1979) describes two Chinese bilingual classrooms in which the Chinese language is used to reinforce content matter presented in the English language. Guthrie (1985) also observed a Chinese bilingual program which did not receive strong support from Chinese speaking parents who, for the most part, felt it was a waste of time to teach in the Chinese language and far more important to teach in the English language.

There is some reluctance on the part of bilingual teachers to use fully bilingual programs for Asian and Pacific Island students. The schools are also facing a number of logistics problems as they attempt to develop bilingual programs for Asian American students. To provide instructional services in English and in a number of primary languages for Asian and Pacific Islander students is vastly more complicated than to offer classes in Spanish and English. Given the longer history of Spanish language bilingual programs and the larger numbers of native Spanish speakers, the Spanish/English bilingual programs have received the most attention and support. Furthermore, in the face of the greater maturity and sophistication of Spanish/English programs, questions are raised by Asian and Pacific Islander bilingual professionals about the appropriateness of programs and instructional approaches for language minority students from Asian and Pacific Island background.

Concluding Thoughts

In clear contrast with the pervasive 'model minority' image which identifies Asian Americans as high achievers, and the little attention and concern to actively provide primary language-based programs and other services to help Asian students adjust to schools and society, Hsia (1986) and other researchers have noted that greater variations in performance exist within ethnic groups than between groups, Asians not withstanding. Tsang's observations (1988) of math performances of Asian foreign-born students likewise points out a great diversity of individual performances even in the face of what seems to be superior math scores. Rather than basing policies solely on ethnic categories, one needs to develop policies which address the educational needs of all children, including the vast array of Asian and Pacific Islander language minority children who appear to be falling through the cracks of existing programs. Hence, we need to look beyond stereotypes directly to students in need of improved services. Cazden and Mehan (1989) stress the need for an understanding of the instructional processes which elevate or downgrade students, not by emphasizing solely the cultural dimensions, but also by focusing on the interaction between teacher and student. They suggest the need to understand how to manage instruction as well as the social levels of classroom organization which channel students towards success or failure. They also caution us about the implied stereo-typing which accompanies our reliance on inventories of students' cultural patterns, learning styles, communication styles, perhaps with the unrealis-tic intent of matching them with teacher and communication styles in the classroom.

A problem with the 'model minority' theme is the apparent contra-diction between the appearance of academic excellence among Asian and Pacific Islander language minority youth and their US-born compatriots versus the performance of many Asian or Pacific Islanders viewed in school as at-risk of failure. A comparison between Asian and Pacific Islanders and Spanish-speaking language minority students, in general, reveals that Asian American students appear to be making the transition into the English language more successfully than Spanish language speakers (Chan, K.S., 1983; Baratz-Snoden and Duran, 1987). Even controlling for length of stay in the US, Asian and Pacific Islander language minority students perform better on standard English verbal tests than their Spanish language counterparts and seem less affected negatively by their primary language. In addition, it is also observed that the level and intensity of home language instruction is considerably less for Asians and Pacific Islanders than for Hispanics. Assuming these observations are correct, even controlling for social class and other resources, does this suggest that less attention is needed for Asian and Pacific Islander language minority students? The insistence that Asians are doing better than Spanish speakers in the acqui-sition of the English language as well as in subject matter, preempts opportunities for Asian and Pacific Islander minority students to participate in, and benefit from, bilingual programs.

Where do Asians and Pacific Islanders fit into bilingual education? A theoretical framework is found in the California State Department of Education supported document, *Schooling and Language Minority Students* (California State Department of Education, 1981). This theoretical work is based on data from international sources on the phenomenon of second lan-guage acquisition, such as the famous Canadian studies of French language acquisition of children from English-speaking homes (Lambert and Tucker, 1972). There are numerous theoretical developments regarding how second language is acquired and how effective methods and political considerations in developing bilingual services, especially the works of Cummins and Krashen, span the recent past (see Cummins, 1989; Krashen and Biber, 1988). The end results are theoretical statements promoting the development of the student's primary language, the positive academic benefits of bilingualism, the importance of comprehensible inputs and a positive recognition of a student's social standing. Krashen and Biber (1988) cite successful bilingual programs, based principally on experiences with Spanish language programs. They interpret the data as support for the preferability of developing literacy in the primary language before transferring students into all English language-based classes.

The theoretical frameworks, in their abstract forms, appear to be principles equally applicable to all Asian American and other language minority students. Yet there exists an uneasiness with these theoretical claims due in large part to the translation of these ideas into actions at the school site affecting Asian and Pacific Islander language minority students. There is little transition from theory to action in terms of materials development, staff development and training and curriculum, which supports primary language services to these populations. There were some efforts in developing Chinese language services, but since its initial development, such services have atrophied. For example, San Francisco Unified School District has only one fully bilingual elementary school, but for the most part offers an English-based transition program, in spite of having a large number of Chinese-speaking Limited English Proficient students. Thus, though the theoretical framework takes into account a full range of alternatives ranging from full primary language maintenance program to English-only programs, there remains an uneasy connection between theory and application, especially in programs serving the Asian or Pacific Islander language minority student. (For additional information on Filipino, Japanese, Vietnamese, Korean and Chinese students, see the various handbooks produced by the Bilingual Education Office, of the California State Department of Education, 1983a, 1983b, 1984, 1986, 1987).

The data presented here not only bring to light the striking cultural and linguistic differences among Asian and Pacific Islander groups, but invite reflection on the fundamental role of home language maintenance in order to achieve in schools. What are the consequences of home language loss in these communities who depend so much on each other and hold high family values? Why is bilingualism an asset not just for the nation's increased linguistic resources, but for the individuals who have skills in several languages? What is the role of schools in helping children and communities maintain their native languages? What kinds of programs should be developed to meet the specific needs of Asian and Asian Pacific Islanders?

American schools in California, and throughout the nation, are beginning to take a closer look at the future of our country in which cultural diversity is best seen as an asset, and hatred-motivated crimes, racism, and intolerance for diversity are seen as a serious social handicap. To learn this lesson, however, it is important to underline the socio-economic, political and educational contexts of schooling in America. Increasing uncertainty about where the country is going as a whole, uncertainty about what American culture is, and how to get ahead and succeed in the sense of the American economic and political success of the previous decades, makes schooling difficult and the job of teachers unfulfilling. We know that technically, militarily, economically, morally and educationally our success is in the hands of the teachers, but they alone cannot do it. The pervasive feeling that cultural diversity is deeply connected to the 'ethnic problem', and that xenophobic tendencies against anything looking 'ethnic' would discourage public support, keeps schools and teachers from innovating and advancing their goals. School personnel need a strong social support from all Americans. Mainstream society must take a firm step in stopping the tacit discontent with increased waves of immigrants and their alleged abuse of the American economic bonanza, employment and political and religious tolerance. Indeed, mainstream Americans ought to count their blessing and pick as a target of their attacks public ignorance and prejudice. Or do we want the kinds of ethnic success illustrated by individuals like Richard Rodriguez (see p. 74) who was ashamed of his family and native language? The irony of the confessions by Richard Rodriguez is that they show he became so isolated, so lonely, and so crippled psychologically that he sought intimacy through text with unknown readers and shared with them his most painful personal feelings. Alienated from his family, his peers, his community, he attacked the public use of home languages (especially the instructional use) and saw self-rejection as the means to become a good American (Rodriguez, 1982). As Suárez-Orozco eloquently puts it 'To give up Spanish to acquire English represents a symbolic act of ethnic renunciation: it is giving up the mother tongue for the instrumental tongue of the dominant group.' (Suárez-Orozco, M.M. and Suárez-Orozco, C., 1991). Is such a person an example of American success? Is becoming upper-middle class, fluent in English and educated the only criterion of success in America? Isn't retaining the home language and acquiring a second, third or fourth language an enrichment that should make Americans proud? The psychological traumas resulting from self-rejection, the break with ethnic community and family are a real tragedy that probably prevents many ethnic persons from fully developing their talents.

Chapter 3

Academic Achievement of Asian Minorities

There are a substantial number of studies documenting how minority groups use different approaches to resolve cultural conflicts and select various strategies to adapt to the United States' schools and society. These studies focus, for example, on the Japanese, Koreans (DeVos, 1967, 1973, 1980, 1982, 1988), Chinese (Guthrie, 1985, Wong-Fillmore, 1985), Indochinese (Trueba, Jacobs, and Kirton, 1990), Hawaiians (Au, 1980, 1981; Boggs, 1985; Jordan and Tharp, 1979) Mexicans (Ogbu and Matute-Bianchi, 1986; Carter and Segura, 1979; Delgado-Gaitan, 1986a, 1986b, 1990; San Miguel, 1987; Trueba, 1987a, 1987b; 1988a, 1988b; Delgado-Gaitan and Trueba, 1991) Central Americans (Suárez-Orozco, 1987, 1989); East Indians, specifically Punjabis (Gibson, 1987), native Americans (Mohatt and Erickson, 1981; Philips, 1982; Macias 1987), Indochinese (Trueba, Jacobs and Kirton, 1990); with the castelike minorities, Hawaiians, Mexican, native Americans and blacks (Ogbu, 1974, 1978, 1982, 1983, 1987, 1989); with all minority groups in a cross-cultural perspective (G. Spindler, 1987a, 1987b, 1987c; Spindler and Spindler, 1987a, 1987b; 1990; Trueba, 1989).

We have learned from these and other studies that the intergroup differences are at times as significant as the intragroup differences. We have also learned that the psychodynamics of motivation to acculturate, achieve or adapt in other fashions is as related to the transmission of the home culture as it is to the immediate context of the individual and the inter-actional circle in which he/she is socialized. Therefore, studies on the processes of socialization for academic achievement are becoming increas-ingly more important, but not without regard to the historical and cultural contexts of the larger groups. In light of these studies, we want to discuss the real or imputed success of Asian minorities in this country, and illustrate the discussion with some specific findings for several studies in California.

Articles in the popular press frequently point to the success story of Asian American students. However, educational statistics reveal that not all students from Asia and the Pacific Islands are successful in school (Hirschman and Morrison, 1986; Tsang and Wing, 1985). Success may be measured by performance on norm-reference test instruments or grade point average (Hsia, 1983; Lee, Y., 1984; Tsang and Wing, 1985). Examples of low achievement can be identified. The psychological isolation, and the perception of being ignored (Olsen, 1988), often lead Asian and Pacific Island students to drop out, engage in criminal activities and fail in school (Galang, 1988; Rumbaut and Ima, 1988).

The lack of services for Asian and Pacific Island students is related to teacher perception that these students do not need any help. No one denies that there is a relationship between school services and achievement outcomes, but just how these services and outcomes are interconnected remains an open question. The relationship between student services and achievement is also affected by students' socioeconomic and cultural background.

The Role of Home Languages in Academic Success

Achievement measures are varied, complex and imperfect reflections of long-term academic success. Indeed, these measures not only assume comparability of curriculum and testing skills, but they also reflect an aggregation of the home-learning experiences with those of the school. Consequently, from a longitudinal perspective, high performance in achievement tests does not necessarily reflect academic success, nor does low performance indicate failure. Furthermore, performance is domain specific. For example, studies citing the high grade point averages of Asian students also cite their low performances in English tests.

The role of primary language development in the acquisition of a second language, as well as in facilitating the educational achievement of language minority students, is discussed by Cummins (1981a, 1986, 1989). His studies became the cornerstone of the theoretical foundations for building bilingual instructional programs in California. The development of primary language skills beyond a minimum threshold, not only for conversational use but also for rigorous academic work, critical thinking and cognitive structuring is at the heart of bilingual education. Yet, in order to transfer knowledge and cognitive skills to another language, and in order to acquire sufficient proficiency in a second language for academic purposes, it is essential not only to be exposed to that language but also to receive a substantial amount of support and guidance in both languages. Because language is not acquired in cultural isolation, it is important to examine possible cultural conflicts that prevent the acquisition of a second language (see Chapter 1). Focusing on verb morphology, Galang reviewed (1988) six studies on the acquisition of Tagalog (or Pilipino) by Filipino children, and concluded that progress in language acquisition reflects linguistic processes (related to the mastery of syntactic structures, lexicon, semantic ranges, etc.) as much as non-linguistic processes (the internalization of cultural values, attitudes, and behaviors). It was also concluded from these studies that social and cognitive skills determine the domains, proficiency and the pace of language acquisition.

The processes of language acquisition and language and culture maintenance reflect an intimate relationship between language, culture and learning. In an ethnographic study of a sixth grade Chinese Title VII bilingual program conducted in an urban West Coast immigrant community, Guthrie (1985) describes students in terms of length of residence in the United States, their language abilities, and socioeconomic status. She also points out the difficulties associated with Chinese literacy encountered by teachers, and concludes that, unless there is sufficient evidence that maintenance of Chinese is both feasible and practical, it remains unlikely that the teachers will emphasize home language maintenance. These teachers are not alone in emphasizing English language proficiency as a practical solution to problems in communication and the acquisition of a high level of literacy for academic purposes.

English Language Proficiency

Adequate proficiency in English, requiring not only basic interpersonal communication skills, but also cognitive academic language proficiency (to use Cummins' terms), is essential for successful schooling in the United States. Studies conducted by DeAvila and Havassy (1974) and Duncan and DeAvila (1979) indicate that English proficiency is the most consistent predictor of academic achievement for language minority groups. If we add to English proficiency other variables, such as teacher judgment, then predictions of academic achievement are the most accurate. Rumbaut and Ima (1988) found English proficiency, as measured by the California Tests of Basic Skills (CTBS) reading scores, to be a significant predictor of grade point average among Southeast Asian students. However, going beyond the DeAvila study, they also found that the CTBS math scores were an even better predictor of grade point average. This observation reflects not only the greater variance in the math scores among Southeast Asian students, but also that the acquisition of English for the foreign-born is a long and painful process.

Achievement differences among various Chinese and other Asian language minority groups are related to their differential proficiency in English (DeAvila and Duncan, 1980). However, limited English language proficiency is not necessarily related to cognitive ability. The problems of English proficiency among Asian American students are a major concern to educators and Asian communities. Scholars have discussed some of these problems. Lum (1971), for example, discusses the isolation of Asian Americans as related to their 'traditionally quiet character' and their lack of knowledge of the English language and American social etiquette. Along the same lines, To (1979) discusses the problems faced by immigrant children and youth in the US. In his opinion proficiency in English can not only help immigrant children (especially Indochinese) raise their school achievement, but can also help them to better adjust to American society. Problems that Korean-speaking children and adults have in pronouncing English words are identified by Robson (1985).

According to Niyekawa (1986), children from the Pacific Islands, Laotian rural groups, and Montagnards from Vietnam have dual handicaps, since they come from countries with oral traditions and little or no exposure to written materials in their own language. Therefore, these children have problems differentiating the appropriate use of written language forms as used in the classroom from the oral forms of communication used in the playground. Other problems associated with the acquisition of English by Asian students in the context of English as a Second Language (ESL) classes are discussed by Liem (1980) and by Osborne-Wilson, Sinatra and Baratta (1989). Their observations cover topics concerning morphemics, syntax, semantics, phonology and discourse. Little systematic documentation and few strategies for the teaching of English to Asian or Pacific Island language minorities are available for teachers. Some linguists have emphasized contrastive and error analysis of Asian student English language use. These efforts have had little acceptance because of their limited application to practice and their controversial theoretical basis. Hakuta observes:

> Those interested in the universal aspects of second language acqui-sition have emphasized the similarities between learners of different language backgrounds learning the same target language. On the other hand, those interested in particulars have focused on the evid-ence of transfer specific to the learner's native language structure (Hakuta, 1986:237–238).

S. Wong (1987) supports a universal pattern in which linguists of the contrastive analysis viewpoint support particular differences between two or three different language groups. This debate is of key importance in the use of particular pedagogical approaches for specific language groups, in contrast with a universal approach to the teaching of English (or other mainstream language) for all language groups. In their critique of contrastive analysis, Dulay and Burt (1975) demonstrate that, in the process of language acqui-sition, errors made by first language learners are similar to the errors made by second language learners. Consequently, contrastive language analysis explains less intergroup variance than individual learning patterns. The critique of contrastive analysis is more a signal of change of theoretical emphases than an absolute rejection of a linguistic methodology. Similar arguments are made by Wong, who examines the work of Alfred Bloom, Matthew Chen and others who remain strong supporters of contrastive analysis. There remains the question of the 'weighting' of relative usefullness of assessing linguistic differences as a basis for judging successful acquisition of a second language, especially in view of the attacks against contrastive analysis. There is some evidence that both the grammar and phonetics of the home language tend to affect the acquisition of a new grammar and phonetic system (especially within certain age groups); this is so-called 'interference phenomena'. As Hakuta noticed: 'Evidence for transfer from the native language provides a fascinating avenue for the study of language universals and linguistic relativism, however, and should not be ignored' (Hakuta, 1986:233). Obviously, there is an urgent need for further study of how the child's primary language, particularly in the case of Asian and Pacific Island students, affects the acquisition of a second mainstream language. Some studies (see Hakuta, 1986) stress that: 1) bilingual children are cognitively more flexible than monolingual children, and 2) the process of becoming bilingual creates cognitive flexibility, but not the other way around (cognitive flexibility does not produce bilingualism). The effective use of a rich linguistic environment, one in which several languages are used in their appropriate contexts, seems to enhance the acquisition of additional languages. From a study conducted among 356 Spanish and Chinese children, Dulay and Burt (1975) note their creative construction, and their complex and strategic approaches to language learning, especially as children acquire new syntactic structures.

English as a Second Language

For some Asian immigrants, the acquisition of the English language is a relatively quick and easy task, executed without experiencing much trouble in keeping up with grade level academic content. Dependency on their primary language to continue learning seems unneccessary to many Asians because of their command of certain subject matters (especially mathematics and the sciences), which is often above the average of their US counterparts. The principle that a solid background in one's primary language forms a strong base for the acquisition of a second language has been defended by many scholars (Cummins, 1980, 1981a, 1981b, 1983, 1986, and 1989; Hakuta, 1986, and others). Can we assume from this body of literature that Asian students should be able to acquire English very quickly? The prevailing public image of Asian newcomer students is based on those who are successful in acquiring English language skills, but unfortunately, they do not represent the full range of Asian newcomer students. Many Asian newcomers never learn English well enough to enter mainstream classrooms, and many drop out of school prior to high school graduation because of language problems. These failures (often hidden), as well as the many successes of Asian students, need to be addressed in order to serve the full range of Asian American students. We will explore the variety of Asian responses to education in the US as well as the factors associated with success. In general, if we compare Asian American students with other immigrant students who have been in this country the same number of years, Asian American students seem to make the transition to the English language in a shorter amount of time and with more efficiency. There is, however, a wide range of paces and performances in the acquisition of English by Asian students. The following vignettes are illustrative of the differences noticed.

Nung Zou, the child of a Chinese PhD immigrated to the US is in her sophomore year of high school. In the beginning she could not speak or write the English language. The school counselor, failing to recognize that she came into the US academically above her American peers, placed her in the lowest level math and English classes. The placement in a lower level math class was especially ironic given her competence in both algebra and geometry. Soon she was moved to a higher level math class. Within a year, she made a successful transition into the English language, competing with US-born students in classes requiring high levels of content comprehension. Her language skills developed while she performed well in mathematics.

A-Bo came to the US from Taiwan at the age of 15 and knew very little English, but she had been an excellent student in Taiwan. She entered the San Jose public school and was placed in an ESL class. She excelled in her other classes to the point that she could assist her teacher in solving mathematical problems. Her self-esteem was very high. Her previous academic success laid a solid foundation for her US school success. In one year's time, she was not only fluent in English but also was leading class discussions and participating on the debate team. She is currently finishing her masters' program at the University of California, Davis. Although the previous two cases repeated time and again, we also find situations of the following case where the student failed to achieve. One needs to pay attention to diverse educational and personal needs of each student.

Shia-chi moved to Los Angeles when she was 15 years old. Her parents own a clothing factory in Taipei. They felt that Shia-chi would be able to receive a better education in the US and that she would have the opportunity to attend college. Shia-chi was a below-average student in her middle school. Although she had had three years of English, she came to US without having the ability to communicate, read or write. She was staying with her aunt, who owned a restaurant in Santa Monica. Her aunt was almost never home in the evenings or during the weekend. Shia-chi went home from school every afternoon and watched TV. She had a great deal of difficulty understanding what was going on in her classes. She attended ESL classes but did not do well in them. She had a few friends, but they were all Chinese-speaking. During weekends, Shia-chi would go to her friend's house, watch videos, dance and occasionally drink. After two years, Shia-chi is still doing poorly in classes and has exited from the ESL program. She is Limited English Proficient and is considered by educators to be an 'LEP forever' student. She will be graduating this summer and intends to go to a community college. How will she survive the academic and social demands of college?

Table 3.1 Educational under-representation by ethnicity, place of birth and language background

	Per cent under-represented			
	English language background		Non-English language background	
	Native-born	Foreign-born	Native-born	Foreign-born
Asian	16	5	11	68
White	9	1	7	2
Hispanics	10	1	48	41

Source: Cardenas, J.A., Robledo, M., and Waggoner, D. (1988) *The Undereducation of American Youth*, San Antonio, TX: Intercultural Development Research Association, Center for the Prevention and Recovery of Dropouts.

The information cannot be generalized and may be misleading, since many limited-English proficient (LEP) students struggle, do not succeed and often linger in 'LEP Foreverland' where they never achieve English language proficiency. There are many reasons why these students do not succeed, and educators need to be informed of the major differences between East and West orientations. Furthermore, questions need to be raised regarding education policy and equity. The following section illustrates the major match/mismatch of East vs. West aspects of education.

The foreign-born Asian groups, which were not exposed to the English language prior to their arrival in the US represent at-risk groups, perhaps the most neglected groups in America. This observation leads us to believe that there is a bimodal distribution of educational attainment among Asian groups, illustrated by the Chinese in one extreme (high achievers) and the Southeast Asians on the other (low achievers). Table 3.1 illustrates this bimodality in achievement distributions.

In a comparative analysis of the 1970 and 1980 Censuses, Kan and Liu (1986) observed this bimodal distribution. In the 1970 Census, Japanese, Chinese and Filipinos exceeded whites in the number of schooling years, but the achievement of the Chinese was far superior to that of the Filipinos. In 1970, the mainstream American population had more years of schooling than Asian minorities. For example, while only 4.5 per cent of whites had 4 years or less of schooling, 16.2 per cent of Chinese and 15.1 per cent of Filipinos had that level. By 1980, however, almost all Asian groups, except the Vietnamese, had more schooling than whites (among whom 20 per cent had four years or more of college): Chinese with four years of college or more 37 per cent, Japanese 26.3 per cent, Filipino 36.9 per cent, Korean 33.9 per cent, Asian Indian 51.5 per cent, Vietnamese 12.5 per cent. The increase in educational attainment for Asian immigrants between 1970 and 1980 was due to real increases in schooling and immigration of more educated Asians. During the years from 1965 to 1975 there was a dramatic increase in the number of immigrants with college degrees. However, since 1975 this number had declined due to the efforts among educated immigrants to bring

Table 3.2   Ethnicity and percentage distribution of number of schooling years

	Number of years of completed schooling		
	Less than 5 years per cent	5–8 years per cent	9–11 years per cent
Asian	15	24	60
White	3	17	80
Hispanic	10	34	56

Source: Cardenas, J.A., Robledo, M., and Waggoner, D. (1988) *The Undereducation of American Youth*, San Antonio, TX: Intercultural Development Research Association, Center for the Prevention and Recovery of Dropouts.

Table 3.3   Work status of undereducated youth by ethnicity

	Armed forces per cent	Civilian employed per cent	Civilian unemployed per cent	Not in labor force per cent
Asians	5	53	10	32
Blacks	5	39	18	39
Hispanics	3	64	13	20
Whites	5	61	16	18

Source: Cardenas, J.A., Robledo, M., and Waggoner, D. (1988) *The Undereducation of American Youth*, San Antonio, TX: Intercultural Development Research Association, Center for the Prevention and Recovery of Dropouts.

in their less educated relatives through family reunification and sponsorship programs.

Another way of looking at the bimodality of education among Asians is to look at the percentage distribution of years of schooling by race and ethnicity as shown in Table 3.2, which corresponds to the figures shown above on the various home language groups discussed earlier (see Table 3.1).

As a consequence of this bimodal distribution of educational levels, we find in the labor force large percentages of undereducated Asian young men, approaching those of black laborers, and larger percentages of unemployed Asians than those of whites (non-Hispanic) and Hispanics (see Table 3.3).

Asian undereducated young men are more likely not to enter the labor force, especially if high skills are required or the job has some prestige. Many Asian undereducated youth are often employed 'under the table' by fellow Asians in exploitive conditions (low wages and long hours) as waiters or garment workers. Official unemployment figures for Asians are higher than those for whites and Hispanics, and they approach the figures for blacks, which are the highest (32 per cent). The unemployment problems and poverty conditions of the Asian communities are normally ignored, but keep Asians at the bottom of the social structure — for example, the deplorable conditions of some ghetto areas of San Francisco's Chinatown.

Undereducation of some, and their ensuring exploitation, is not the only

Table 3.4   Dropout rates by ethnicity and grade

	Grade 10 per cent	Grade 11 per cent	Grade 12 per cent	Average per cent
Asian	4.0	4.1	5.5	4.4
Pacific Islander	8.1	7.9	35.6	14.9
Filipino	4.2	4.7	7.5	5.2
Hispanic	12.3	10.4	13.9	11.6
Black	12.8	10.5	14.1	11.9
White	5.0	5.6	7.9	5.9
Total	7.6	7.0	9.5	7.7

Source: California Department of Education. (1989) *Language Census Report 1988*, Sacramento, CA: California Department of Education.

problem faced by Asians in California. Figures on K-12 school dropout rates were generally low for Asians during the academic year 1986–1987, with the exception of Pacific Islanders. This high level of Pacific Islander dropout was also noted in San Diego City Schools. These figures, however, do not take into consideration Asians who arrived to this country with little education and have not continued onto higher grade levels.

A serious flaw in this data is that the category Asian covers a heterogeneous set of groups, each with its own unique problems of dropouts. Cambodians have the highest and Hmong the lowest dropout rate in San Diego. While there is no evidence of these trends in other cities with large Southeast Asian refugee youth, there are some indications that the overall dropout statistics mask at-risk pockets, especially notable among the Pacific Islanders that arrived most recently.

Data on high academic performance of Asians and Pacific Islanders is further complicated by the arbitrary aggregation across groups whose performance is lower. Therefore, in order to identify at-risk students, for example Filipino males, it is necessary to calculate achievement outcomes for separate groups in the various geographical areas, by sex and generation, and to consider the recency of arrival in the United States.

Asian and Pacific Islanders in Post-Secondary Schools

We would be remiss if we did not examine one of the bright spots in the educational outcomes for Asians and Pacific Islanders. The data reveals once more that academic success does not characterize all groups. Asian postsecondary enrollment increased two-fold from 1976 to 1986 (from 1.8 per cent to 3.6 per cent). The overall increase in educational attainment between 1970 and 1980 was due both to genuine improvement in school attendance and to the immigration of Asians with more schooling. The 1965–75 period saw a dramatic increase in the percentage of immigrants with college degrees. In contrast, since 1975 school attainment decreased due to the large proportion of Asians and Pacific Island immigrants with less education.

At both the undergraduate and graduate levels, the fields of study selected by Asians were predominantly engineering, physical sciences, mathematics, and computer sciences. At the graduate level, in addition to these fields, Asians chose dentistry, medicine, optometry and pharmacy. Few of them, however, became lawyers, chiropractors, theologians, philosophers or veterinarians. Asian students pursue occupations they perceive as having higher status and ones in which communicative language skills are less required. This pattern raises questions as to the reasons why Asian students limit their career possibilities.

Another way to measure the overall success of Asians and Pacific Islanders, other than schooling and academic achievement, is to study their placement in the workplace. The analysis of the occupational profile of Asians shows that they reach occupational levels commensurate with education, regardless of age. Asians have generally more schooling than whites and other persons holding the same or similar jobs. While other ethnic groups have to confront this problem, it would appear that Asians need to have more schooling than other ethnic groups in order to obtain and hold a professional position. School officials tend to measure school success with graduation or with the number of school years completed, without taking into consideration other skills required to hold these jobs, or the biases of the labor market against ethnic persons, especially Asians. Overeducation as a requirement to obtain and hold professional occupations affects especially the foreign-born workers.

Despite the fact that Asians overall are more highly educated than their white counterparts and are in many cases more qualified to hold professional jobs, they tend to be underrepresented at managerial levels. Instead, they are put in technical and non-supervisory positions in which they are overqualified. In California, while 67.9 per cent of all college-educated white people obtain professional, administrative or managerial positions, only 48.4 per cent of the Koreans, 49.5 per cent of the Filipino, 50.6 per cent of the Vietnamese, 61.6 per cent of the Chinese and 63.7 per cent of the Japanese obtain such jobs. There is, indeed, substantial documentation of the high performance of Asian language minority students as measured by above-average grade point average, above-average standardized test scores (especially in mathematics); of greater likelihood of taking college preparatory courses, and lower rates of suspensions or referrals; of higher attendance rates/lower truancy rates, and higher graduation rates and lower dropout rates (Baratz-Snoden and Duran, 1987; Broadman and Wood (1978); Caplan, Whitmore, Bui, and Trautmann, 1985; Hsia, 1983; Kan and Liu, 1986; Rumbaut and Ima, 1988; So, 1986, and many others). Other scholars, however, in examining the mathematics achievement characteristics of Asian American students, especially immigrants, found a wider standard deviation of Asian performance, including a disproportionate number of low performers, in comparison with other groups Tsang (1983, 1988). He pointed out that their approach to learning seemed to overemphasize the mechanical and not the conceptual understanding of mathematics. In effect, the appearance of general high performance serves to mask the persistent bimodality or differential distribution of achievement among the various groups, and to raise serious doubts about the level of understanding and critical thinking among Asian and Pacific Island language minority students.

The generally favorable academic attainments of Southeast Asian refugee students in San Diego should not hide the fact that there are greater variations of academic attainment with each group than between groups related to ethnicity, age, time of arrival, parents' educational background and parents' mental health (Rumbaut and Ima, 1988). The following contextual information is relevant to the issue of Asian achievement in San Diego:

1 Immigrants and refugees in the United States, whether from Asia, Europe, or Latin America, systematically outperform all native-born American students in grade point averages (GPAs) despite initial (or even persisting) problems in English.

2 Southeast Asian youth have GPAs above those of white students, as well as of all other ethnic minority students, except Chinese, Japanese and Korean students.

3 Among the Southeast Asian students, the Khmer and the Lao have a GPA below that of white majority students. In contrast, the GPA of Vietnamese and Chinese-Vietnamese students is well above the average GPA of white students; and, contrary to expectations, Hmong students' average GPA is above the white majority student average.

4 Test scores of Southeast Asian students are above average in national standardized math test scores, in essentially the same GPA rank order noted in 3), except that the Khmer rank last.

5 Southeast Asian students have below national average standardized verbal (reading and vocabulary) test scores, in the following rank order: Vietnamese, Chinese-Vietnamese, Khmer, Lao and Hmong.

What are the factors of the differential achievement within and between Asian groups? To what extent are these factors the same as those presumed to explain differences of academic achievement among mainstream populations? Socioeconomic status, social class, educational background of parents, cultural values associated with achievement motivation, and others are listed as key factors.

Socioeconomic Status

Parents' higher income and educational level, higher occupational status, urban versus rural origin, and overall higher quality of the family learning environment are considered important factors in successful academic achievement. When teachers are asked to identify key factors associated with the performance of their pupils, they often point to the child's family. English-learning among refugees was correlated with the years of schooling parents had in their home country, their literacy level, the length of time they lived in the United States, and the amount or dominance of English as the language spoken at home (Stephany, 1984). In their study of 53 US born 9–10-year-old Chinese students, Yee and La Forge (1974) found that social class was associated with six subtests WISC performance levels. A study by Guiany (1980) of third and fifth grade Filipino students suggests that the child's home environment correlated with reading achievement, and that the parents' economic and educational characteristics were related to achievement, although this finding was not statistically significant.

While the educational level of parents and their current employment and income levels are important, they are not the sole or even main determinants of academic performance. The social class and cultural values (presumably associated with achievement motivation, literacy and participation in social institutions) have a determinant impact on academic achievement. This finding may suggest that upper-class socialization and value orientation in the home country leads to a more effective use of resources in the host country.

Upper-class socialization may often bring more years of formal schooling in the home country, and additional home language development which are transferred to the new linguistic and cultural environment. The study by Lopez (1982) suggests that the higher academic performance of Asians in contrast with Hispanics is consistent with the fact that 31 per cent of Asians had training in English prior to their arrival to the United States, in contrast with only 3 per cent of the Hispanics, and that the socioeconomic status of Asians is consequently higher upon arrival to this country.

This is not a complete explanation, however, if we compare the Punjabis with the Mexican American within the same geographical area. Gibson (1987) indicates that most of the Northern California Punjabi Sikhs she studied, some 6000 of them in 1981, had come from Northwest India and had lived in small rural villages of less than 1000 persons. They came in search of economic opportunities (like most immigrants). Gibson states:

> Most appear to believe that if they work hard enough they can succeed in school, regardless of all other obstacles. *Age on arrival and length of residence* appears also to be closely related to the school performance of linguistic minority immigrant children. Language minority students who arrive in the new country by age 6 or 7 tend to do better academically than those who arrive in the upper elementary and junior high years. . . .In general, those who receive all of their schooling in the new country gain sufficient proficiency in the dominant language to be competitive in their academic classes (Gibson, 1987:271).

Two important characteristics set apart the Punjabi; 1) they do not assimilate into mainstream society, but keep their ethnic identity separate and their own cultural values and traditions; and 2) they handle cultural conflict with tenacity and with strong support from their families. The following description by Gibson gives us some insights into the barriers overcome by the Punjabi:

> Punjabi students, even those who are American-born or who arrive in this country at an early age, have far from an easy time in school. Most of those who I sampled had started school knowing little or no English, and, prior to high school, had received no special assistance in learning English. In addition, the Punjabi students had to cope both with severe prejudice and with sharp conflicts between home values and those promoted by the school. Valleyside is 'redneck' country, and some white residents are extremely hostile toward immigrants who look different, act different, and speak a different language. In school, Punjabi teenagers are told they stink, directly by white students and indirectly by their teachers. They are told to go back to India. They are accused of being illegals. They are physically abused by majority students, who spit at them, refuse to sit by them in class or buses, crowd in front of them in line, stick them with pins, throw food at them, and worse. They are labeled troublemakers if they defend themselves. Only a minority of white youths participate actively in the harassment, but the majority either condones their classmates' behavior, or feels powerless to alter the status quo (Gibson, 1987:268).

The opposition and hostility shown to Indochinese and other Asian students may not be as severe as the case of the Punjabi. What is significant, however, is that both the Punjabi, the Indochinese and other Asian people adjust to the United States with similar adaptive strategies which result in higher academic achievement even in the midst of serious difficulties in school.

Cultural conflict seems to be handled differently by the various Asian and Pacific Island groups. For example, E.W. Lee (1988) found wide variations among reclassified Asian immigrants and refugee students in their California Tests of Basic Skills (CTBS) achievement scores. Those from Hong Kong and Taiwan fared better than those from mainland China and Vietnam. Most scholars seem to point at the same factors affecting the ability of immigrant children to achieve, such as age of arrival, social class, income, length of residence in the United States, home cultural values, and family support (Rumbaut and Ima, 1988; Hakuta, 1986; Carter and Segura, 1979; Gibson, 1987; Suárez-Orozco, 1987, 1989; and others). The literature on immigrant academic achievement is intimately related with the study of motivation to achieve. Suárez-Orozco, using a combination of ethnographic

Table 3.5   Competency in home and host languages and cultures

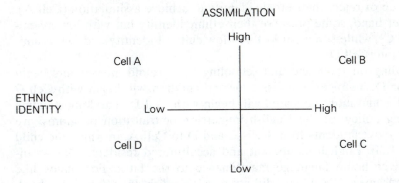

High Level of Competence: Highly acculturated individuals, with high levels of both English and home language proficiency, as well as with substantial cultural knowledge of both the home and the host cultures.

Low Level of Competence: Unacculturated individuals with a low level of skills in both English and the home language as well as with limited cultural knowledge about the home and host cultures.

and projective techniques, documents cases of Central Americans whose motivation was central to their school achievement. One of these cases is that of Rodolfo:

> Little Rodolfo had to work since the age of five to buy food. His poor mother was sick, his father left them. Rodolfo paused to medi-tate about his future and concluded that there was a fundamental difference between the street and school: Knowledge. Knowledge represents a capacity to tell good from bad. Rodolfo thus chooses to go to school over street life. He tells his poor, sick mother not to worry because he will take care of both: he will study and work. He becomes a model student and chooses a career to help as many poor kids as possible (Suárez-Orozco, 1987:297).

Suárez-Orozco's work (1987, 1989) eloquently describes a strong motivation to succeed, which embodies the refugee working ethic and the view that schooling is a precious opportunity not to be wasted.

Throughout the above discussion, little mention has been made of the alternative outcomes for these newcomers. Table 3.5 suggests beginnings, outcomes and paths between beginnings and outcomes. Though the fourfold table provides only four discrete possibilities, as with other heuristic devices, this does not literally mean that there are only four options. In reality, there are probably gradations along both major dimensions; but for the sake of thinking about language options, this simplified Table 3.5 is a useful peda-gogical device. According to Kitano and Daniels (1988), some people are highly assimilated and still retain high ethnic identity (Cell B), whereas others give up or reject their ethnic identity to achieve assimilation (Cell A). On the other hand, some preserve their ethnic identity but with low assimilation (Cell C), while some get lost in a low cultural identity and low assimilation situation (Cell D).

Depending on their age and schooling background, newcomers begin in Cell C or D. Younger and less educated children will begin with Cell C and the older and more educated will begin with Cell D. The long-standing US schooling policy, or the English immersion or transition programs, are designed to move students from Cells C and D to Cell A, in which the child becomes a fully English competent and acculturated resident. This acculturation leaves home language maintenance to the fates. For many, like Richard Rodriguez (1982), who did not speak English upon entering school, the choice was clear — either be an English speaker or a Spanish speaker; Cell A or C. Many Spanish-speaking persons tell stories about how their parents had a choice to make — either to encourage their children to be English-language competent or to be Spanish-language competent, but not both, since that was viewed as impossible; the choice was considered crucial in terms of 'making it in America'. If one chose English, then one could have a chance at succeeding, or realizing the American Dream. If one chose Spanish, then one was destined to remain at the bottom of the social ladder.

The same choice befell Asians, such as Japanese Americans, who by the second generation (the first US born generation) had lost fluency in Japanese and rarely acquired literacy in the Japanese language. This preference for the English language is sometimes used to explain their success, clearly reinforcing Rodriguez' thesis (see p. 59). Given the US language history of preferring mono-lingual English speaking citizens and discouraging non-English language usage, it is little wonder that foreign language speaking US citizens are so rare by world standards. Consequently, the ambitious among immigrants would not only embrace the English language, but also abandon their home language, since the latter was viewed as detrimental to success.

Is this the same choice facing Asian newcomers? Between the time of Rodriguez' schooling experiences and the current time, thinking regarding the importance of the primary language has changed. Hakuta, among other researchers of language acquisition, has argued about the benefits of becoming bilingual; rather than bearing a burden by having such skills, bilingualism enhances cognitive development and general intellectual skills. Then numerous research findings suggest that the choice Rodriguez made is not necessary and that primary language retention while acquiring a second language is highly desirable. Elite immigrants have always known the virtues of bilingual skills and were among the small proportion of immigrants who could have it both ways, contrary to the experiences of Rodriguez. In effect, elite immigrants have always considered option B as not only desirable but also practically beneficial to their children. To be sure, one of the motivations among the elite was the prospect of going back to or visiting their home country, which would require home language competence. Today, the children of Japanese national businessmen, who have temporary assignment in the US, are schooled in both oral and literate skills of the Japanese language because their prospects of entering college in Japan would be seriously undermined without those competencies.

The Cuban American experience in Miami is an instance which supports the bilingual option B. There Cuban children become bilingual, possessing both oral and literacy skills in English and Spanish. One may argue that these children come from elite backgrounds and, therefore, this argument may be less viable when dealing with those from more modest backgrounds, such as Puerto Ricans. Additionally, the Miami experience may be unique in the sheer concentration of Spanish-language speakers and the availability of both languages in the public arena of advertising, newspapers, radios, television and so forth.

While the Asian newcomers do not come from a single language group and their numbers may be relatively small, the above examples on the possibility of option B as well as the traditional option A, gives us a framework for reviewing the possible outcomes and trajectories of those students. The following materials are organized along the lines of the four-fold typology; whether or not options A, B or C are desirable or realistic will remain open for debate.

Concluding Comparative Reflections

Nidorf (1985) notes the higher at-risk of failure among Southeast Asian refugees who enter this country as unaccompanied youth. They not only carry the burden of having to succeed in the US for family members back home, but also have to cope with difficult situations without the support of parents and close family members. Rumbaut and Ima (1988) observed the greater likelihood of unaccompanied youth to be more at-risk of becoming juvenile delinquents than those with parents in the US. The refugee experience generates not only separation from parents, but also disruption of extended family and other support systems. Again, this is one of the factors identified by Schuman as undermining progress in schooling. Rumbaut and Ima observed that students with intact families were more likely to do well in school than those students with disrupted families.

A study comparing Chinese and Hispanic students' performance in school (Ogbu and Matute-Bianchi, 1986), finds important differences in their strategies to cope with school demands. Among Chinese students, there is a high emphasis on individual, personal responsibility, in contrast with the sense of collective responsibility and collaborative strategies preferred by Hispanic students. Additionally, Chinese students appear to accept a prolonged childhood associated with the legitimacy and desirability to stay in school, versus a view of a shortened adolescence in which students accept both the responsibility and desirability of being able to provide for the support of families at an earlier age. Boardman and Aloyd (1978) observed Asian students as having a more positive attitude towards education than Puerto Ricans; the latter students did not view school achievement as important.

Japanese American students were more likely to accept the desirability of education as a means to higher achievement in society than Mexican American students, especially those identified as 'Cholos', who tended to view school as a foreign institution attempting to deprive them from their ethnic identity. Cholos seem to take a more confrontative stance towards schooling, treating those who accepted schooling as 'school boys' or individuals who should be rejected by their peer group. This study may support some of the ideas advanced by Ogbu regarding the tendency of some groups, or segments in those groups, (he calls them involuntary or castelike) to define their cultural identity in opposition to the culture of mainstream groups (see Chapter 1 for a discussion of these issues). This tendency conflicts with other segments or entire ethnic groups who have no problem conforming to the American cultural values of school achievement as a means to gain other benefits (social and economic status, etc.). Nevertheless, in the comparison of Asian groups with Mexican American groups, Ogbu and Matute-Bianchi are careful to identify the variety of Hispanic groups, some placing more emphasis on schooling than others; this cautionary note raises questions about the role of culture versus socio-economic factors.

Gibson's work (1987, 1988) with Punjabis (East Indians) in California's Central Valley is advanced by her in support of Ogbu's cultural ecological position, but more concretely as a kind of adaption strategy that excludes acculturation and emphasizes the retention of the home language and culture without excluding scholastic achievement. She observed that rural Sikhs of modest educational origins wanted their children to succeed in American schools, without losing their cultural values. The strategies used by the Punjabis remind us of some of the strategies adopted by the Hutterites and Amish who found themselves in the same situation. The most important difference between Punjabis and Amish or Hutterites, is that the former did not create separate schools, but only separate communities, and that the latter, being from European groups (ethnically and racially) had a much more difficult time keeping their youngsters from assimilating to the surrounding American mainstream world. Apparently, they viewed schooling as a pragmatic option to working in lower income and less desirable jobs. Punjabis did not view themselves in conflict with schools and welcomed school authorities, but kept to themselves outside of school. This is what Gibson called 'accommodation without assimilation'. They emphasized persistence and accommodations to school settings and even surpassed the performance of mainstream students.

Scholars working with a large literature on Pacific Islanders in American schools (Au, 1980, 1981; Boggs, 1985; Jordan and Tharp, 1979; and Jordan, Au and Joseting, 1983) conclude that the discourse patterns used by

Hawaiian children reveal a special set of cultural values that were compatible with the teaching of reading and writing, and that could enhance academic achievement. Attempts to force Pacific Islanders to learn through techniques, curricula and discourse styles peculiar to mainstream American children was counterproductive and could undermine their motivation to learn. The use of Hawaiian 'talk story' in the Kamehameha schools, that is, peculiar ways of collective participation in social and academic endeavors, resulted in significant achievement gains. The issue of sociocultural compatibility between the home and the school learning environments is a complex issue for Asians and Pacific Islanders whose cultures and lifestyle are so varied. How could schools design curricula and teaching techniques congruent with the home cultures and languages? How specific would the accommodations have to be? Would these accommodations be made on the basis that the school personnel have all of the burden of restructuring curricula and teaching materials, while the children will remain culturally unchanged? The evidence from other studies (including that of Mohatt and Erickson, 1981) suggests that children can also accommodate, and that they actually change in the process of being schooled. Another set of problems is associated with the actual implementation of the Kamehameha model; that is, the resulting curriculum and teaching techniques may not necessarily work with some Hawaiians whose social class and home learning environments are vastly different from those used in the initial studies. Of course, this observation made by recent researchers (personal communication with Cathy Jordan), only stresses the notion that the cultural characteristics of some groups (including those manifested in discourse patterns) are not shared by all the segments of these groups. Intragroup differences resulting from differential exposure to learning environments in which literacy plays a key role in daily activities are as important as the presumed historically based characteristics of castelike groups. Or perhaps, could we say that the castelike status disappears as soon as the home learning environment becomes more supportive of academic achievements? If this is so, then the theories of empowerment require further attention, and the castelike hypotheses need to be qualified.

So far we have dealt with comparative studies of performance of Asian and non-Asian groups in the United States, and the possible explanations for their differential performance. What do we know about the differential performance of ethnic groups in situations where schools are highly diversified, and where most minority groups are equally exposed to similar treatment? In the last two decades a number of studies compared the performance of ethnic groups in ethnically and racially diversified schools. Schwartz (1971) attributes the high achievement of Asian students in these settings to cultural values, especially those associated with collective vs. individual orientation, and on generation-based linear authority of family members over students. A Los Angeles sample of 6th, 9th and 12th graders in twenty-three racially mixed schools was the basis of his research. Motivation to achieve is related not only to the use of authority by family members, but also to the nature of rewards offered to children. According to Bit (1981), adequate rewards were given to Cambodian bilingual children in the Oakland schools. These children performed better under cooperative settings with collective rewards than in the competitive settings with individual rewards. Children who come from backgrounds heavily influenced by Confucian philosophy, as Chinese and Indochinese children, are more likely to respond more positively to collective rewards than to individual rewards. By the same token, studies among the Filipino (Gomez, 1981), as was the case in the work alluded to earlier by Suárez-Orozco with Central Americans (1987, 1989), indicate that achievement motivation is deeply rooted in family values and the commitment to help one's own relatives. Gomez's study with 259 Filipino fifth graders focused on the family cultural values of solidarity, human concern, shame, and pride. The stronger predictor of academic achievement was 'human concern' or *Pakikipagkapuwa*. A similar study by Rebecca (1981) suggests that:

1　Filipinos scored higher on values of expressive orientation, formal school compliance, idealized school goals, instrumental orientation, faith in human nature and self esteem.
2　Achievement scores are associated with formal school compliance, idealized school goals and instrumental orientation, confidence in mankind, collective vs. self orientation.

In contrast with Rebecca's study of Asian American children who followed the strategy of 'accommodation without acculturation' alluded to by Gibson (1987, 1988), E. Lee and M. Lee's (1980) study suggests that acculturation is a factor of academic achievement because it permits children to display appropriate school behavior. This study may not be in contradiction with the observations by Rebecca and Gibson. Indeed, Gibson shows that the longer Punjabi children have been exposed to American society and school, and the more English they learned, the better they perform in school. However, one of the means for Punjabi children to cope with school demands is to draw upon their cultural values for motivation to achieve in a very hostile environment. Formal school compliance as selective acculturation is one strategy for obtaining the right to participate in other benefits offered by American society. Successful schooling is seen as a means to an end; a means of bringing economic security to the family, and as compatible with keeping one's own central cultural values as reflected in traditional beliefs and collective rituals. The comparative study by Lee was conducted on eighty Headstart children, and concluded the following:

1　Parents' backgrounds and teaching styles were unrelated to outcomes.
2　Chinese children were passive in play, but engaged in task-oriented

activities and were more likely to ask for adult help than other children, especially black children.

3 Black children were socialized through peer interaction and oriented to conform to peer behaviors.

4 US-born Chinese, in contrast with immigrant Chinese children, are more likely to participate in group activities and to receive minor reprimands more often than their immigrant counterparts.

Obviously, there is no single determinant factor of achievement for minority groups, nor a single best strategy to succeed in the adaptation to school and society. Yet the explanation for the apparent success of Asian Americans continues to be of interest to scholars. The theories based on the relationship between positive teacher attitudes and behavior toward Asians and pupil achievement obviously presuppose that Asian children's home environment is very supportive of school. For example, children's time on tasks, development of inquiry skills, motivation to achieve and dedicated academic efforts over long periods of time are due to the socialization in the home, parental modeling, rewards in the home for appropriate behaviors, and the underlying cultural values that facilitate the home socialization process for academic success.

Social bias in favor of Asians is a crucial factor in their academic success. Generally speaking, attitudes of school personnel towards Asians are a social response to the model minority image held by most Americans. For example, teachers imputed (impute) middle-class status to the Southeast Asian refugees and spoke positively of these students' performance. In contrast, they downgraded the performance of blacks and Hispanics. Y. Lee (1984), in his study of two Chicago area schools, observes that both teachers and non-Asian students ascribe even higher academic expectations to Asian students than those students ascribe to themselves. Wong-Fillmore (1980) not only made observations of how the teachers' perception of Chinese Limited English Proficient (LEP) students as being more responsive to teachers than Hispanic students, but she also documented the behavior of the Chinese students as being more in accord with teachers' expectations. Goldstein's study of Hmong students (1985), another group of API/LEP students, also reports that Hmong children received more favorable assessments by teachers than other minorities.

While there is evidence that student behavior matches teachers' expectations, it stands to reason that students' actual performance can reinforce teachers' expectations, and that favoritism has limits. There are limiting consequences in the Asian student behavior of absolute compliance with authority, especially if this compliance is associated with social isolation. Asian children are less likely to acquire the networking and social skills associated with mainstream individuals who advance in the workplace. As one foreign-born Chinese engineer put it, 'we are twentieth century Coolies'. His comments suggest that compliance with teacher authority and the acquisition of educational credentials does not guarantee success in the workplace, in large part because they seem to lack the social skills which have not been cultivated among this population. Other studies point out the passivity of API students and the persistent ignoring of this matter as long as they don't seem to cause trouble for teachers (Sato, 1982).

Accounts of trauma in the home country and in refugee camps, or associated with the departure, are also important in order to understand differential achievement of children and their choice of adaptation strategies in the host country. Masuda, Lin and Tazuma (1979, 1980) documented the problems of Vietnamese refugees and the high levels of physical and mental dysfunctions among them. Kinzie, Sack, Angell, Manson and Rath (1986) recorded the psychiatric effects of massive trauma on Cambodian children and found over half of a high school student population was suffering from severe emotional crisis, while the rest of the students, though traumatized, appeared to be functioning as regular students. Trueba, Jacobs and Kirton (1990) described the traumatic experiences suffered by Hmong families in their journey from home to the United States and the consequences of such experiences. The psychological problems of Indochinese associated with excessive stress, for example, the levels of depressive symptomatology exhibited by the Cambodians (significantly higher than the levels observed for any other group) and the mental sufferings of Khmer mothers (with the highest degree of depression among Indochinese observed) have been discussed by Rumbaut (1985). The longitudinal data in his sample of 500 suggest that the most severely affected by these disorders are the Khmer (the depressive symptoms are chronic, not merely transient mood or affective disorders), followed by the Hmong and the Lao, and lastly by the Chinese-Vietnamese and the Vietnamese. Overall, mothers are significantly more depressed than fathers, except for the Hmong, where levels of depression are identical for both fathers and mothers. Rumbaut and Ima (1988) and Ima and Rumbaut (1989) not only confirmed the existence of a high level of emotional traumas among Cambodians, as well as all of the other refugee groups (measuring between three to four times the level of psychological depression among the average American population), but also found evidence that the consequences of the trauma were linked to school dropouts and academic performances. Those students whose mothers were highly traumatized were less likely to do well in school.

In brief, what have we learned about the Asian and Pacific Islander language minority students can be summarized as follows:

1 The growth of the Asian and Pacific Islander language minority population has been substantial and is expected to continue increasing into the near future.
2 The majority of Asian and Pacific Islander individuals will come from language minority homes, and the issue of English language

proficiency remains a fundamental problem, even for those who are classified as fluent English proficient.

3 The diversity of this population includes hidden at-risk Asian and Pacific Islander student pockets, which are masked by socio-economic statistics on their well-being. The persistence of the bimodal distributions of Asian and Pacific Islanders along a wide variety of indicators are significant facets of their school failures — a frequently hidden side of this population.

4 US schools have not provided adequate language services, which approximate services given to native English speaking students, to this population. Serious and appropriate educational programs are lacking for these students, including identification of language needs, programs, staffing and counseling/guidance.

5 The academic performance of Asian and Pacific Island students is good as measured by traditional benchmarks of grades and math scores, but in spite of these academic marks, there are significant pockets of the undereducated and the persistent weakness in language scores among a large proportion of all Asian and Pacific Island language minority students.

6 There are identifiable factors associated with low performing Asian and Pacific Island student.

7 There is a dearth of research, theory and working models on these populations which can be used to design appropriate programs, including both linguistic and non-linguistic issues.

Chapter 4

Conflict and Adaptation:
Child, Family and Community

Culturally diverse immigrant, refugee and other minority families are described by George and Louise Spindler (1987a and b) as facing cultural conflict and developing adaptive strategies in order to cope with the conflict. According to these authors, for example, many of the native American communities, such as the Menominee, choose to reaffirm their ethnic cultural orientation and to resist acculturation; others remain as transitional between the mainstream culture and their native culture, and finally others acculturate.

Among the various adaptive strategies that are used as mechanisms of adjustment to the new culture by the Asian Americans are the following: assimilation, acculturation, integration, alienation and rejection. These behaviors are observable among all immigrant populations coming to a foreign country. What adjustments must take place before immigrants and refugees blend into mainstream culture? (Gollnick and Chinn, 1986).

There are general issues which reflect different philosophical positions regarding assimilation of this population. A trend toward Anglo conformity has been developing during the past decade. The underlying idea of freedom of individual choice may be ideologically desirable, but is unrealistic for many new Americans. In discussing assimilation, it is enlightening to look back to older Japanese or Chinese immigrants who have been in the US for many years. The Hawaiian Chinese community celebrated the 200th year anniversary of their habitation on the island of Oahu. Chinese, Japanese, Filipino, and Korean immigrants have been in the United States for many generations. There are records of Filipinos living in Louisiana even before its sale to the United States in 1803. However, full assimilation has yet to take place for these groups. Takaki (1989) clearly documents that Asians remain foreigners to some extent, even after three or more generations on American soil. As a Japanese individual, people continually ask him, 'Where are you from?' Although he is acculturated, observable Asian features still place him in a separate category. The issue of race limits assimilation and persists over generational boundaries. The cultures of Southeast Asian newcomers (the

Indochinese) have been heavily influenced by the two major cultures of Asia, namely, the Chinese and Indian cultures. Many aspects of the Chinese culture have been integrated into the Vietnamese, the Chinese-Vietnamese and Hmong cultures. The Indian culture has influenced the Lao and Khmer cultures. Such cultural integration is a result of many generations of close contact. These newcomers are now experiencing new values and beliefs of the US culture.

Choices in Acculturation

In terms of acculturation to the American way of life, there are four possible ways in which immigrant children can choose to live. One is to develop bicultural/multicultural competency. This includes competency in the home as well as in the outside environment. The child must learn to juggle these two settings. This is the best, but also the most difficult solution.

Some individuals keep the two environments separate with no crossing over whatsoever. There are those who refuse to acquire the new culture, but instead maintain only their home culture. They may speak the new language, yet their cultural ways remain the same as in the old country without any serious acceptance of the American mainstream culture. They may eat only their own ethnic food, watch television programs, movies and videos in their home language, and read newspapers, magazines and books written in their home language. They will socialize only with people from their same ethnic groups, go to church where their home language is used, and celebrate holidays according to their home traditions. They are unfamiliar with local politics, and are not involved with local community work. They have established a close network of friends, who are supportive of each other. In sum, their social circle encourages a limited life-style, and they prefer it this way.

The third manner of acculturation includes those who reject their home culture entirely and wholeheartedly embrace behaviors which they perceive to be consistent with the American culture. These individuals will speak only English, refuse to speak their home language, and will often even deny any knowledge of their home language. They often despise their own ethnic food and prefer to eat American hamburgers or steaks. They follow trendy fashions, and often refer to themselves as 100 per cent American. They reject their home language and culture in all aspects and attempt to break into the mainstream circle. All too often, however, they are unsuccessful.

The fourth profile consists of those who are comfortable neither with their home culture nor with their school culture and find themselves in an in-between world. The question remains, 'What factors cause people to develop into one of these types, and what are the consequences for education?' This simplified model suggests a fourfold strategy which is far from exhaustive. By using this model, we can identify a diversity of adjustment strategies among people. The upper-class tend to develop a bicultural strategy in which their degree of comfort in the mainstream American culture and home culture are at a relatively high level. They successfully juggle the two. They continue to be nurtured in both contexts and often enlarge their social circles to include multicultural/multilingual/multiethnic groups of friends and associates.

Those coming from the lower ranks either reject US culture or fall into a kind of no man's land in which they're neither one nor the other. They're often referred to as the marginal people. As an illustration, let us examine the case of a Vietnamese youth who belongs to neither side. His Vietnamese language is very poor; his English is poor, also. The only people with whom he can interact are Vietnamese of his own age group. These children use a mixture of English and Vietnamese; their Vietnamese is substandard and their English is equally bad. They are stuck in an in-between land, not codeswitching, but codemixing, and there is a lack of grammatical accuracy in both languages. This behavior presents a real problem in communication with most people. In the streets, there exists a small community of these types of people which may become members of the underclass. They pose a problem for themselves as well as society. These are the abandoned juveniles who may, in all probability, become criminals or enter the welfare ranks.

The 'Killing Field' Experience

If we are to have a truly multicultural society, we need to reexamine the curriculum and academic expectations regarding what is accepted as valid. The concepts of gender and age equity are fundamentally at odds within the child's home and school culture. Questions are being raised about experiences of trauma that may affect immigrants' adaptation to the new country. Those coming as refugees from Cambodia are more likely to have had traumatic experiences such as witnessing the killing of babies and children during their escape to Thailand. This affects survival strategies in the US. Emotional traumas are common among all individuals who worked with the military. The refugees came to the US confused and scared. They need to redevelop trust and gain reassurance before acculturation can begin.

For children born after this period, it is unclear what consequences the trauma has brought, but surely we must investigate the effects. There are students who cannot forget the past, and preoccupation with it undermines their attention in school. In some cases, individuals gravitate towards peer groups that share similar experiences and find solace in their company. This may involve drinking, smoking or just talking with each other. A large number become runaways and status offenders.

Among Cambodians, 25 per cent of all adult females are widows whose husbands were killed during or after the Pol Pot period. A report about a group of Khmer women claiming disability due to blindness revealed that these women have no neurological evidence of visual impairment, and yet they insist they cannot see and are disabled. After their application of disability was denied, they continued to claim they were blind. Such cases may be labeled as 'conversion blindness', which is typically associated with witnessing severe trauma. On the average, Cambodians are four times more likely to suffer severe emotional distress than the average US adult resident. Over half of them experience post-traumatic stress disorder (PTSD), which is an emotionally disabling condition. Not only have many parents been distressed but many, if not most, have had disrupted families, such as the death of a father; and this affects the way their children behave in and out of school.

Emotional survival from day to day is a main concern. Graduating from high school, going to college or getting As and Bs is often not considered a priority. Coping with each day's struggles is an energy-consuming task. We can discuss academic concerns in terms of linguistics or social psychosocial issues, but if one has underlying psychological problems, such as dealing with nightmares, then schooling takes a back seat. Without stable mental health, all other academic problems are secondary. If children cannot deal with repeated nightmares, they cannot deal with authority or concentrate on their school work. As well as dealing with his own problems, children may have to deal with the emotional problems of their next of kin.

A Khmer widow whose husband was killed during the Pol Pot period was not able to cope with the daily demand of getting food on the table. The children went to school hungry, dirty, without sleep, without care, and without a nurturer, parent or guardian. The mother needed therapy and the children suffered because their mother was not functioning normally. Eventually, a teacher had to call child protective authorities, provides care, as well as housekeeping. These are some of the hidden aspects of the adjustment of Asian newcomers to American schools and strongly suggest the necessity to develop counseling and guidance services for students and to develop networks with community based agencies.

Group Identity vs. Marginality

Many Vietnamese eventually stop receiving welfare, enter the job market and become home-owners. What are the contributing factors that lead toward independence? The Vietnamese are sophisticated with respect to material goods and value their acquisition. The cultural attitude among the Lao, in contrast, is that to have too much is not good. One should have a moderate amount of goods, which is nothing to be embarrassed about. The desire to acquire more, whether schooling or material possessions, is valued among both the Vietnamese and the Chinese. The desire to keep minimal standards and stay in the same social class is more appropriate for the Lao and Khmer. Their culture emphasizes moderation and punishes those who are immodest.

Immigrants come to the US to gain more freedom, more material goods and greater knowledge. Refugees, on the other hand, come because of fear of political persecution; a small percentage come for economic reasons, though it is increasingly a combination of the two motives. Overall, most immigrants come for better living conditions and better education in order to be more marketable. Hence, they get better jobs and acquire more material goods. Vietnamese and Chinese people are well aware of status possessions such as cars and educational degrees. Many of them own a BMW or a Mercedes Benz and live in nice houses, not only because they are more valuable, but also because status is conferred onto them through such possessions. While traditional values of the Chinese emphasize moderation, things have changed among the Chinese in South China, where there is considerable acquisitiveness. In Hong Kong there is also a high level of acquisitiveness and preoccupation with accumulation. Clothes bought from boutiques, high fashion styles, watches and name brand accessories are considered highly desirable.

Cultural Conflicts

Traditional culture is in conflict with industrialization. Hong Kong is a commercial port where material goods, which people work to obtain, are plentiful. The purpose of the system is to enable people to purchase more. The traditional value of being modest is still a hidden cultural value, but it is certainly not as valued as was once the case. However, there remain a large group of Chinese who choose not to live by the principle of trying to acquire more material goods. Status is a separate issue. If one wants to acquire more social status, one can do so by becoming involved in politics, gaining some position of power, or going into research to gain scholarly recognition. It is desirable for the children of the elite or the near elite of Confucian-based countries to go to Ivy League schools, preferably Harvard, Yale, Brown, Oxford or Cambridge. There is considerable drive among these children to succeed in getting into these elite schools. Parents sacrifice personal needs in order to send their children to private universities; children, in turn, are expected to take care of their parents and show filial piety by obeying their parents' wishes. These are status considerations, but they are purely incompatible with welfare dependency.

The middle-class Asian Americans seem to be interested in accumulating material goods for their own sake rather than for status reasons. Middle-class Vietnamese and Chinese reflect in their life styles prevailing social class and educational values learned from their exposure to Western cultures. This is also true of the middle-class Lao, Khmer and Hmong educated in Western school systems, and affects their strategies in dealing with the American society. Southeast Asians and their diverse strategies reflect not only their culture but also the kind of life experiences and expectations they bring with them. Educational policies that attempt to change these strategies must first address issues related to the culture of the Southeast Asians.

Sung (1987) addresses the bicultural conflict that Asians experience upon arrival to the United States. Below are just a few of the types of conflicts that many newcomers must resolve and incorporate into their assimilation patterns:

1   Asian children are raised to divert aggressive behavior, whereas a masculine 'macho' image prevails in the US. Asian males, in particular, are faced with this bicultural conflict.
2   Sexual appeal has a subtleness in the Asian culture, whereas in the US sexual appeal is overtly stressed. Teenage Asian females are most affected in this aspect.
3   Asian children are quick to report wrong-doings of themselves and/or their peers to authoritative figures; their American peers will be quick to dub a reporter as a 'tattler'.
4   Asian children who have become familiar with the American social life are attracted to the public physical expressions of love but they are inhibited from such displays of affection by their upbringing. This may cause confusion leading them to wonder if the love their parents show is less than the overt love they see in their peers' families.
5   Greater value is placed on scholastic achievement in Asian cultures than in American cultures.
6   To be thrifty is a valuable trait in the Asian community, whereas conspicuous consumption is practiced in the American culture. These two extreme opposites stir up confusion in Asian children.
7   Immigrant Asian parents discourage their children from becoming independent and from socializing outside of the family until a much later age than other ethnic groups.
8   Immigrant Asian children struggle with the fact that in the US authoritative figures are not shown great respect by their inferiors. They find this to be especially true in the relationship between students and their teachers.
9   Asians become heroes and heroines because of their superb moral caliber. Americans become heroes because of wealth and material possessions — they are often sport players and entertainers.
10 The Asian views himself in terms of his relations to other people. His success and happiness are dependent upon others; the American culture stresses individualism.

Cultural Maintenance and Communication

How can grandchildren communicate with their grandparents if each speaks a different language? How can children talk with aunts, uncles and cousins from their home country? Determining what is ideal and what is practical goes beyond a matter of personal choice to the question of language utility and family cohesion. Wong-Fillmore (in press) pointed out the difficulties children have when they cannot fully express what they want to say to their parents, causing communication breakdown and misunderstanding.

Linguists (Grosjean, 1982; Hakuta, 1986, and McLaughlin, 1984) suggest that parents should use the highest quality of language in the home setting and expect children to converse in the home language. It is ineffective to use a defective form of language as a model for children. English competency is not just knowing the rules of grammar, vocabulary, or pronunciation, but includes competency in discourse (Heath, 1983, 1986; and Lund and Duchan, 1988). This is sometimes overlooked. Heath's *Ways With Words* helps to explain the consequences of acquiring home discourse patterns which contrast with standard or school patterns.

The main factor in dealing with competency in a particular language may be a cultural issue. In the culture of the United States, verbalization is extremely important. In the Chinese culture, excessive verbalization is seen as bad manners. It is clear that there is social class variation, and the kind of discourse one learns is very critical. There are rules governing the discourse patterns: when to speak, who speaks first, what to talk about, what not to talk about, what is considered appropriate, what is considered rude, how to initiate a conversation and when to terminate a conversation, what is considered complimentary and what is considered insulting, what is considered polite and what is considered rude, etc. These rules have to be learned and cultural variations need to be addressed. Since language minority children do not have models that they can look up to in the home environment, such rules need to be clearly taught at school, and the teachers need to expose students to the various rules that dictate the discourse. This part of the added curriculum can be referred to as the hidden curriculum.

Looking at cultural issues, one immediately recognizes the fact that different cultures place importance on different forms of language. For example, in the Japanese language the use of the word *I* is a critical matter. One must know when to use the polite form of *watakushi* and when to use the colloquial *watachi*. Among young Japanese children, there is even a differentiation by gender, whereby boys are encouraged to use the informal *boku* form for *I*, whereas girls are encouraged to use the polite form '*watakushi*'. In the Chinese language, there are also different terms of address. There is the polite form, or the form that has honorific attachment to it, and there is the more casual form or more intimate form.

In English, the words *you and I* are all encompassing. In any type of discourse, because of the variety of social settings, one has to learn the rules for the different kinds of social settings. If someone has been exposed to a kind of formality in cultural attitude, then his or her focus is going to be quite different from someone who has been exposed to a less formal way of addressing people. Calling everybody by his or her first name rather than by a title, such as Mr., Dr., or Professor, might not be appropriate. This type of cultural difference actually influences the overall social discourse in terms of one's orientation of social distance and how much to say, to whom, or about what. All of this is learned from the variety of social encounters to which one is exposed; because of this, people coming from different social classes are exposed to very different social functions. As a result, the variety of discourses to which one is exposed will eventually be reflected in one's way of speaking. This is what Heath talks about in her 'ways with words' in terms of different communities. The consequences for Asian newcomers may be extreme by their shift towards a simplified pronomial use, which causes complaints by parents and other adults that the child has lost not only the ability to use proper honorific titles but also the proper respect for elders, as is indicated by the use of a familiar form of *you* with adults rather than a more formal *you*, which implies respect.

This is a sociolinguistic issue, but it is clear that the topic of English language acquisition and how well students are doing in school involves the whole spectrum of discourse competencies. The ability to think abstractly and to deal with a variety of situations is cultivated in formal academic English in which everything has to be laid out precisely. In more colloquial speech, much of it could be simply taken for granted or inferred. Many Asian newcomers are simply not taught to articulate in the same fashion, and so they have to learn not only the English language but also a variety of discourse forms, which are essential for social and conversational competence and are part of the broad definition of 'well-roundedness'.

Well-roundedness

The definition of well-roundedness is difficult, since individuals from diverse backgrounds have different definitions. In general, the definition implies that the person is knowledgeable about a variety of topics ranging from sports to politics, from movies to operas, from African geography to Chinese history, from gourmet cooking to high fashion, from contemporary literature to ancient archives, from environmental issues to computer languages, from law to medicine, etc. Many newcomers neither comment about their ignorance of such esoteric topics nor seem to be able to manage American verbal nuances, such as humor. How one acquires such knowledge is puzzling and challenging. Such information can be shared with classroom teachers for the development of well-rounded individuals who are multiculturally literate, but for the most part, Asian newcomers miss out because the notions are assumed rather than specifically articulated in classroom settings. In a sense, one has to be a cultural 'native' to possess the notions of well-roundedness, since it is a hidden cultural agenda.

According to Chinese tradition, people are not supposed to talk much during dinner. If anyone must talk, it will be the parents who speak *to* their child but not *with* their child. It is a one-way discourse. American discourse structure violates some of the social pragmatic rules that have dictated Chinese tradition for thousands of years. It is very difficult for parents to change roles when communicating with their children. Observing what the child brings home from school is not stressed in Chinese cultures. Parents continually wrestle with conflicting rules of pragmatic social conduct. They must become bicultural and understand that different rules dictate accepted discourse in a variety of environments. Exposure to all aspects of communication is not available merely in the home environment.

For parents to change or make great modification in their usual style of discourse is usually very difficult, if not impossible, because it is so ingrained into their cultural background. To ask for modification, educators must provide workable strategies that are culturally acceptable and relevant. Suggestions that parents talk with their child at home carries very little weight or practicality. School districts often provide workshops for parents. A one-day workshop is not sufficient for bringing about real change with these parents. Responsible teacher/parent communication, although difficult to accomplish given the time constraints of teachers, is crucial. Communication through a support system of biculturally competent parents is more effective than the best planned workshops.

It is clear that we cannot single out language as the only issue that must be dealt with regarding new Americans in our schools. Embedded in the language issue are a multiplicity of psychosocial factors, such as school adjustment and mental health. First, let us deal with some background information that will help support discussion regarding adjustment of this diverse population.

The California State Department of Education documented language acquisition of LEP students and reported on bilingual students. In 1986, they produced *Beyond Language*, which identified additional factors besides linguistic issues as causes for school problems. Of primary concern in these documents were the problems of Hispanic children. Only in a cursory fashion were Asian or Pacific Islander children addressed. Asia as a continent has many diverse countries, peoples, cultures, and languages. The groups with which educators in the US deal most often are the Vietnamese, Laotians and Cambodians. Thailand and Burma are excluded since there is not a large influx of refugees or immigrants into this area. China alone has more than 55 different ethnic groups, with more than 88 different languages. The Philippines has more than 7000 islands and 80 different languages. The diversity of languages, people, religious beliefs and background is such that one must examine many varied factors before dealing with an individuals' psychosocial and mental health concerns. People come to the United States with very different kinds of cultural and linguistic backgrounds; kinship systems and religious folk beliefs are all very different. One cannot stereotype any person from the Asian and Pacific Group as being from the same homogeneous groups of people or even from the same language family.

Throughout this text we place emphasis on the Chinese perspective, since it has shaped the traditions of Hong Kong, Japan, Korea, Taiwan, Singapore, Vietnam and other Asian nations. Nevertheless, the reader should be alerted to those countries shaped by the Indian tradition, such as Burma, Cambodia, Indonesia, Laos, Malaysia and Thailand, as well as by the Pacific Islanders form other groups including Melanesians, Micronesians and Polynesians. Finally, the Philippines form a uniquely separate culture that was shaped by the cultures of indigenous Malayan groups, Chinese immigrants, Spain, and the United States.

Family Context: Parents Pursuing the American Dream

How can parents enhance school success which, in turn, leads to social success? There are basically three means. The first is parental knowledge of access to resources. This may include IQ tests, language schools, special programs, such as Gifted and Talented Education (GATE), etc. The second means is home teaching by the parents of academic subjects taught in school. This can be provided directly by the parents themselves or by the use of tutorial services. The third means is auxillary learning and includes extra-curricular activities, such as music, dance, acting lessons, sports and travel.

Home teaching or tutoring is becoming increasingly popular as Asian parents become increasingly concerned that their children receive after-school practice in the academic skills taught in school. A San Jose mother, born and educated in Japan, has two children attending private schools. Her English language competence is very low. Because she wants to make sure that her children are at the top of their class in school, she hires a tutor to come to their home to read and do math with them every afternoon. A chemist from Taiwan, who received his PhD from the University of Pennsylvania daily gets up at 4:00 a.m. so he can arrive at his office by 6:00 a.m. Every afternoon he comes home early from work and picks up his first grade son from school. Together, they read, write, and do math. This type of home teaching is very common among Asians and is not class linked.

Parents who have little schooling can provide educational opportunities for their children as well. An example is a Chinese family, in which the parents are the owners of a restaurant in Los Angeles. The mother has a fifth grade education and the father finished middle school. Because of their business, they have very little time to spare. Their child, who is 11-years-old, has had a tutor since she was seven. The tutor, a major in journalism, reads with her, works with her on school projects, takes her to the library to check out books and also takes her to different school activities. Although the parents are incapable of personally providing academic education at home, they make certain that they provide the best possible home tutoring for their child. After the tutor had worked with the daughter, her grades went from Cs to As. She is also taking music and karate lessons.

Asian parents who are wealthy, but not necessarily well educated, usually realize that their children need to get ahead and that they cannot help them personally. These parents often hire tutors for their children. Parents who are in business and have limited time at home also make every attempt to give their children an academically stimulating environment. There are many middle-class Asians who hire college students, rather than typical teen-age babysitters, during the summer to care for their children.

Most Chinese immigrants emphasize education at home. They feel that American schools are not demanding enough, so they create their own homework to augment their children's education. Mei-lin is taught the Chinese script at home by her parents. In math, she is above grade level and at the top of her class, because her father tutors her in many areas of math before it is introduced to her class. His attitude is that since she must compete, he wants her to be 'number one' and will insure her success with personal tutoring. He expects her to go to medical school and will support her if she wants to go to Stanford or Harvard. This is the least her parents expect of her.

It can be observed that most parents, regardless of their cultural background, maintain common goals for educational success. The above examples identify important differences, not only in attitudes, but also in strategies that parents use to achieve their goals. The approach of the Chinese parents is very specific. They identify specific goals, with emphasis upon certain skills, such as reciting multiplication tables one through five in under five minutes, or the colors of the rainbow in the order they occur in nature. The skills required of children are typically the traditional skills that parents have learned and acquired throughout the years. They want their children to acquire these same skills. It is important for Chinese parents to instill in their children a sense of history and geography. Facts and figures are also very important. Wong-Fillmore (1985) notes that Chinese parents focus on the acquisition of factual knowledge. She further states that parents de-emphasize any type of fantasy or exploratory studies. Instruction is explicit and direct. Skills are outlined sequentially and categorically. Knowledge is equated with facts and figures. A knowledgeable person is one who has memorized a great deal of information. Part of the rigorous Chinese training includes the recitation of poems, rhymes and pieces of articles from the first word to the last. These kinds of activities are considered rigorous learning exercises.

Chinese parents would feel that simply presenting the child with different types of leaves for them to study and memorize is an efficient way of gaining knowledge; they may question the importance of going to a zoo to see animals or to a forest to search for different kinds of leaves. It is deemed sufficient for children to learn their names and the way they look from a book. Chinese teaching philosophy is contradictory to that found in American schools because of the different emphases. The Chinese philosophy emphasizes recitation and rote memory of knowledge that is fixed and factual, whereas the American philosophy values creativity, exploration and innovation. American children are reinforced and praised for individualism and uniqueness.

Auxiliary Education

Anything dealing with learning aside from what is required in the schools is defined as auxiliary learning. Music lessons, art instruction, sports and travel would be considered auxiliary learning opportunities. Historically, Asian students have emphasized traditional academic subject matters, such as math and language, with little regard for auxiliary subjects. As a result, Asian students have been criticized for not having command of these areas. Auxiliary learning plays a role in the overall education of the child. It provides access to hidden parts of the culture that are not normally available through traditional academic exposure.

In general, American society, at least within the realm of higher education, values a person who is not only excellent in academic areas but also well-rounded. Leadership, social skills, self-confidence and self-awareness are all important aspects of American cultural tradition. The hidden curriculum is something that Asians are just beginning to discover, as this complementary aspect insures that Asian children succeed in getting into 'the best schools'. Admission standards have been studied carefully; it has been found that a good SAT score does not guarantee entrance into the best schools. Emphasis on auxiliary learning is not a cultural tradition, but has been discovered as a means of getting into the best schools. The hidden curriculum is being uncovered by parents who may not have an overwhelming appreciation for music or art, but who consider it a means to an end and treat it as an important curricular activity.

In the European tradition of social stratification, one of the marks of where you are placed is your knowledge of culture and of the fine arts. Exposure to auxiliary learning gives access to what is valued by upper and upper-middle classes who are the gate keepers. Sometimes such knowledge helps one get through the gates and is an instrumental aspect of socialization. A number of Chinese, Korean, and Japanese have recently entered the world of the arts. How do Asian parents view musicians such as Yo Yo Ma or Seiji Ozawa? Some have penetrated the world of sports. Michael Chang and Kristi Yamaguchi are two newcomers. Do Asians ever comment about them? Is importance afforded to music, arts or sports?

These different forms of art have not been traditional indications of a learned person, but there has been a recent shift of opinion. In general, people are very proud of Ito, Chen and Yamaguchi (famous ice skaters), Yo Yo Ma (a classical musician), Michael Chang (a tennis star) and other young artists. Exposing children to auxiliary learning, even as a motive for covering the hidden agenda, has resulted in exceptional cases in which youngsters do excel in the various forms of art. Proportionally, the number is very small. Major emphasis remains on academics. They know that success in sports, art, etc. is of short duration. The financial rewards of becoming famous as an artist or as a sports figure have warranted new perspectives. Michael Chang, through his endorsements, has made a lot of money and Kristi Yamaguchi, the Olympic and World Champion Skater, is able to enjoy fame as well as prosperity because of her skating skills. The success of these and other artists are beginning to penetrate the Asian consciousness. The traditional mind set still sees these forms as unimportant in terms of achievement. A person who gets the Nobel Prize in Physics has much higher prestige than Michael Chang, who may win the Wimbledon tennis tournament. For example, Yang, Lee, and Ting are Nobel laureates — they are held up as models to emulate.

Auxiliary learning is mainly seen as an aid to achievement. Auxiliary learning for groups such as the Pacific Islanders, Cambodians, or Laotians is valued and accepted due to differing traditions. Chinese have acquired and accepted the importance of certain auxiliary learning experiences, such as family vacations, visiting museums, etc. Such experiences are in concert with the tradition of and appreciation for history and geography. In China there exists a tradition of travel to famous places and historical sites, but hiking on forest trails does not have as high a priority as going to Tienamen Square or to a memorial park. A historical outing as a group or with a tour is usually preferred to a picnic. Travel has become more popular because of relatively recent affluence. When someone has a lot of money to spare, a good way to use it is to travel; it is very common, accepted and quite valued. Travel is perceived primarily as a family event, to visit someone you know, not just travel for the sake of travelling. Sports, on the other hand, is not as valued by Asians, although getting children into Little League baseball is now seen as an indication of success. Soccer is important to a lot of Southeast Asians, but not of highest priority. Most social gatherings tend to have a family orientation, that is, a family dinner, wedding, or birthday of a family member. Parties in which a lot of friends socialize are not frequently given.

One problem is the difference between poorer refugees and well-to-do Taiwanese immigrants. The well-to-do are very much influenced by international, particularly Euro-based, culture. The upper-middle classes try to emulate fashions and cultures of the international set. Travelling to different places also enhances this perception. For example, in Taipei, a trip to Paris is considered an impressive status symbol. With the accumulation of wealth, many Asians begin to think of ways to use their money to do things commonly done by the rich and famous. They imitate their behavior, style of dress, and buy the same style cars. These activities reveal that children and parents are becoming increasingly knowledgeable about the world.

Another type of auxiliary learning is language. Children are exposed to language, either the home language of their parents or another language, such as French or Spanish. Many children attend classes, including language courses after school. In San Francisco, for example, most Asian children go to three night courses a week after school, while many Asian children in Boston, San Diego, New York and Los Angeles go to school on weekends. The purpose of such schools is that the children maintain their home language while being exposed to different languages. Parents often force their children to attend these schools in the belief that the more languages the children know, the more qualified they are to compete in higher education. In many disciplines, a second or third language is a requirement for a doctoral degree. Therefore, this type of auxiliary learning facilitates and enhances future success.

The above analysis reflects the world of the 'brain drain' Asian new-comers and does not, in general, reflect the average Asian newcomer. The average Asian newcomer's world is much more mundane and is similar to that of others who are on the bottom of the social scale and who have little luxury of thinking about auxiliary learning. For them, the primary goal is to have enough money to get by, to learn the English language, to acquire skills which will give them a good job and then, possibly, to acquire social status. A fuller description of the average immigrant and refugee will be provided later in this chapter to demonstrate the wide range of socio-economic statuses and backgrounds that our newcomers bring to us.

School after School

At the time of World War II when people who were competent in the Japanese language were being recruited, American-born Japanese youth were asked whether they knew how to speak Japanese. It was estimated that approximately 95 per cent could not pass Japanese standardized tests. In spite of having attended Japanese schools throughout childhood, these youth were not competent in Japanese. Similar situations exist with regards to the Chinese schools. It would be surprising if, in general, the level of competence in the Chinese language among these students was above the sixth-grade level.

The question is whether or not children who have attended Chinese language schools being sponsored by the upper-middle class have higher levels of Chinese competence than those of traditional Cantonese-based schools. Children, whose parents spend time working with them on their Chinese homework, show a higher level of Chinese competence than those children whose parents do not. Parents who conscientiously make sure that the primary language is spoken at home also make a great difference in their child's education. The main thesis of the presentation given by Wong-Fillmore and Britsch (1988) on the price paid for maintaining primary language was an argument against early transition into English without any attention paid to the primary language. A policy of 'English only' could be destructive to families.

The above remarks reflect the 'functional' and 'informed' Chinese immigrant parent. What about the less 'functional' parent, such as many found among the ranks of refugees? Many of them are not only illiterate in their home language as well as in the English language, but also untutored with regard to education in the first place. What advice should be given to such a parent regarding home-based education?

As previously mentioned, though the Chinese model is applicable to many Asian newcomers, some will not have backgrounds which reflect that model, and some refugees may not have any schooling. Therefore, it is necessary to ascertain from the students what kind of schooling they have had. As we will see, the traditional Chinese education, while not the same style as American education, can be adapted for use in the American schools.

Bridging Cultural Gaps in Learning Approaches

The Chinese learning philosophy closely resembles that of lower-class whites in their emphasis of recitation and rote memory of facts and figures. This style is in direct contrast to the upper-middle class Anglo style most often taught in schools — problem solving, creativity, and innovation. In spite of differences in systems, Chinese influenced children seem to do quite well in US schools.

How do we account for this apparent contradiction? The benefit of rote learning to children is that if they memorize facts, they will eventually be able to use their memory to come up with answers to many of the questions asked in school. The Chinese believe in giving information to children and having them memorize it, even though they might not be able to comprehend it. Later, through study and maturity, they will begin to comprehend what they have been memorizing. Therefore, comprehension is not seen as a requirement or prerequisite to learning. For example, in Confucius' document of the *Analect*, there are hundreds of verses that children must memorize. They may not know what these verses mean, but they are able to recite them from memory and write them out. As they mature, they begin to understand their meaning. The underlying presumption is that the child is capable of 'learning' or memorizing information, and in time the child will gain wisdom. Thus, in contrast to the US working class, who may share similar rote learning approaches, the assumption Asians have is that education is a meaningful and worthwhile endeavor which will eventually pay off.

Chinese students do very well in competitions that require knowledge of facts (such as spelling bees and mathematics drills). Homework is considered very valuable and necessary to the Chinese, Japanese, Korean and Vietnamese cultures. To learn the many logographs of the Chinese language takes time and memorization. There is no short cut to escape the hard work required. Homework is essential because one cannot write Chinese properly without writing it many, many times. In contrast, there are only fifty-two letters (twenty-six small and twenty-six large) of the English alphabet for a child to master. Thus, by investing the time necessary to learn the Chinese logographs, Asian children gain a discipline from their early experience that is carried with them throughout their lives.

In Chinese schools, pages of writing are given to children to take home to practice and memorize. In contrast, most schools in the US do not give students in lower grades much homework. This presents a problem for parents who expect their children to work hard and become literate. This is one reason why many parents send their children to after-school programs to make up for the 'deficiencies' of American schools.

There exists today a common perception that American society has de-emphasized discipline — the very virtue honored by the Chinese, Japanese, Korean and Vietnamese. Discipline is seen as part of hard work, a virtue imbued from early childhood. In a curious manner, pain and hard work are seen as conditions which produce strong morals. Traditional child-rearing practices among the Chinese and Vietnamese put heavy emphasis on the necessity that parents avoid spoiling their children. Thus, severe physical punishments for infractions are not seen as child abuse, but as expressions of parental love and responsibility in raising the child. Rather than assume that the child inherently knows right from wrong, American parents feel that the child is highly moldable and that close supervision and socialization is necessary. By contrast, Asian newcomer parents feel that too much latitude is afforded the US-born children, and that these children lack discipline. Asian newcomers bring to school a discipline and database of knowledge frequently admired by teachers who lament the loss of the work ethic in America.

Even though Asians newcomers bring many positive qualities with them, they may be unfamiliar with the American system that utilizes creativity, critical thinking and comprehensions. If tutorial services in the schools can stimulate creativity and comprehension, then the child's chances for success will increase. Parents, who are aware of what was missing in their own training and thus of their limitations in helping their children make adjustments, will be motivated to find the best assistance for their children's needs. Many parents have entered the US educational system at the graduate school level. Upon entering graduate school, they realized that book knowledge would not earn a doctoral degree; the breadth and depth of knowledge and the process of inquiry and analysis are of utmost importance when turning doctorate degrees into realities. Because they did not learn this through experience in their own country, many Asians suffer a great deal in American society. Thus, they hire tutors for their children to compensate for what the parents cannot do, or cannot do very well.

There is a hidden factor that is not often discussed regarding transitions of Chinese immigrants. Prior to 1950, many Chinese students from Taiwan and China came to the United States to attend the best institutions, such as the University of Chicago, Harvard, and Yale. They did very well, received advanced degrees, and many of them now teach in universities. Others do research work. Most of them studied disciplines such as engineering, hard sciences, math, and physics. Few studied or received degrees in the areas of sociology, anthropology, or literature. Why was there a disproportionately high amount of immigrant students who studied science and math disciplines? Certainly, there was a linguistic barrier, and less language is required for these disciplines. Also, in disciplines such as engineering and chemistry, the work is very prescriptive, which the Chinese are trained to do. On the other hand, there were those few who studied in areas requiring more creativity and exploration and who did not do as well academically as the Chinese who were studying in the sciences. These graduates often became professors and teachers, but are not considered the best teachers; their students often complain about their teaching style. Is it because of their lack of knowledge, or is because they have been educated differently and teach in a style not compatible with their students? Their teaching style reflects the Chinese learning system, which contradicts the learning style of their students. Throughout the educational strata, there is a conflict between teachers who have been educated in the US and immigrant/refugee students who have had exposure to the educational system in their homeland prior to attending school in America. In order for parents to help resolve this conflict, they must enhance what is missing in their children's previous educational experiences. How can Asian parents empower their children with the ability to succeed in school when they themselves have an educational background which is weak in some areas? Many of them hire tutors, while others provide volunteer work in the schools. By volunteering, parents learn more about the system and better understand what is needed for their children. They can then more efficiently provide needed access to their children. They may visit the school and observe the teacher and the classroom in order to replicate and enhance that environment at home.

Coping with Daily Survival: Preliteracy and Illiteracy

The refugee population brings with it varying levels of literacy experiences. The Hmong population, for example, does not have a high literacy rate, but has a developed oral tradition instead. The other refugee groups have sporadic schooling. In the home environment, literacy skills may not be regarded as highly desirable or necessary. After they arrive in the US and their children are placed in school, literacy becomes an educational priority.

The topics previously covered include acculturation and psychosocial adjustments of the Asian population. Acculturation to a new country presents conflicts that may be dealt with in three typical ways: immigrants may try to maintain the old culture; they may gravitate towards the US culture; and they may be caught in-between, never fully accepting either culture. Refugees who have experienced trauma tend toward issues of survival, such as mental health issues and effects on language/literacy acquisition, as exemplified by the Cambodians and the Lao community.

San Diego social workers have noticed an emergence of a second generation of refugee children maintaining welfare status rather than moving on to the job market, as had been expected. It takes them longer to learn English, get high school degrees, get into the job market and get off welfare. This raises some fundamental concerns. In general, the population is thought to be the model for other minorities to emulate, but experience with these new Asian groups indicates that adjustment is very complex and of quite diverse character. To compare blacks with Asians would be inappropriate without qualifiers, and to treat Asians as a single group is also wrong. When we compare Asian groups with each other, we find factors which differentiate them from each other.

In the next century, a main societal concern will be the permanent underclass. It has been about fifteen years since the first wave of Southeast Asian refugees came to this country, resulting in a decade and a half of study of the population. Second and third waves came much later. Many immigrant children in school today were born here. Their experiences are not the same as their parents' home country experiences. Since their parents are receiving welfare, the children are considered members of the underclass. They know of no other way of life, and feel they have no alternatives. They share a similar world view of hopelessness and helplessness.

The purpose of education is to empower every individual to become vocationally and professionally prepared, but somehow some cannot escape entrapment in an underclass. Once they get to the age where they are eligible for social welfare, they continue to take it. Perhaps this indicates a failure to some extent of the American social system to empower these recipients, to educate and guide them, so that their children may get out of this cycle and be prepared to enter the working force. This trend is a tragedy for these individuals, their families, their culture and for society as well.

Within the refugee population, the vast majority enter the welfare system initially. The Vietnamese, although they choose welfare as a practical solution, ultimately work themselves out of welfare, because they have other approaches to survival in the US. Obtaining home ownership, relocating to a better area for the schooling of their children, and moving up in the world for status reasons is very important to them. The Vietnamese are somewhat akin to the Chinese, in that although they may come in at lower socioeconomic levels, they have the concepts most appropriate to a capitalistic system, especially the goal of accumulating capital.

Lao and Cambodians who enter as refugees come with different historical backgrounds. Many were peasants with very little experience dealing with a modern economy. Although Chinese-based cultures tend to direct people away from welfare, the experience of the Lao and the Cambodians makes them more vulnerable to welfare dependency from the start. Cultures such as the Cambodians and Lao emphasize patron-client relationships such as those found in the welfare system. Taking welfare is not considered a loss of face. In fact, some refugees who work are considered fools, because they get less money than those who receive welfare. Sadly, it is true, that often one actually can make more money on welfare than at entry level labor jobs. Educational level and other variables affect the decisions to receive welfare. The consequences for the children of welfare recipients is yet unknown, but many questions are being raised with regard to this issue. Teachers need to be alerted to potential problems that may result, such as the following:

1   *Psychosocial issues.* The circumstances of newcomers are extremely complex, as they involve adjustment to life in a new country and culture. Some newcomers bring with them a history of trauma and have to seek counseling and psychosocial therapy. Many individuals' problems remain undiscovered due to their lack of knowledge of resources and language barriers. Many cases have been reported in areas where there is a large concentration of refugees, such as Los Angeles, San Diego, Minneapolis, San Francisco, and Fresno.

2   *Family Disintegration.* There are three main types of family organization when immigrants come to the US. The most common type is the whole family that comes together and settles in a city. They then sponsor other members of their family through petitions, usually taking up to ten years to bring the whole extended family to the US. The second type of immigration is when one person comes first, either to study or to travel, chooses to stay and petitions for immigration. Included in this category are young students who come to the US to study English, to attend high school or college. These individuals are often unsupervised. Some stay with a host family, others share an apartment and some may stay with a friend or relative. The third type is most common for refugee groups. An individual or a group of people may emigrate to the US using refugee status and are sponsored by either a church group or other organization. Refugees come as individuals or with their family. Frequently, the family of a refugee is disintegrated due to war, separation and death. This third type of family commonly replaces family with friends. It is not unusual to find an apartment occupied by friends who work together as a family unit. Each member takes on a particular role.

3   *Role Shifts.* When immigrant/refugee groups come to the US, they usually experience great shifts in roles, often leading to stress and family unrest. The following is such a situation.

Ping came to the US from Hong Kong with his wife and two teenage children. They decided to leave for fear of the 1997 takeover of Hong Kong by the Communist Chinese. Ping had a managerial position in the Post Office, and his wife Wen was a Principal at a primary school. They were in their mid-forties and were hoping to find employment in the US. They brought their life savings with them and used a large portion to buy a four bedroom house with the expectation that their parents and other members of their families would come and stay with them.

Ping and Wen went to adult education classes to learn English, which proved to be difficult. They were also desperately looking for jobs. After many rejections and disappointments, they finally chose to learn technical skills and found employment in a factory that manufactures computer disks. Ping and Wen worked examining computer disks. They often had to work long hours including overtime. They chose the grave-yard shift and often worked during the weekend. They had practically no social life and still could not communicate very well in English.

When they had lived in Hong Kong, the family would go out in the weekend with friends, play mahjong, and have dinner parties. Ping loved to cook and entertain at his home. Now in the US they did not have a social circle, and Ping and Wen felt isolated and depressed. Ping lost interest in cooking, they often ate fast food, and seldom went out. After working in the factory for several years, both Ping and Wen developed back and elbow problems that required physical therapy. They were in constant pain and felt even more depressed. Meanwhile, Wen's parents and sister came to stay with them. Wen's sister, divorced with three young children, could not find a job. Tension began to build and, eventually, Ping had to ask Wen's sister and her family to move out.

The above example highlights several important points: the change in social status and job mobility; the social isolation and physical isolation from friends; the loss of self-esteem and the burden of sponsoring family members without other forms of social support.

The following illustrates the problems of multiple-role shifts. Tran and his family (his wife, mother, mother-in-law and two children) came to the US after the fall of Saigon in 1975. He was a physician and his wife did not work outside the home in Vietnam. When they first came, they were on welfare. Tran tried to obtain a job to no avail. His wife received training at a local community college and found a job as a nurse's aide in a nearby hospital; she also learned to drive and became quite independent. Her job had a rotating schedule that required her to work late, which often resulted in her absence at home during dinner. Both his mother and his mother-in-law were in poor health, so Tran began to buy the groceries, prepare the meals, change diapers and clean the house. Such duties were not part of his experience, and he resented them deeply; he still expected his wife to serve him whenever she was not working. She felt fatigued, overextended, and resented the fact that she had to be the breadwinner and still carry the full load of housework whenever she was home. She began attending social functions and leaving her husband at home. Tran had no social life and felt very depressed. Their son was doing well in school and often served as the family interpreter. This young son began to take on the responsibilities of going to the immigration office.

Tran and his wife began to fight, and they were very unhappy. He started to drink heavily and play cards all day. His younger son stayed at home and watched TV all day. The son, mother-in-law and mother were left by themselves during the day, eating meals consisting mainly of bread and milk. The younger son who was five and could not talk much, also seemed depressed. The older son would come home from school and cook for his family. He felt the burden of family responsibilities and resented the fact that he had to play the role of son, brother, father, cook and student.

The above illustrates role-shifts and the difficulties which accompany them for many newcomers. Such problems may be resolved by the community leaders, thus problems of dysfunctional families are sometimes resolved. A closer look at the community organization may help us understand how a community facilitates interaction and provides resolutions.

Community Resources: The Chinese Community

The following section describes the social organization of Chinese immigrant communities, including an analysis of the San Diego, California Chinese community (See Map 4.1). The principle of social organization is the development of reciprocal relations with a variety of social networks. No single support system is isolated from a wide variety of particularistic relations. Those relations provide information on survival in the US, information on schooling, and information on the exchange of goods and services. The root model of all social relations is the family and its associated obligations. Thus, entering these relations entails both rights and responsibilities. The wide variety of support groups have common reciprocal ties, and a serious violation of obligations in one relationship is likely to have repercussions in other ones. Thus, a person who is seen as 'unethical' may find him or herself ostracized from the whole Chinese community.

The Chinese community has a highly developed social system based on three aspects. The first is the church. Most people go to church to worship and also to socialize and get information. They find out where the best restaurants are, the best schools, the best piano teacher, and other information. The second is grouped according to language/dialect. Those who speak Cantonese belong to the Cantonese group, those who speak Taiwanese make up another group, and those who speak Mandarin yet another. People from Taiwan, Hong Kong, or Singapore may not only share the same language but may also be able to exchange information about business, money, investments or may even collaborate on projects. The third is vocation or profession. In large cities, people of the same profession may become associates. We find, for example, that people in engineering form relationships with one another just as motel or restaurant owners form their own groups. These groups are defined by profession, business, or vocation; members usually share the same ethnic background. There is a wealth of

Map 4.1   *San Diego, California*

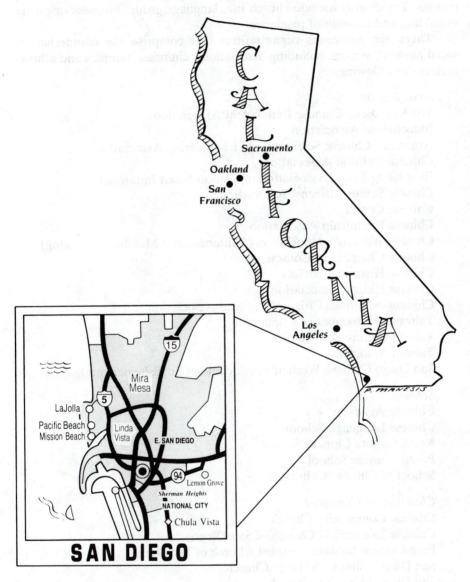

Source: Peter Manesis

information to be shared. Aspects of a parent's life may be shared with other parents. Topics may include church life, language group, business or professional life, and location of residence.

There are numerous organizations that comprise the comprehensive social network system, including associations, churches, temples and schools, such as the following:

Associations
The San Diego Chinese Benevolent Association
Indochinese Association
American-Chinese Scientists and Engineering Association
Chinese Cultural Association
Bing Kong Tong (Association of Canton-based Immigrants)
Chinese Senior Citizens' Association
Chinese Center
Chinese Friendship Association
Chinese Women's Association (Cantonese and Mandarin-speaking)
Chinese Chamber of Commerce
Chinese Historical Society
Chinese Elders' Association
Chinese-American Citizens' Political Association
Taiwanese Chamber of Commerce
Taiwan Culture Association
Taiwan Association
San Diego Chinese Women's Association (English-speaking).

Schools
Chinese Academy
Chinese Language School
North County Chinese School
Po-Ai Chinese School
School of Chinese Culture

Churches and Temples
Chinese Community Church
Chinese Evangelical Church of San Diego
First Chinese Southern Baptist Church of San Diego
San Diego Chinese Alliance Church
San Diego Mandarin Church
San Diego Taiwanese Christian Church
San Diego Taiwanese Evangelical Church
Southern California Chinese Christian Church
East Clairemont Baptist Mission
First Chinese Southern Baptist Mission
Western Temple
Ten-ho Temple

There are also social/recreational groups, such as the Chinese Peking Opera Group, Chinese Choir and Chinese Marshal Arts. Furthermore, there is an organization that supports political activities. These formal organizations meet regularly and sponsor a variety of activities, including the Chinese New Year Bazaar, and the International Festival.

Traditional Social Support: Friends, Family

The social support system of Southeast Asians includes aspects of the social control system. Hence, the question of social support is also a question of social control. In their home country, what were Asian support systems like, and how did communities maintain social control over youth? Can we rely on the same support systems in the United States?

The traditional Southeast Asian family commonly includes the extended family and consists of members belonging to several generations, most of whom live under the same roof or in the same community. The Vietnamese family system consists of several layers forming a well-defined hierarchy. At the base is the immediate family which resembles, to a certain extent, the American nuclear family. Beyond this is the extended family, which consists of members born of the same parents and grandparents. The extended family exerts strong control over the immediate family and individuals. Members of the extended families do not necessarily live under the same roof, or even in the same community. Even when they live far away from one another, members of extended families still feel close and exert influence on one another. They are expected to give moral, material, and financial assistance to other members, especially in times of crisis. The Southeast Asian family usually provides to its members many services which, in the United States, are provided by government or private agencies, such as loans, baby sitting services, unemployment benefits, and senior citizen care.

Each member of the Vietnamese extended family has a special role to play, a responsibility to assume, and a special authority to exercise vis-a-vis other members. The dynamics of Vietnamese familial relationships are reflected in their rather complicated kinship terminology. Different kinds of uncles, for instance, will be designated by different labels which confer different responsibilities and authorities. More important than the extended family is the clan-type family, which remains strong in rural areas but has become very weak in urban settings where members of the clan often move and become detached from one another. The role of the clan is still strong among the Hmong. Hmong people cannot marry members of the same clan, although a Hmong widow usually marries the brother of her deceased husband. This custom, referred to as levirate, is not practiced by other Southeast Asian groups.

Although the husband is the head of the family in Southeast Asian cultures, the wife has considerable power in the family. She has more power than women in many other Asian cultures. Husbands and wives are bound by collective and bilateral responsibilities. Vietnamese women, in particular, have the power of the purse. As they grow older and become mothers and grandmothers their power increases. In the eyes of her children, the Vietnamese mother has the same status as the father. She is also seen as the embodiment of love and the spirit of self-denial and sacrifice.

Southeast Asian parents consider it an important responsibility to train their children. Children are taught to love, respect and obey their parents. Talking back or acting contrary to parents' teaching is not tolerated. The children are also taught, by way of their parents' example, to show solicitude and support to their parents in their old age. Southeast Asian elderly people never live alone or in nursing homes. They live with one of their children, usually the oldest son in Vietnam and Cambodia and the youngest son or daughter in Laos.

Respect and love are demanded of young people to members of the parental generation and above. Uncles and aunts must be treated with the same respect shown to one's own parents. Older children in the family, especially the oldest son, expect respect and obedience from their younger siblings. The eldest son is entrusted with a heavy responsibility, that of substituting for the parents in emergencies. His brothers and sisters think of him as their leader, who has the responsibility to provide them with advice and guidance. In Vietnam and Cambodia, it is customary for the eldest son to have the largest part of the family inheritance. In Laos, on the contrary, it is the youngest child who has the largest part, usually the parents' house.

Dating is not accepted in Southeast Asian societies. Children do not usually tell their parents if they have a boyfriend or girlfriend. This is especially true of girls. One of the main reasons that dating is not accepted is that it often distracts children from their school work. 'There is ample time for them to date after they have graduated', parents often argue. There are, however, many opportunities for boys and girls, especially in Cambodia and Laos, to socialize and date.

Prearranged marriages are no longer highly favored in Southeast Asian countries. Usually children have the freedom to choose their own mates, but the choice must be approved by their parents. If they act against their parents' wishes, it is considered a rebellious act, which is not accepted by members of the extended family or the community. Traditional wedding ceremonies are usually held in the bride's home. In Vietnam, a civil ceremony is held and the local record-keeper is invited to notarize the marriage certificate. Catholics celebrate their weddings in churches, in addition to the civil ceremony at the bride's home. In Cambodia and Laos, the wedding is also celebrated in the bride's home, where Buddhist monks usually give blessings to the married couple. In Vietnam and Cambodia, it is customary for the married couple to live with the groom's family, while in Laos it is standard for the married couple to live with the bride's family for a period of time. The first child will also be born in the home of the bride's parents.

In Southeast Asian cultures, it is the family, not the individual, that is the basic unit of society. This structure was created to perpetuate society and provide protection to the individual. Although the above analysis identifies variations in family form, let us examine more analytically the differences between the family forms of the Chinese and Indian cultural traditions.

Most outsiders assume that all Southeast Asian families function in the same manner as Vietnamese families. This is incorrect. Both the Khmer and the Lao (Luangpraseut, 1987) have been more influenced by Indian civilization, whereas the Vietnamese and Chinese-Vietnamese (and the Hmong to a lesser extent) have been decisively influenced by Chinese, especially the Confucian tradition. The Chinese model is based on vertically-organized, hierarchical, patriarchal, highly disciplined extended-family systems which instill deeply felt norms of filial piety and ancestoral worship. These deference norms are part of a system of mutually reciprocated obligations, including the expectation of extraordinary parental self-sacrifice. This ensures, in the US context, that the children will go as far as possible in pursuit of their education in order to ultimately honor and support the parents financially, thus making good on the parents' investment (Duong, 1981, and Te, 1987a and b). Furthermore, this Confucian model reflects an adaptive style that is active, pragmatic and instrumental, based on a work ethic of personal effort and an 'internal locus of control' orientation to problem-solving.

In contrast, the Lao and Khmer generally share a common religion (Theravada Buddhism) and common linguistic and cultural roots. More importantly, they do not have the kinds of patriarchal, extended family systems found in the Chinese model. Instead, family organization tends to be more nuclear, neolocal, bilateral and matrifocal — curiously more akin to American kinship patterns. Where one finds extended families among the Lao and Khmer, these families tend to reflect optional and individualistic rather than obligatory or deeply institutionalized obligations. Their emphasis has a spiritual element and a preoccupation with feelings. Several Khmer respondents, when interviewed, illustrated this perspective by asserting their need to establish a household separate from their parents, reinforcing the idea of family relationships as conditional and voluntaristic, based on individual feelings rather than collective obligations. In parent-child relationships, one finds looser social controls and less emphasis on filial piety among the Lao and Khmer, with less parental pressure to achieve, less of a sense of obligation to parents and emphasis on material achievement. Curiously, this view is compatible with the current American ideal of individual happiness.

The Hmong occupy an intermediate position, largely because of the relative absence of social class resources among preliterate parents (although in those cases where parents had some educational advantage or other human capital, this difference is positively reflected in children's attainment patterns). Instead, Hmong family and clan organizational resources may be more predictive of future self-sufficiency outcomes, despite obstacles posed by the scattered communities of this population as well as by the severely disadvantaged labor-market position of the first generation. Clan and family structure are manifested most notably in the discipline and attention Hmong youth give to authorities. They are highly motivated to avoid negative comment or sanctions and clan members will go to great lengths to avoid shame and to save face and their family name.

Although these characterizations of the Chinese, Indian and Hmong models of social life are themselves broad oversimplifications, they point out the necessity of recognizing ethnocultural diversity of Southeast Asians and its effects on adjustment patterns, including delinquency and response to school authorities. In all groups, the circle of people who live in the same location, whether village or urban neighborhood, form a system of social support and social control. This type of living is typical of many American small towns. In American cities we might associate these images with ethnic enclaves, such as Latino barrios. Although the idea of a circle of intimates who share the same physical space is similar to the refugee experience of community, there are important differences to recognize among which are:

1) *Village*: Village life consists of inhabitants living in close proximity sharing feeling of being a mutually responsible collective body, whose aim is to control not only youth but also each other through gossiping and ostracism. All adults feel they have the right to control any youth of the village. Additionally, the whole village feels an obligation to support all youth. Among the Khmer and the Lao the community contributes to the temple which feeds, clothes and shelters youths without parents. Among the Lao the organization of adjacent households are called *ban*, and the leader of the group is known as *po-ban*. Similar forms occur in other groups as well, but there are differences in the relative importance of kin versus community. Among the Hmong the family unit is the clan; among the Vietnamese and Sino-Vietnamese the family takes precedence over all other group allegiances.

2) *City*: In the city, various neighborhoods function as villages within an urban context, though the extent of close social control is considerably less than that found in villages. In cities such as Saigon, urban neighborhoods are closer in style to the metropolitan way of life of San Diego than to villages. Nevertheless, the system of community social control among these groups is considerably stronger than that found in present-day San Diego.

In general, whether in the village or city, punishment is often informal but invariably swift, which means that violators see a direct relation between their actions and consequences. This emphasis on social control, even to the point of what Americans would call violation of individual rights, is very effective, leaving little likelihood the repeated offenses. It is this background of heavy-handed punishments which undermines a respect for the US legal system. People in general perceive little connection between criminal activities and punishments. For example, a first-time juvenile offender may be released without punishment from the US legal system and given the impression that 'crime may pay'. Adult refugees recognize that US laws prevail and have given US authorities the right to establish social control. This control, however, does not replace traditional systems. For example, use of severe physical punishment was commonplace in the home country, but under US child abuse laws, refugee parents would be prosecuted for using traditional forms of punishment. There is a collective sense among adults that they have lost a system of social control and cannot rely upon each other to reinforce their beliefs.

Changes in Support and Community Issues

Living in the United States means a potential for losing not only support systems, but social control as well. When refugees come to the US, they bring with them the institutions of family, neighborhood, village, etc. Observations of persistence of Laotian social support systems (including village organization) even after repeated relocations in Southeast Asia, contrast with the apparent dissolution upon arrival to the United States. It is not that Laotians have lost all aspects of their organization, but the strangeness of a new land and a new people who have interfered with the ability to guide and control its members, especially the young. Some incarcerated youth are those who would be compliant with Laotian norms even in the relocated villages of Laos or Thailand. What have they lost, and what are we to think about reconstituting a social order which would either prevent youth from becoming delinquents or redirect deliquents away from deviancy? The same problems of cultural continuity and social control are present among the Khmer, Hmong and Vietnamese.

Many refugee families are experiencing a crisis over the loss of control of children, a problem facing many immigrants as well. Here are some issues facing these families: disrupted families, absence of parents, single-parent households, and working parents. Most individuals experience some disruption of family organization, whether it be the loss of a parent or, as in the case of unaccompanied minors, a total loss of family. Most young people have some sort of family in this country, but they are usually less complete than they would have been if they had not been refugees. The absence of both mother and father causes extreme disruption, and has especially for the Vietnamese.

Children who know English gain control over parents who do not. As in any family situation, relations between child and parent may become a battleground over the differing needs of the two, for example, decisions regarding times for coming home. Though many refugee adults know conversational English, a large percentage rely on their children to translate letters, phone calls and other contacts with non-refugees. In some instances, a child is asked to translate messages between parents and teachers over questions of his or her discipline problems. This situation creates a role reversal in which the child gains control over relations with parents by being able to manipulate translation. Control of communication channels means power. This condition undermines the ability of parents to control their children.

Since children acculturate faster and more completely into American customs than their parents do, disagreements result over a wide array of issues, including decisions on dating, mate selection, career choice, and hours of leaving and coming home. One effect of these conflicts is the resulting role of third parties, especially US authority figures. Refugees are subject to laws and expectations of the American legal system and norms, which are frequently in conflict with home-country laws and norms, such as the use of physical punishment on children. Teachers and other American authority figures enter into parent-child relations, often without realizing their role. In some instances, children have used American teachers to bring the police into their homes because of a dispute with parents. When parents use physical restraints and threaten children with physical punishments, children, remembering what their teachers tell them about child abuse laws, frequently warn their parents that they may go to jail if they hit them. Consequently, parents may feel intimidated and over-react to this threat by abandoning discipline altogether. Clearly both parents and children may abuse each other through the invocation of threats that bring American authorities into the home.

Even though refugees often live near each other, they do not experience the same level of collective responsibility and mutual support. Among them are people who are non-refugees or people who do not share the same sociocultural backgrounds. As community institutions do not travel well, traditional villages and neighborhood social organization have deteriorated. This is observed in the continuity of the Lao *ban* (or Lao village) as they moved from place to place within Southeast Asia. When village groups moved to the United States, they were unsuccessful in transporting their *ban* with them. Within San Diego there are groupings of individuals who live in adjacent apartments and homes who form a *ban*, but not one which retains the power of organization like those found in Southeast Asia. For example, the *poban* (formal village leader) no longer has the power to influence individual families and individuals as he once did. One can find quasi-*pobans*, but they are, in most instances, holders of fragile influence. Why didn't the Lao *ban* form of organization survive trans-oceanic travel? A major factor is the different types of surroundings. In Southeast Asia, no matter where Lao villagers moved, they found similar geography and physical arrangements, even when they moved to urban places. In the United States, individuals are no longer dependent upon fellow villagers and can, more or less, go their own way. Children are especially prone to disregard the feelings of fellow *ban* members, except those in their own peer group, who may not be drawn exclusively from the same neighborhood.

American Institutional Support: School, Community and Family

Refugees frequently look to American authorities to solve their problems, but they are often disabused of this idea when so-called authority figures release their youth without apparent punishment. Eventually some adjustments will have to be made between their expectations and the US system, but, in the meantime, the gap creates conditions for continuing troubles for these communities. Added to the lack of traditional support and control systems, these individuals face several problems in their adjustment to the United States, including learning the English language, finding work, and loss of control over their children.

In general, communities and institutions have been fragmented, and only those refugees who have continuing functional families are at a low risk of being in trouble. It is striking how we focus on the characteristics of individual youth to ascertain reasons for delinquency; perhaps, one might ask whether or not the community itself is encouraging delinquency. Some adults have been known for their welfare cheating, gambling, buying known stolen merchandise and substance abuse. In Southeast Asia these behaviors may have less negative consequences on the youth, because the mechanisms of social control are more likely to be intact. However, in the United States, especially under the welfare system, one wonders how these indiscretions may influence not only delinquency but also longer term maladjustments. For example, some youth are encouraged to steal cars, which through a series of exchanges, end up in the hands of a refugee with legal documents. In this case, the youth is actively encouraged by adults to violate the law for financial gain. Under these circumstances, attention should be paid to the enabling adults as well as the youth. Both adults and children are responsible and should be held accountable.

We are aware of over-simplification contained in the above analyses but find these analyses to be sufficient guidelines for ordering approaches to these populations. Nevertheless, we recognize variations within each group and the following list is an attempt to introduce guidelines for recognizing such variations. The educated have greater resources to keep control. Those individuals with a higher education are also more likely to be westernized, and thus, more prepared for adjustment to the US. The longer one is in the US the more likely adjustments can be made, but patterns are further complicated depending on continuity or discontinuity of cultural orientations. There were the serious consequences of war; the more severe trauma was experienced, the more difficult adjustment in the US.

When resources are limited, people may pool their money together to co-own a car or a house. This is a common occurrence among refugee families. This system of mutual assistance becomes a resource for upward social mobility and can be an asset. On the other hand, collective solutions can inhibit upward mobility, as exemplified by the Samoans. Pooling resources demands individual sacrifices of further educational experience. The Samoan child is likely to drop out of school and go to work in order to contribute to the collective. In the case of the Vietnamese, collective monies are used to support individuals who continue their education. Among Cambodian and Lao, the tendency to pool resources is not as strong as among the Vietnamese. This is primarily because the Vietnamese kinship system and ideology allow a rationale for pooling resources. The Cambodian and the Lao have a bilateral system, and the rationale for pooling resources, although existent, is not as persuasive. The strategy for pooling resources can be positive if used for the purpose of upward mobility or higher education.

What is the composition of a typical Asian family? There is a family living in a high rent district of northern San Diego that consists of a Vietnamese couple who are both in their early thirties. Both of them came to the US in their teens. One came with parents and one with another Vietnamese. Both of them were educated here and eventually moved into the medical field. The husband is working in a hospital. His wife could not find a job in San Diego, so she works in Orange County and commutes. The wife's mother and the husband's mother, both older women who do not speak English, live with the family and care for the couple's two children. They also have a distant relative living with them. This pooling of resources has enabled the family to move from being recipients of social welfare to owning their own house and multiple automobiles.

As people try to find better houses, they may go from East San Diego or Linda Vista to Mira Mesa and then to Poway or Rancho Penasquitos or further north to Rancho Bernardo. To finance better housing they pool their resources; again, there may be three generations in a single household. Large households are actually preferred to prevent loneliness. Among the Vietnamese, it's not unusual to find large households. In response to a question about how many bedrooms were in his house, a Vietnamese child replied, 'Every room is a bedroom.' There was no bedroom concept because every room was a room for sleeping.

For many of these people, mainstream culture is not part of their everyday living. All household members live out of every room, and privacy for them means something very different than it does for us, because they are used to living in more crowded quarters. They share their goods and pool resources and help out with the labor. There is a case of a Hmong girl who cooked for eighteen people every single day. Even though they lived in several separate apartments, they all got together for mealtimes. This is commonplace, especially among the Vietnamese and the Hmong who both have large household sizes. Furthermore, both of these groups reflect the importance of the patriarchal system, where male dominance and lineage is considered the key to life. Other groups, although they also live in extended households, have ideas about household formation which are somewhat different.

The Cambodian idea of a household is of joint households, not limited to family members, but including people they consider close to them sharing the same quarters. There is a greater fluidity in household formation among the Cambodians than the Vietnamese. The ease and frequency of sharing households with non-kin reflects the relative ease of creating a closeness of relations. It is not associated with long-term or permanent commitment. Cambodians form and reform joint households with greater frequency, because there is not the same long-term commitment as embodied in the Confucian system, where one is obligated to kin for life.

In a Khmer family, a woman lost her husband and was left to raise her five children. Would she be considered the head of the household or would there be other resources and support for this woman who might be experiencing mental health problems? Obviously, officials would try to find an adult male who is related and could help out, such as a brother or an uncle. If that didn't work out, the children might be left on their own to struggle and figure out what school and community means of help are available for them.

Implied in the operation of the mutual support system is the relationship to the child and how adults collectively have control over children. There is a different concept of child rearing among the Cambodians. Each child is thought to have his/her own Karma and will come into his/her own being as has been preordained. Although the Chinese believe in previous lives, they tend to shape their current lives by will rather than by preordained principles. Hence, the traditional child-rearing practices are the exception rather than the rule. The Cambodians have more relaxed child rearing practices because of different assumptions about the nature of the child. This has ramifications for teaching. These children come in with much looser attitudes regarding relationships. They are less uptight, but also much less disciplined.

The Stockton School Massacre

The following is a summary of the Stockton school massacre and illustrates how children, family and community can work together in a moment of crisis. On January 17, 1989, a young man carrying an AK 47 semi-automatic machine gun went to Cleveland School in Stockton, California and opened fire. He killed five children and wounded others. All five children came from Vietnam and Cambodia. The school and the community were in mourning. First some facts: The victims were Vietnamese and Cambodian children. Interestingly, this incident struck fear in the hearts of the Cambodians across California, but not the Vietnamese. The Cambodians, whether in Oakland or San Diego, felt personally threatened by what happened in Stockton, as if they themselves were going to be next. Why would this massacre in Stockton affect those living in Long Beach or San Diego? It has to do with their belief system. The second thing to note about this incident is that parents kept their children away from this school, and school officials had difficulty getting parents to let their children go back to school. This was a big issue. The Cambodian population believes in spirits, and life and death issues revolve around spirits. They believed that the Stockton children were killed because of spirits running loose, loose spirits which inflict bad consequences on people. How does one console the spirits of the dead? To get the children back into school the authorities had to deal with their ideas of spirits.

The school personnel were not aware of the beliefs, thus did not know that such fear existed. Their immediate reaction was, 'these kids are not coming to school, what do we do?' Field workers told parents in effect, 'We want your kids to come back to school. It's the law, it's safe, there's no longer any gunman there. The police are on the school ground.' But that wasn't really the answer. The field workers were focused on the safety of the children who were not hurt, but the community's focus was on the spirits of those who died. Field workers from the same culture group eventually found out about their concern. Outsiders, who were not employees of that district, came up with the solution. They suggested a ceremony on the school grounds to console the spirits.

School officials followed this suggestion made by outside consultants who were culturally aware of the concern. Officials were willing to accept having a religious ceremony on the school site, in spite of the long standing legal separation of church and state. With this intervention the children then came back to school. Parents were invited to the ceremony to witness the making of peace with the spirits and a Monk was invited to console the spirits.

This incident clearly illustrates the need for school authorities to understand, respect, and be sensitive to the beliefs of students and their parents. It took a consultant who was a well-respected member of the community to resolve the situation. This Stockton school example gives important educational implications for other school districts that educate Southeast Asian newcomers throughout the country. Reputation, respect and long standing trust are necessary for successful school interventions.

We discussed the adjustment of newcomers. Some fare well and others experience hardships, emotional traumas, family breakdowns, financial difficulties, language barriers, and social isolation. The so-called success stories cannot blind our vision and mislead us into thinking that the Asian newcomers do well and have relatively few problems. Contrary to this common belief, Asian newcomers experience extreme hardship, and many have to fight against high odds for survival and maintenance of family harmony and cohesion. In summary, when the school, community, and family work together, they can create a better tomorrow for all.

Chapter 5

Asian Minorities at Risk: Education, Delinquency and Labor Force

Asian groups are generally stereotyped as the successful, law-abiding and high-achieving minorities. This stereotype has important positive effects for most Asian students, and it is reinforced by the actual performance of most of these students. Southeast Asian communities, especially the Vietnamese community, are very aware of their image in the broader American society and seek to instill a sterling image of valedictorians and super achievers. On the other hand, if Asian students are viewed as instant successes, there is less justification for paying any attention to them or directing resources to assist those of them who may need help. The result is negligence in school, isolation, delinquency, and poor preparation for the labor market. This chapter describes in their historical context the various waves of Asian, particularly Southeast Asian, migrations to the United States, the consequences of inadequate education received by immigrant youth in the form of delinquency, and the role of teachers and community members in addressing education and delinquency problems.

In general, refugee adjustment has been laudable, as reflected in the majority of first-wave refugees who are self-sufficient, but there are many refugees who remain on welfare and are in need of special support. Asian groups, Southeast Asians in particular, like previous immigration waves in America, have had their share of problems. Examination of delinquency among immigrants and refugees is not intended to defame them but to seek a better understanding of their problems in order to find adequate solutions. Much of what is presented here is part of a local study in San Diego (Rumbaut and Ima, 1988), but its findings support the findings of other scholars in California, and with the overall historical picture of Asian immigrations in the West Coast.

Every major population movement inevitably seems to involve youth adjustment problems beyond those experienced by normal youth making their way to adulthood. Although the percentage of Southeast Asian refugee youths facing the American juvenile justice system appears to be below the national average, recently there have been increasing numbers of Southeast Asians youngsters charged with misdemeanors and crimes.

Historical Context of Southeast Asian Migrations

During the beginnings of Asian migration in the nineteenth and early twentieth centuries, Asians were depicted as dirty, with amoral sexual habits, opium addicted, dishonest and, were, in general, characterized as undesirables. Nevertheless, studies have documented the relatively low levels of crime and delinquency among Asians, and these low rates of criminal involvement have persisted up to the present time (Beach, 1932; Kitano, 1985; Kitano and Daniels, 1988; Misaki, 1933; and Strong, 1934).

In spite of overall low rates of criminal deviance, early histories of the Chinese and Japanese reveal that criminal behavior was associated with communities composed largely of single males. Such behaviors included prostitution and gambling. Among the Chinese, criminal behavior was linked to secret societies, which were a reflection of the Chinese search for social support systems, otherwise lacking, pertaining especially to a weak clan, provincial, or family organization (Lyman, 1974). Similarly, criminal activities among Japanese immigrants were linked to pre-1907 migrants of predominantly young male sojourners who sought recreation in drinking and gambling, so common in a frontier society.

Once the family formation stage began among the Japanese (1907–24), pool halls, gambling halls and drinking establishments diminished, reflecting a transition of the community toward more conventional behaviors such as family formation, child reproduction and development of an educational system (Miyamoto, 1939). In general, once in the family formation and reproduction stage, social control of individuals became a central preoccupation, since deviancy was seen to reflect poorly on families and thus communities. In effect, the Japanese American and Chinese American families became extensions of the communities in which they lived. In more recent years (1965 to present), the Chinese community has experienced a resurgence of juvenile delinquency, reflecting the influx of new immigrants. This resembles the early days when newcomers, who were dissociated from stable social networks, sought out companions who could fulfill their needs for identity and security. In a sense, the influx of dissociated individuals created conditions for the formation of new 'secret societies' which behaved like gangs. Their collective behavior frequently involves illegal activities.

The first wave of Southeast Asian refugees has been here only fifteen years and the bulk of the second wave refugees have been here less than ten years. The adjustment of previous immigrants and the manifestations of maladjustment in terms of delinquency were developed over several decades. In contrast, recent waves of immigrants seem to either rapidly fit into the American lifestyle and to adopt American cultural values, or to reject them and become isolated, alienated and even delinquent. Does speed of change foreshadow a different pattern of juvenile delinquency? Are the Asian refugees comparable to the older Chinese, Japanese and Korean communities, or is America, in fact, dealing with entirely different communities?

Among the Southeast Asian Chinese-speaking refugees, especially those who speak Cantonese, having an established social support network similar to the secret societies of many decades ago is attractive. This attraction to the new secret societies is due to their difficult time in finding a financially and emotionally secure niche in this new society. The prior existence of this network, which was also rooted historically in Chinese history, establishes a model not only for the Chinese-speaking refugees, but also for other refugees. At this time, the relative newness of the refugee population means that the most developed 'deviant' refugees will be the Chinese, since they have by association inherited networks of Hong Kong and Taiwan-based secret societies. The Chinese Vietnamese, in turn, have begun to socialize Vietnamese and other refugee youths into the ways of street life and strategies for survival including car burglaries, in that setting. The patterns of deviancy are at variance with gang behavior found in the black and Hispanic communities, since each group appears to have different social histories and cultural patterns. For example, the assumption that gangs are territorial is correct for black and Hispanic gangs, but not so with Asian gangs, at least for the most part.

We surmise that a similar motivation occurs for the refugees as it probably occurred for previous Asian immigrants — the search for money and security in a new society whose challenges seem insurmountable through the conventional channels of education and work. The youth, especially those who arrive in their post-puberty years with little schooling and few marketable occupational skills, are vulnerable to delinquency. Our examination of the Southeast Asian youth rests on the idea that maladjustments to the new society motivate many of those youths to seek deviant solutions. These observations were relevant to prior newly arrived Asian residents, especially those with few economic resources and access to the main economy, and we suspect a recapitulation of the same process among the Southeast Asian refugees.

In the 1970s and 1980s, Southeast Asians came to the United States as refugees, not as immigrants (see Chapter 2, pp. 25–29). They arrived in three waves. The first wave of people came between the fall of Saigon and the onset of the boat people (1975–79). They were primarily Vietnamese and individuals with higher than average social resources, including higher levels of schooling, professional and managerial occupational experiences, familiarity with urban life and so forth, when compared with their fellow countrymen.

The second wave, the boat people (1979–1982), began arriving after the Vietnamese communist invasion of Cambodia which precipitated a flow of refugees from Cambodia, Laos and Vietnam. From Cambodia came many individuals who were fleeing both the Vietnamese and the Khmer Rouge or the Cambodian communists; the war between Cambodia and Vietnam gave many individuals the chance to flee the 'killing fields' of Cambodia. The conflict between Vietnam and China over the Cambodian conflict resulted in persecution of Vietnamese persons of Chinese extraction. Many of these individuals fled across the northern border or in boats across the South China Seas and the Gulf of Thailand. Joining the Chinese-Vietnamese were many other Vietnamese individuals who had endured persecution from the communists, and some who were fleeing from the extremes of poverty. Thus, this second wave included not only a wide mixture of ethnic groups including Cambodian, Chinese, Hmong, Lao and Vietnamese, but also a wide mixture of persons from diverse socioeconomic backgrounds, especially including those from more modest backgrounds, such as farmers and fishermen. These individuals were not only less likely to be educated and to have fewer trans-ferable job skills, but were also less likely to know English. In general, they were less prepared for survival in the US.

The third wave (1982-present) have been affected by changes in the US refugee policies. The US government, in collaboration with the Vietnamese government, established an orderly departure program (ODP) which permit-ted some Vietnamese nationals to leave Vietnam as immigrants rather than refugees. Though the motives to leave Vietnam may in actuality still be politically-based, such as for those individuals who have been freed from re-education camps, people now have the possibility of being admitted to the US with immigrant status. Most of these cases are ones of family reunification or in the instances of Amerasian youth, cases of implied US citizenship by virtue of having a biological American father. This third wave continues to consist of boat people and individuals whose lives have been threatened physically. For this reason the US government grants them refu-gee status. Thus, the diversity of individuals in terms of ethnicity and social class backgrounds and the changes in the processes of leaving continue in the third wave. As the Vietnamese society continues to fail to feed, clothe, house and educate its citizens, many individuals now accepted for admissions into the United States have even fewer social resources than the earlier waves, including education, work skills and urban experiences. Especially notable are the Amerasian youth who are the least likely to have had schooling or worked in jobs which provide transferable occupational skills.

Areas of initial refugee settlement generally have lower rents and hous-ing costs, but over time, refugees move into single family dwellings in the next higher cost range. The first area of settlement in the San Diego area was Linda Vista. (See map 4.1, p. 103). In 1975, the Vietnamese moved into the area followed by the Lao and Hmong. In those early years overt conflict erupted between refugees and older residents, especially with individuals from black and Hispanic groups and those from lower income groups. Currently, the conflict has eased and the community has stabilized with little increase in the number of Southeast Asians. Not only has the population mix stabilized, but the level of criminal activity and intergroup violence has also decreased as the refugees and other residents have adapted to one another.

After 1979 and an increase in the number of refugees, a secondary area of settlement in East San Diego occurred with a dramatic growth of all Southeast Asian groups (Cambodian, Hmong, Lao and Vietnamese), especially Cambodians. This area lacks the geographic boundaries which define and limit Linda Vista. East San Diego appears to be a geographically ill-defined area with high residential turnover of persons from all backgrounds, resulting in an appearance of high residential mobility. Additionally, the area has had an increase in the number of prostitutes from Southeast Asia and there is a sense that the area is a no-man's land. During the 70s, it became an extension of San Diego's zone of transition, resulting in an upward trend of crime and police surveillance. In this rapidly changing and unstable area is a wide mixture of ethnic groups who not only harbor ill feelings towards each other, but also seem to be willing to physically and verbally confront each other.

The third major area of refugee settlement includes the corridor of housing along Highway 94, beginning in the heavily Hispanic area of Sherman Heights and continuing to the Black-dominated area at the Lemon Grove border. In the Sherman and central residential areas are Cambodians with a sprinkling of Lao; around the Gompers Middle and Senior High School area, close to Euclid Avenue, is a large settlement of Lao. This latter area is the location of the Lao Buddhist temple. There are also a large number of Lao near the Educational Cultural Complex near the National City boundary. The presence of Lao is evidenced by the increasing numbers of Lao students in Lincoln High School and its feeder schools.

Mira Mesa and the surrounding suburbs are the latest areas of settlement. They are the second point of residence of earlier waves who have been able to afford more expensive housing and are likely to be from the earlier groups of refugees, especially the Vietnamese. Many families have begun to seek housing outside of San Diego's inner city neighborhoods for two reasons: better housing areas and better schools. Though the main bulk of the population live in these four areas, one can find refugees in other areas throughout San Diego County.

After working with dozens of youngsters who committed petty theft and other small offenses, the repetition of the same stories raised questions about possible patterns of involvement with the criminal justice system, especially as the tales reflected similar stresses, such as the traumas of departure and the disruption of traditional family relations. Questions were raised about the representation of these cases, since it could easily be assumed that the courts were sending only the most serious cases for evaluation and counseling.

After reviewing case files, major themes and parameters were identified. These reports were psychological descriptions and analyses used by the court to decide the disposition of cases. The reports include 1) interviews with defendants and others in the defendant's immediate social environment, 2) review of police reports, 3) psychological testing, 4) reason for referral, background information and social history, 5) clinical observations including intellectual and emotional functioning — cultural values and beliefs which impinge on understanding the defendant's functioning, 6) defendant's accounts of the event, and 7) conclusions and recommendations.

Permission was obtained to read the records for all delinquents from the San Diego County Probation Department's juvenile files. We identified all Southeast Asian delinquents for 1984 and 1986 and were able to read and code their files; they represent the complete record of all Southeast Asian juvenile delinquents who were formally charged with a crime during 1984 (n = 90) and 1986 (n = 132) in San Diego County. We developed a coding instrument based on the previously mentioned case files and a review of the probation department files. We were especially careful to develop codes which would enable us to compare both studies, thus permitting us to make comparisons between white and other non-refugee minority delinquents.

The probation department files were found to be irregular and frequently lacking any in depth materials, except in the most serious cases, where special clinical investigations were made. These special clinical files contained extensive observations as in the initial set of files. These files offer an unusually rich source of insights albeit confined to only a small portion of the total number of Southeast Asian delinquents. Some of the conclusions cited below came from those enriched files, for example, the issue of youths being older than their official age. The problems resulting from the age disparity is not commonly mentioned in the probation files except in some of the enriched files. Therefore, the overall statistical results and the details from select files complement each other; the latter are used for interpreting the resulting statistical patterns.

Since all of our materials are drawn from San Diego, we cannot make strong claims about Southeast Asian delinquents in other cities; however, we suspect that the patterns we have found in San Diego are parallel with those in other areas, for example, there is a greater likelihood of Vietnamese youths becoming delinquents than Hmong youths.

When referring to the refugees, the terms Indochinese or Southeast Asian refugees are used in their restricted meaning and include only people coming from Cambodia, Laos and Vietnam. These people came to this country for political asylum, not primarily for economic reasons. They escaped because of fear of persecution when the communists took over their countries of origin in 1975. They were deeply rooted to their native countries, even their native villages, and were reluctant to resettle in distant lands. Before 1975 there were very few Cambodians, Laotians, or Vietnamese in the United States.

The Case Study of Som

Som's father, who is of Chinese ancestry, immigrated into Laos at the age of 12. He received six years of Chinese education, and by the time he joined the

Lao military, he was learning both English and Lao. Som's grandfather migrated to Laos and eventually to the US as a refugee. He was hired by the Central Intelligence Agency (CIA), which was responsible for interdiction of North Vietnamese supplies along the Ho Chi Minh Trail. In 1975 when the Communists took over, he left the military and hid his association with the CIA. Eventually he became an importer-exporter. Other relatives who were also affiliated with the CIA were not as lucky — they were caught and sent to re-education camps.

Som's mother is a Lao farmer's daughter who received an elementary school education. Like other Lao, she retained close ties with her parents and would go back to her father's farm to help with planting and harvesting or whenever extra help was required. Preoccupation with helping his grand-father who continued farming ran throughout Som's interview. One of his uncles was captured while fighting with the Communists and was later executed. Another uncle was placed in prison for being a member of the CIA forces. Although his father was not identified as a member of those forces, he resented the way he was treated in his business — they unfairly taxed him and confiscated his goods. Som expressed feelings of revenge towards those who hurt his uncle and other members of his family.

Som, the oldest child, was born in 1974 and has two sisters and three brothers, all of whom were born in Laos, with the exception of the youngest brother who was born in the United States. Relatives who had previously moved to the United States wrote to his father about how much better things were. Consequently, in 1983, his father decided they should leave Laos. Although their city was located on the Mekong, they could not cross at that point because there were many Communists guarding the river front. There-fore, they went down the river to cross, and four days later they arrived on the Thai side. They were fortunate to have missed the Communist border guards who arrived on the Laotian side of the river. However, on the other side, the Thai people extorted money by holding the family hostage in a hotel for four days and sending a ransom note to an uncle. The uncle ultimately received money from relatives in the US and was able to pay off the Thai. After the money was paid, they were released and joined an uncle, who had been in a refugee camp for several months. Even though the camps were better because there were 'no Communist', life was still hard. The family of ten could not afford a place to live and were given the use of one room by the uncle. Though some food was supplied, there was rarely enough; lack of money meant that they had last priority for water, supplies, fuel, and all other amenities. They wrote to relatives in the US for money, but it took three months to receive the first payment. They were very angry about the delay and felt that their relatives were holding back. This constant theme of being disappointed and harboring anger toward other people was directed not only toward the Thai people, but also toward their relatives in the US.

Finally, the family was accepted for settlement in the US. Som was happy to be in such a rich country where he could better his life. His immediate family has remained intact since their departure from Laos, and they live in a San Diego apartment which was managed by his uncle. Three black families also lived among the Lao refugees, all of whom came from the same village. They call their new settlement Keng Kok Ban, after the name of their home village.

After he entered elementary school, Som's worries centered on learning the English language, making friends, and getting along with the teachers. He expressed his frustrations by saying, 'I didn't know how to talk. When I talk, the kids, they laugh at me. This makes me want to study hard so they don't laugh no more. When the teacher tell me to read, when I read they start to laugh.' It took him a year before he felt comfortable around his peers. During his integration into the American schooling system, his parents stressed the importance of doing well in school, so he could get a good job and earn enough money to help those relatives still in Laos. In school, Som must study hard, especially in math and English, yet his effort did pay off when he was allowed to skip the eighth grade. His transition to Lincoln High School was marked by his beginning to hang out with other Lao boys; they dressed the same and stood up for one another. Som told about many of his experiences during this transitional period: 'School wasn't hard, but because I got involved with other boys, I didn't do too well. I dropped out of school, stole cars and had fun thinking about being tough. I wore black clothes like other Lao boys. I didn't think we were gangs.' He tells about one instance when a friend, after stealing a car, came to his house and gave him driving lessons in a nearby parking lot. When his friend hit a trash can, someone called the police and a chase ensued. Som drove the car to a dead end and attempted to outrun the police. Nonetheless, Som was caught and his entanglement with the law began.

There was another incident during lunch at Lincoln when a Mexican boy began verbally attacking a group of Lao boys, saying: 'Chinese don't know how to fight', 'dumb Nip, Jap', etc. He pushed the Lao boys, and in spite of a preliminary attempt at allaying the hostility, the harassment continued and resulted in a fight. The fight established a bond between the Lao boys; the violence initiated a foundation for their close friendship. Som's affiliation with these boys who skipped school and stole cars further continued his bad relations with the local police. For instance, Som was arrested alongside his friend, who stole a car. In jail, Som lied about his name because he thought that they would harm his family. In spite of his seeming concern for his family, Som failed to listen to his father's advice to be good and to stay away from trouble. Som preferred to be part of the group; he wished to be tough and to have a lot of money.

After the Lao New Year, Som joined the Oriental Killers gang. Several other episodes occurred, and Som was arrested numerous times. He spent many months in jail, served time in juvenile hall, and even spent six weeks at Campo Detention Center. Som was sent far from his family, which made it difficult for them to visit Som, who felt lonely. His father scolded him and asked, 'Why didn't you want to be good?' When the authorities took him to the Padres San Diego baseball game, he escaped and went home. His mother cried, and his father told him to return; the next day he did. He was given an extra year term for the escape. Following that event, he tried hard to do the right thing. In the fall he was sent to the Youth Day Center in San Diego for two months; in December he was granted probation on an early release. Presently, he is at Summit School and wishes to go to college to study engineering. He has cut his ties with the other Lao boys, has decided to go straight, realizing that being bad will do him no good. He even talked to another boy in his housing complex about not hanging out with the 'bad' Lao boys. He wants to make sure that other Lao boys do not have to go through similar experiences.

Characteristics of At-Risk Asian Groups

Within the Asian groups, there are subpopulations sharing language, culture and experiences, and connected by family ties. This is especially notable among the immigrant and refugee populations which enter this country at puberty and are placed in various public schools. These youngsters also share similar problems, which are related to their pre-arrival experiences. These at-risk characteristics used for guidance and counselling are listed below:

- disrupted schooling
- disrupted family support system
- experience of trauma
- long duration at refugee camps
- poor health
- lack of prior schooling
- poor school attendance
- lack of participation in class
- lack of supervision at home (possibly no parents)
- lack of progress in English
- lack of participation in extra curricular activities
- lack of guidance and counseling for career/life goals

Clearly there are Asian at-risk students that need to be identified. Foreign-born Asians need to be better prepared for the job market and must recognize nonacademic issues that will affect their future, such as accent and the importance of networking. These issues definitely should be included in any curriculum dealing with this population, so that they can translate academic success into occupational success. We need to stress educational needs of the foreign born population in terms of social competencies. Having barely survived the school system, they have to be prepared for life outside the school set-up, and enter directly into the work force. They are basically an invisible social stratum (often the lowest in the stratification of an ethnic group) and we hardly hear about them. Many work in factories doing computer chip work, manufacturing and other occupations requiring manual skills. There is also a group of entrepreneurs who make money by working very hard and become successful business people, but who have very little political clout. Another group of the at-risk drop out of school. They don't seem to break from the vicious cycle of isolation and illiteracy. These are the permanent Limited English Proficiency, or 'LEP forever' students. They are unable to find adequately paying jobs and seem to continue to receive welfare or take odd jobs when they are available. Among the at-risk group is the delinquency group. These students do not master the English language and have difficulty dealing with academic issues. They may also be the learning disabled, mentally retarded or language impaired in their home language.

Their failure is a clear indication of the lack of adequate educational policies to accommodate their needs. They need a total support system that will not only make them more successful in acquiring the ABCs at school but will also give them skills required to become competent citizens outside the school domain. How do you get these children to participate fully in extracurricular activities? How do you prepare the parents to become members of the school community and provide opportunities for the growth and development of social skills? Social skills are required in order to participate in learning activities, and to acquire the knowledge necessary to compete in the labor force.

The following story illustrates the need for preparing Asian immigrants and refugees to acquire the necessary skills in order to protect themselves and deal with the world around them:

A man and his wife, restaurant owners, were accustomed to carrying home their cash in a money pouch every night. Money was counted at the end of the day, placed in a pouch and then taken home for deposit the next day. One night, the couple drove home and as they got out of their car, two Asians approached them with a gun and tried to rob the pouch from the wife. She resisted and, consequently, was shot. Because she was injured, she dropped the pouch and the men were able to grab it and run away. They were never caught. From the description, it was indicated they were Asian, probably Vietnamese because of the accent they used when they spoke English. The owners of the restaurant had been seen taking the money pouch home every night. The casual observers informed others, which resulted in the robbery and injury. The woman was taken to the hospital, and they called their friends to come to the hospital to help them explain to the police the details of the robbery. They also learned from their friends how to file insurance claims. Although they are illiterate, they found ways to get information through their friends. Robbery and car thefts are the most common kinds of crimes. Not many crimes involve drug trafficking, prostitution or gambling.

The Indochinese community of San Diego has both the highest level of academic performance, and one of the juvenile delinquent rates (Rumbaut and Ima, 1988). This is not unique to the Vietnamese. The Chinese community also shows a wide range of subgroups. This range creates a barrier in schooling, because teachers often assume that all Indochinese or Chinese can perform well in class. Those who are involved in crime tend also to come from disrupted homes. The home setting cannot control them and provide supervision.

A critical issue is understanding the home life. In Chinese and Vietnamese homes, guidelines are laid out by parents, especially the father. When there is no male model available for discipline and guidance, children are more likely to become involved in crime. Another problem are the runaways and the teenage pregnancies that often follow. Coming and going at will is considered part of life for some Indochinese. However, for other groups running away from home has severe emotional consequences. The runaway population is higher among the Cambodians and the Lao than the Vietnamese. In looking at crime statistics, we notice that a larger percentage of delinquents in the refugee population go to school outside San Diego county. This may indicate that the Asian youth population is somewhat mobile. Hmong have the lowest rate of runaways, something that may have to do with their tight family organization. Lao and Cambodians seem to have a looser family structure. Children are not ostracized if they run away. In Chinese and Vietnamese families, the penalties can be very high; parents may say, 'We disown you.' This is very unlikely to happen among other Indochinese. They don't see running away as a serious problem. There are no statistical figures on Asian teenage pregnancies, but we have heard statements from youth indicating that premarital sex is becoming more commonplace. Some Indochinese families do not consider pregnancies out of wedlock a disgrace for the family, in contrast with most Chinese families for whom this would be a terrible stain on their family name.

In dealing with acculturation, self image is an important factor to consider. Many children would like to be like their peers. When they dress, speak, eat and behave differently, they may feel a sense of alienation and isolation. This can cause problems for the students as well as for teachers because a sense of alienation and social isolation may hinder school progress. The students will have to wrestle with the fact that their parents look different, talk strangely, and do not conform to American, mores and manners. Students face many concerns. Should they go with friends and imitate the group in terms of dressing, verbal mannerisms, and ways of dealing with people? Do they live by the rules of their home that imply strict obedience, compliance, and acquiescence? These are conflicts that most Asian immigrant youngsters cannot verbalize but truly feel. They may reject the notion of belonging to an ethnic group because they feel they will not be accepted by the mainstream. They may socialize only with others like themselves and form their own groups. In some circumstances, these can develop into gang groups.

The Role of Teachers in Preventing Delinquency

Teachers may bring to the classroom certain assumptions about their students. Teachers explain the rules of the classroom with the expectation that they will be followed by the students. LEP/NEP students may need extra help in learning the rules and often learn by imitation and observation.

There are culturally understood rules that are generally assumed by teachers, such as how to use a fork and knife, the use of tissue paper, personal hygiene, etc. The following episodes demonstrate how such implicit rules may also need to be explained.

Episode 1:

A-Dong's (a 5-year-old Vietnamese boy) mother received a phone from Mr. L. the principal of the school. He said that A-Dong went to the bathroom in the playground near a bush. Mrs. T was puzzled by this phone call, since she often took A-Dong to a bush for his urination. So she asked what was wrong. Mr. L. explained to her that little children should go to the bathroom to urinate and not do it in the playground near the bush. Mrs. T. said she would talk to A-Dong.

Episode 2:

Ms. D. was trying to help Hong Thong (a Lao boy) in the bathroom since this was his first day in school. She helped him unzip his blue jeans and found out that Hong Thong had no underpants. She did not know what to do and asked the bilingual aide to explain to Hong Thong's parents that he needed to wear underpants. Mr. Hong Thong was contacted, he didn't know what underpants were, so the aide explained to him what they were and where to purchase them.

Episode 3:

Blia's (6-year-old 1st grade Hmong) parents were called by her teacher and informed that a parent-teacher conference was scheduled to discuss her placement for the next school year. When Mr. and Mrs. C. arrived at the school, they found six people sitting in a conference room, including the teacher, the principal, the speech-language pathologist, the resource teacher, the school psychologist and the school nurse. The teacher, Mrs. J., said that she felt Blia should be held back because she seemed very shy and unsociable. Blia seemed to get tired very easily. Furthermore, she felt that Blia was not interested in learning the letters of the alphabet or reading. She asked Mrs. C. what bedtime stories were read to Blia. Mrs. C. was not able to respond, since she could not read and did not know that other parents read bedtime stories to their children.

What does school success mean? How can individuals who are at-risk or in need of intervention become empowered to succeed in school? In the traditional sense, one type of school success is academic, which is determined by subject-matter competency, defined by school curriculum and class texts. The second type of success is extracurricular, which involves student extracurricular activities, such as student government, social clubs, volunteer work, sports, and music. Such activities can be measured by participation and popularity. The third category of school success is social. This may be measured by how popular the child is, how many parties he's been invited to, how many friends he has, or what kinds of after-school social life he/she conducts. This category involves skills of social networking — to be acculturated to a point where one knows what to do in a social gathering, whatever the event.

The fourth aspect of assuring school success is parent participation, where parents support their child's education outside the school setting. We can categorize parental support into three different areas:

1   Parents can have knowledge of access to resources that enhance school success in their children. These resources include: testing, the Gifted and Talented Education (GATE) program, and summer enrichment programs, among others.
2   Parents can help their children with homework assignments, or may provide tutors who are capable and understand the educational system.
3   Parents can provide auxiliary education within the home environment by getting their children involved in music lessons, art lessons, sports, or foreign language learning. Auxiliary learning also comes from travelling. Learning about geography, social customs and history of different areas within the state, country, and other parts of the world are all benefits of travel. Included in these experiences are weekend visits to performances, art exhibits, museums, aquariums, and zoos.

Parents can play a big part in ensuring their child's school success. However, not all parents are willing or able to assist their children's education to such great extents. How can we assist a student who may be at-risk? First of all, we must define success; which depends on certain student attributes, for example, with children entering kindergarten success is viewed as making a successful transition to the English language, being able to attain an average or above-average grade point average (GPA), and having average or above-average standardized test scores. They should have no suspensions and no delinquencies. Teenage newcomers who enter American schools at the post-puberty level with very little formal education have special problems. The ability to manage rudimentary English in order to get through a job interview or to ask where the bathroom is is necessary in order to function within society.

In terms of education and success, we want to deal with the aggregate as a whole. If equity is the objective, then it would be desirable for immigrant student scores to match the school and statewide percentage in which the measure of success is one aggregate against another. Asians, in general, far exceed others in most traditional measures of success — graduation from high school, eligibility to enter the University of California or University of San Diego system, having an acceptable GPA, passing standardized test scores, etc. The issue for these Americans is their preparation to deal with the job world beyond traditional measures. This would include social competency and the ability to deal with racism and the 'glass ceiling' or invisible barrier to upward mobility problem (See pp. 75–80 for further discussion). These are issues raised from Asian American perspectives and are not a part of the school curriculum.

There have been reports about the success stories of Asian students, such as one student in 1989 who went through the Preliminary Student Achievement Test (PSAT) and received 99th percentile ranking. There are also case reports of many Asians, specifically Chinese, Japanese and Vietnamese young scholars who are recipients of scholarships from General Motors, Ford and IBM. These success stories are wonderful, in the sense that they portray Asian youth as model students who have no problems. But we cannot make generalizations. The question is, once these model students graduate from medical, engineering or law schools, where do they go? In the work force, how many of them are decision makers? Where are they placed in terms of academic hierarchy? What are the hidden barriers to their success? What are some of the obvious barriers, and how can we remove them? What are the issues beyond academic success?

Consequences of Inadequate Education

We are trying to not only clarify the consequences of education but also to define what educators can do to rectify the problem. The problem being raised, although conservatively, is a serious one. It involves trying to prepare Asian students for 'cracking the glass ceiling', removing limitations associated with cultural selection, language proficiency and the misunderstanding of American cultural values. This goes beyond simply making structural changes. Educators ought to better equip Asian students to deal with the artificially imposed limitations. Strategies being proposed for the parents include auxiliary learning, and special tutoring. Will base strategies be as important for cracking the ceiling as parents think? We also have to deal with historical developments that follow due to demographic changes of the population. The social system is political; recognition of Asians will begin by the conscious recruitment of Asians into management and decision-making positions.

A competent, working Vietnamese woman once remarked, 'I don't know how to order in a restaurant.' Others have made comments about feeling lost in a department store, etc. Such difficulties in social settings present a problem, and it is sometimes viewed as a lack of social competency. Another concern is participation in national and state politics. Not many foreigners or foreign-born Asians know the history or politics of the United States. We draw from our previous experiences the relevant information necessary to maintain a topic. These people are limited in social competency, although they may be proficient in the English language. They are at a loss when it comes to social gatherings and shy away; consequently they are left out of the decision-making process.

Most teachers feel that it is important to teach standard English and basic social skills in order to facilitate the participation of Asian children in daily interaction, such as asking for directions, ordering in a restaurant, or shopping. This can be called social and multicultural literacy. It is important that multicultural literacy become a part of the school curriculum. The teacher can facilitate multicultural literacy by having certain kinds of social gatherings in the classroom, such as birthday, Christmas, Thanksgiving, and Halloween parties. Some children do not experience these parties at home. They don't exchange gifts. They have never seen a pumpkin being carved or a cake being baked. Some teachers have incorporated such activities in their curriculum. However, extra efforts need to be made in educating teachers about the social and historical contexts of these interactions. Teachers can empower the parents by talking to them about these extracurricular activities. In interviews with successful and highly-educated Asian parents, we find they are competent in professional areas but may lack social competency.

Parent participation in the school system is not viewed by Asians as very desirable. It is often viewed as interference. Parents shy away from making decisions for the school or from telling teachers what to do or what they think ought to be done. In the US, parent participation is regarded as highly desirable and, furthermore, it is expected. It is understood among parents that involvement in school activities will enhance their child's opportunities and potential for success. Studies indicate that within the American context, the academic well-being of the child is directly influenced by parent participation. Parental expectations are one of the primary factors in how well a student does in school. In most Asian families, especially those from Confucian-based homes, parents have a crucial role, but the manner in which they influence their children will be different from that of the US-born parent. Their primary role as parents is to teach their children to be good students, obey the teacher, respect authority, and take responsibility for the outcome of their behavior. A whole set of value reinforcements have been developed even before the child gets to school.

Participation in the education of their children is one area often overlooked by immigrant parents. Home tutoring and home teaching are excellent examples of how parents can help assist the school system, but many parents are affected by the glass ceiling and have not cracked the system themselves. As a result, they don't have strategies to share or the ability to empower their children. They do their best by giving their children linguistic cultural orientations based on what they know and on what the community can support. There is still a part missing — the social life. Networking becomes essential. How does one build a system of interrelated networks? How does one build a social circle? Certainly, it starts in very early childhood. Attending preschool, interacting with neighbors and going through primary school are some ways.

Many Chinese parents feel that sending their children to the best school will provide them with better network situations. The La Jolla Country Day School is one example where children learn early socialization skills. When they are not in school, do they socialize? Do their parents socialize? Do they belong to certain clubs, such as the country club, yacht club, golf club, raquetball club, or health club? Essentially, they involve their children in their own social circle and events, thus exposing them to the intricate system of networking. It is built intentionally and unintentionally but it does happen. Many times corporate chief executive officers (CEOs) talk about their buddies from high school and college who were on football teams with them. The use of sophisticated network systems such as this help a great deal in the corporate sector. Since most parents do not have memberships for these clubs, and nor do they know how to get into them, they look for ways through interacting with parents of their children's friends hoping to learn something about gaining membership. Gaining membership into clubs presents a challenge because of the glass ceiling effect.

The second point has to do with the price one pays for fitting in. People who have been successful at mid-management levels have adopted values and lifestyles similar to their colleagues and, especially, their superiors. They learn to speak the language of their associates. They also understand the need to discuss politics over a golf game, to have a few drinks with their colleagues after work, and how to socialize at parties. Many people who are academically successful still do not know what it takes to host a party from the Anglo point of view or how to become an integral member of an academic unit. Such things are seldom talked about because very few Asians have had the opportunity to be socialized in a variety of social functions. They do not know how to advance themselves further. The future labor force will ideally see a 15 per cent even distribution of Asian representation across all levels of corporate structure throughout California.

Many decisions to hire are not based on individual competence, but on political pressure. Eventually, the solution will come from participation of Asians in the political process through elected officials working as lobbyists. Organizations are not mindless. Decisions are made by people who have their own particular perception of things.

Lack of political involvement has cost the Asian community access to resources and influence. Affirmative action as a policy, for example, was first driven by the needs of affluent Americans. To what extent Asians have been affected by this policy, and how much progress has been made in the last twenty years to bring Asians to universities and businesses remains unclear. Perhaps the bottom line is political visibility and becoming more vocal. Perhaps one of the reasons for Asians' lack of involvement in politics is that they find it difficult to maintain harmony with their cultural tradition of cooperation while being aggressive or assertive in the workplace. This trait presents a conflict for Asians. In order to become bicultural, it is necessary to learn to be inconsistent (from an Asian perspective). Many must face ambivalence when coming to the decision-making crossroads of about how to act in social situations. Perhaps one of the solutions is to foster the development of biculturalism, a reality for many immigrant-group communities, and which permits people to switch from the home context to the school or work context without problems (Spindler and Spindler, 1990; Trueba, Jacobs, and Kirton, 1990).

A Taiwanese professional, who feels that in order to be promoted he must go to country clubs and drink and do other socially acceptable activities, may change his behavior deliberately. Would his change in behavior and daily routine adversely affect relationships with his family or others from Taiwan? These are issues to consider. What is recommended for teachers of Asian children? Teachers should consider the wider picture of an Asian child's life when teaching these children. The more we understand the vantage point from which these children are looking, and weigh the social and personal costs involved in their education, the better adjusted our future generation may be.

Teachers, especially in the primary level, have their daily lesson plans to cope with; facing diverse groups in the classroom is a burden for them. Adding something else to their curriculum to help children begin to understand the importance of social networking may be very difficult due to time constraints. A more practical recommendation might be to look at curriculum reform. If it is already incorporated into a teachers' daily plan by the school system itself to talk about social experiences, this important agenda will surely be brought out and discussed. As stated earlier, most Asians really appreciate explicit explanation and demonstration of things. Mass media can play a very important role in transmitting educational messages, but from the quality of television programs today getting quality messages across is difficult. The school curriculum can certainly portray and convey social experiences that are important for success and that can be framed and contextualized, for example, during social studies classes. What needs to be stressed with bicultural populations is not just their personal struggle and hard work, but how they network with friends, family, and other support systems. Teachers have the power to get to the heart of some important issues that are otherwise omitted totally from the school curriculum.

The mindset of Americans regarding multicultural diversity and its benefits must be changed with respect to Asians. Asians are going to make up a large part of the future labor force and will be decision makers. While at the present time Asians are only 15 per cent of the labor force, given their educational qualifications and training, it is expected that their contributions to the labor force will continue to be indispensable. A certain percentage of employees as supported by affirmative action have attempted to become successful. Getting ahead in a corporate structure and in a technological society requires deeper understanding of cultural values and what empowers Americans to become economically successful. Success can be equated with the number of dollars earned or with a prestigious title.

Recruiting and retaining more people from Asian Pacific backgrounds to join the teacher training core to become future teachers is crucial. Teachers who understand the orientation of Confucian-based families as well as the American culture and society will be better prepared to support children's development of bicultural skills in order to successfully adapt to American society.

Access to Resources Within the School and Community

How do immigrant parents, who are unfamiliar with available educational resources for their children, access these resources? Why are some parents more knowledgeable about their availability than others? Cultural differences, even for immigrants who have received a college education in America, are vast and greater than most native Americans realize. For example, a highly educated Korean woman expressed great reservations about booking airline tickets on the telephone for fear that she might not be understood. There are many things in the American culture that immigrants do not understand which native Americans take for granted. There is so much cultural information for new Americans to understand, yet it is unavailable for them in textbooks, schools, or school curriculum. Trueba (1990) discussed the notion of cultural therapy. It may be a useful tool for bridging cultural gaps. Parents could learn from a friend who is familiar with the culture; however, most Americans do not know what advice to give. If the parents are shy or easily embarrassed, they might not admit to their lack of understanding. Someone must be explicit and inquisitive and understand that new Americans need to feel comfortable before they will expose their lack of knowledge or information and ask for help.

In the GATE program (gifted and talented education), children at the end of the second grade are tested for eligibility, but the program doesn't start until the fourth grade. The program categorizes a group of students who are GATE against another group of children who are not. Children who are in the GATE program have the label of being gifted and talented. Does this imply that other children are not gifted and talented? Some parents take their children to private agencies to orient them to testing procedures. By exposing their children to several types of tests, parents feel that they will have an advantage in competitive school testing situations. The GATE program is based on IQ test scores, and there are only a small number of existing reputable IQ tests. If a child has had prior exposure to these tests, he/she will not be as hesitant at actually taking the test as a child who is unfamiliar with them. He/she will have a head start. How can parents who do not know about the GATE Program, IQ tests and related services available for their children offer them this advantage? Teachers are supposed to identify talented children and inform their parents about this possibility. However, for many Asian parents, communication with the school is minimal. Unless the child is doing exceptionally well, he is not likely to be flagged for the GATE Program.

High Technology Education

There is one added dimension. With regards to auxiliary learning, we must remember that this is the computer era. Children are being exposed to computers both in and out of school. As a result, computer games and programs dealing with computer problem solving (i.e. Nintendo) provide children with opportunities to use computers, but take time away from their studies. Auxiliary learning must include high technology. Many parents are high tech oriented themselves, and their children are getting more exposure. High technology has had an effect on overall auxiliary learning of today's children. Overall socialization of children is affected by the impact of the computer. This is especially true with some communities of Southeast Asian refugees.

Vietnamese consider computer science an important field because it lends itself to other fields well known to them such as programming and electrical engineering. Many girls are encouraged to become computer specialists because it is a reliable source of good income. Most middle-class Chinese and Japanese families have computers in their homes, and many have very sophisticated equipment. High technology will influence the future education of this country. Parents provide auxiliary learning in high technology to enhance their children's academic success.

There is a class issue involved with access to computers. A simple unit may cost approximately $1000 without software. Many Asian people in the US are in the income bracket that can afford a computer. However, among the refugee population, income is considerably lower. In today's market, a Nintendo starting package costs approximately $150. Every additional package costs $40 to $50 extra. If one wanted a library of Ninetendo games, it would easily run about $500. Many people cannot afford this type of luxury. Awareness of computer resources often depends on having sufficient financial resources.

The computer is one of many resources of home-supported education that gives access to information. It is clearly related to class differences. For Asian refugees, learning computer technology requires the same types of learning styles that they traditionally use. Learning computer language requires a well disciplined mind. The strict discipline that the Vietnamese, Chinese and Japanese are brought up with enables them to succeed in these fields. Computer languages change rapidly. It takes great discipline to learn and keep up with these languages.

The Confucian tradition helps to shape this discipline. Parents often stress that school success is gaining entrance into the best colleges and universities. They continually ask their children what they plan to do in the future and guide them into fields in which they think they will find success. Parents make sacrifices for their children and expect performance in return. The importance of discipline is always stressed. What is done at home shapes children's style of and attitude towards learning.

What topics are discussed in the average middle-class Anglo American family? What are their concerns regarding their children? What lifelong goals are given top priority? Many Asian professionals consider themselves coolies, the bitter labor of the twenty-first century. Asian middle-class families share many of the same concerns as other middle-class families, however, when it comes to education, there is more concentration, time, and effort put into schooling and much less emphasis on sports, for example (see p. 93).

Criteria for success changes from generation to generation. In earlier generations, most Asians felt they were second class citizens and were willing to accept less. Within the past two decades, equity is in the forefront of many Asians' minds. White males are widely used by studies as criteria for relative success. Conclusions drawn from these studies indicate great variations in terms of the benefits different Asian groups receive from their respective educational backgrounds. Filipinos seem to get less from their educational achievements than the Chinese. A year of schooling in the Philippines is not equivalent to a year of schooling in the US. In looking at the Cabezas and Kawaguchi (1988) study, we find that in order for Asians to receive the same level of income as a white male, more years of schooling are required. There is a cost factor involved because an advanced degree involves additional years of schooling.

Future Labor Force Supply

In the next twenty to thirty years, Asians will make up approximately 15 per cent of the California labor force. What ramifications will result? Will all students have to be better prepared to do well in the work-place? Will competition for the best jobs increase? There seems to be a systematic bias built into the occupational system against all Asians, whether they are American or foreign born.

In a recent issue of *Amerasia Journal*, there was an article about the glass ceiling. The authors were referring to those born in the United States who had had similar school experiences. Systemically, the glass ceiling was imposed on foreign students. This is an issue of racism. Other ethnic and racially different groups are not excluded from the white mainstream. The glass ceiling is transparent to most, but persons trapped by it know all too well of its stifling effects. Upward mobility is restricted for those who are affected. At entry levels, linguistic, cultural or academic barriers may not exist. All people compete equally. Somewhere along the career pathway, something happens. At higher levels, problems begin to emerge. A topic of great importance which relates to the glass ceiling is preparation of Asian and Pacific Islanders for the job world and factors that facilitate or impede progress in school. The Asian population is known both for its high rate of high school graduates, and also that most are likely to be eligible for college admissions. What happens with this promising group after college? Based on anecdotes of the Southeast Asians who have gone into technical fields, many with engineering degrees have not been employable because of their poor language skills. Even among those who receive college degrees, there are those who won't be able to crack the job market because of their accent or their inability to be fluent or as fluent as employers would like. Many employers hire persons technically prepared for the jobs to be done, who happen to be Filipino or Cambodian. They, however, are kept at very low levels not commensurate with their educational backgrounds. For those highly educated from other countries, for example, Taiwan, some may be able to proceed further up the ladder, but they will also find barriers. An important question to ask is 'why isn't a formal educational certificate translated into equal opportunity and success?'

How does one define equality? Should those with backgrounds similar to any given white male have similar income levels? Should the number of Asians at each level equal those employed from the general population of the United States? Is there an even distribution of Asians across different levels? San Diego County has reached their affirmative action goal with the employment of Asians. However, most Asians are employed in clerical or technical positions. Very few have managerial positions. In the State University system, most Asians are in Professorial positions and not in middle or higher management. Asians are not considered underrepresented by most because there are a lot of Asian faculty. Percentage-wise, affirmative action meets their minority quota. Naturally, some professors do not feel linguistically or culturally confident enough to enter into administration.

Those who were born and educated in the United States have no barriers of language or culture. They should have no problem getting higher level employment, but they do. Here, the glass ceiling phenomenon comes into play. There may be several explanations for this phenomenon. Somehow these individuals do not have the skills required for advancement. In many instances, Asians are screened out of the interview process because they are viewed as being too passive. The apparent passivity which reflects the cultural value of being modest is in direct contrast to what is considered assertive and positive self-image. As a result, the explicit appearance of passivity which implies the cultural value may be a detriment to one's potential for success.

Chapter 6

Equity Issues and Recommendations

Do Asian newcomers feel safe and welcome at school? All students should experience a safe and welcoming school environment. A right to a safe environment is one which includes both the absence of verbal and physical abuse, particularly abuse that is racially motivated, and a positive welcoming school atmosphere. All students should have fair access to schooling resources. By practice, this equity issue applies to populations which have suffered historically; thus policies, such as affirmative action, are written to correct historic wrong-doings. Blacks, Asian Americans, native Americans and Latino Americans have a history of exclusion. Clearly Japanese, Chinese, and other Asian Americans of earlier immigration waves have suffered greatly because of their race. This suffering continues even to this day, albeit at a reduced intensity level. It is equally clear that the recent resurgence of the 'Yellow Peril' fear places the newer Asian arrivals in the same position as those Asians whose parents and grandparents arrived generations ago. Although Asian Pacific Americans from earlier groups (such as Japanese Americans) are seen as 'arrived', those from the later groups, including the Vienamese, Lao and Khmer, face racism and the need to gain a foot-hold at the bottom of the social ladder, as well as English language competency and acculturation to American society. Persons from other minority groups may argue that they have suffered more and that consideration of newer groups is less warranted. In large part, this type of argument is inflammatory, because it degenerates into claims of who had the 'worst' experiences and, consequently, into arguments of priorities which become the basis of ethnic conflicts — a sum-zero game (what you gain, I lose; what I gain, you lose) in which somebody always has to lose.

Beyond the consideration of protected minorities, we are living in a time when there is increasing cultural and racial diversity in America. Furthermore, we are living in a time when our future labor force must be better educated and more skilled, implying that it would be in our best interest to enroll in college those who otherwise would not have entered. Given this view, we need to ask who might be under-served. In all probability, these

populations come from lower socio-economic groups, from minority linguistic backgrounds and also may be a part of the foreign-born — including
both refugees and immigrants. Most Asians or Pacific Islanders are either
foreign-born or children of the foreign-born. By the turn of the century 80
per cent of Asians and Pacific Islanders will be from homes where a
language other than English is spoken.

In effect, we can approach the needs of Asian newcomers by suggesting
that existing institutional mechanisms be reviewed for their effectiveness in
outreaching Asian and Pacific Island students. Further, if these mechanisms
are found, we should seek to improve them; and, if absent, seek to create them.
The issues we need to evaluate for effective changes are discussed below.

We do not have systematic data which records the frequency or trends
of violence against Asians in California, Texas, New York, and other states.
However, many articles in our daily newspapers support the contention of a
pervasive anti-Asian current. The 1986 Attorney General Van de Kamp final
report lists the titles of newspaper articles which cite violence against Asians,
e.g. 'Asians in School: Melting Pot near the Boiling Point', 'Violent Incidents
Against Asian Americans Seen as Part of Racist Pattern', and 'Viet Refugee's Mother Calls His Slaying Racism'. Recent press has alluded to the
changing of colors or faces in America, referring to Asians being the fastest
growing minority group in the US and also to the uneasiness of mainstream
American Groups about this growth. This, in turn, results in an increasing
backlash against Asian immigrants and refugees (see Chua-Eoan (1990:32–
5); Henry (1990:28–31). Olsen (1988) reports instances of Asians being
called inappropriate names and also being physically assaulted in California's
K-12 schools. Many newer Asian resident students confirm the racially
offensive name-calling experience, these names include Chink, Gook, Jap,
Nip, and Yang. Many native-born Americans are unable to distinguish
Asians from one another — often they tell Vietnamese refugees to 'go back
to Japan'. Takaki (1989) in his book *Strangers from a Different Shore*
discusses the covert racism against Asians. For example, Asians are often
asked to join the Foreign Student Club or are asked such questions as,
Where did you learn English?' and 'How did you learn to speak English so
well — you speak without an accent?'

Nation-wide, there have been reports of anti-Asian activities, along with
a general anti-minority sentiment on campuses. Though the number of
reported incidents are few, it is suspected that many incidents are left un-
reported, especially those incidents that have taken place in the various
Asian American communities over the years. Asians are fearful of reporting
crimes because of their bad experiences with the law-enforcement agencies.
Furthermore, the victims are afraid of the criminals, who often come from
their own neighborhoods. What results from the anti-Asian sentiments and
behaviors on campuses? There remains a pervasive sense of being an
outsider and a feeling of being unwelcome. Testimonies at recent hearings
document this climate:

Many Asian American students experience subtle racism, anti-Asian sentiment, the negative effects of the model minority stereotype, and insensitivity. Yet, this is not acknowledged. Most Asian students suffer in silence.

Through personal experience and from talking to other students, I found out that many people do not demonstrate patience, sensitivity and compassion in dealing with students, especially students of different national origins. I wish that I could have had a hidden video camera to tape some of these negative encounters to show those individuals their rude behavior.

The level and intensity of these incidents are difficult to measure given both the reluctance of many Asian and Pacific Island individuals to speak up and the blindness and benign neglect of these experiences by non-Asian and Pacific Island students and staff.

Recommendations for Teachers

Teachers can ask a number of questions to inform themselves better about the Asian students' background. Understanding these students will help in becoming empowered to work with the Asian and Pacific Island students in classrooms. An example of questions regarding language issues are the following:

1　Is the home language of the student the same or similar to English? If not, how different is it?
2　What level of English proficiency is desired before English language evaluation?
3　How do we differentiate between language disorders and language differences?
4　Are the Asian and Pacific Island students willing to learn English in order to function more efficiently in this society?

An example of questions regarding classroom management issues are the following:

1　Assuming they cannot keep up with their classmates due to a lack of English proficiency, what kinds of activities can a regular classroom teacher give Asian or Pacific Island children during regular reading time that will enhance their English skills?
2　How can Asian and Pacific Island students be grouped to facilitate effective learning, and what kinds of service delivery models are most appropriate for special education of Asian and Pacific Island students?
3　What kinds of interaction do these children have with their teachers?

It is important for teachers to find about children's families and previous experiences. The following questions can serve as a guide:

1 What experiences did the newcomer children and their families have prior to their arrival in the US?
2 Might those experiences affect schooling behavior?
3 If they are refugees, the following are critical questions to ask:
    a. When did you leave your country? Can you tell me about your life after the communists took over and before your escape?
    b. Back home, before the communist takeover, were you living in the countryside or the city?
    c. What kind of work did your parents do?
    d. Did you ever go to school back home?
    e. Can you tell me something about your escape? By what means, with whom, who did you encounter along the way, etc.
    f. Was anyone in your group hurt by land or sea pirates?
    g. Describe your life in the refugee camp.
    h. How long have you been in the United States? And when did you arrive?
    i. What is your 'real' age?
    j. With whom are you living now?
    k. If you are living without your parents, what are you most concerned about? (Explore worries, fantasies, ruminations, etc.)
    l. If you are living with your parents, what are you most concerned about?
    m. If it were possible, would you return home to live?
    n. If you had one wish that could come true, what would you wish for — and why?
    o. If you could ask an American several questions about life in the United States, what would you ask?

The ethnicity, country of origin of the adolescent refugee, and the timing of departure will all affect the adjustment of refugee youth. Such information gives insight into the traumatic experiences they may have had. The socioeconomic status of the adolescent's family, the parents' level of schooling, and an urban versus rural background affect the abilities of the refugee in dealing with extraordinary stress.

Information on cultural values and family interdependence are also important. Filial piety, 'face', respect for teachers, elders, and authority, the education of children, spiritual beliefs, stoicism, fatalism, and a world view grounded in Eastern traditions determine much of the behavior of Asian families. The stronger these values, the better refugee youth are in coping with troubles.

The experiences of leaving home affect the adjustment of refugee youth. It is important to find out:

1   With whom did the young person leave? (i.e. with or without parents or family members) Whether or not the youngsters' family remain intact during the migration will affect their subsequent adjustment.
2   The escape or emigration experience. The degree of trauma experienced in this process (e.g. attacks by pirates), especially as that trauma is subjectively interpreted by the youngster. During the escape process there may occur an immutable transformation in the youngster's perception of others, of self, and of the larger universe.
3   The refugee camp experience. This includes the degree to which the camp provided (for some youngsters) a psychosocial moratorium during which they were able to put their flight and plight in perspective.
4   Experiences in the US: The circumstances after arriving in the US will also affect their adjustment, including:
    a. How long has the person lived in the US? When did the person arrive?
    b. With whom does the young person now live? Are the youngsters living with or without biological parents, older siblings, distant relatives, or are they in foster homes?
    c. What is the social fit of the adolescent's resettlement, the compatibility between past and present environments and their current life-style? (For example, what is the pace of life, geography, employment, size of community density, heterogeneity of the population and the presence or absence of established Southeast Asian enclaves in the resettlement area?)
    d. Public experiences. This includes sponsoring agencies, schools, learning the English language, vocational training, friendship, social service and health care agencies, and experiences of racism, if any.

In sum, the following issues need to be answered:

1   Home language(s) — The language(s) spoken in the home may have an affect on the quality of schoolwork produced by students. The extent of the family's acculturation will influence a child's work as well.
2   Birth history — The mother's pregnancy information, birth history concerning a child, and early developmental history is important to help detect problem areas that may occur.
3   Religious beliefs — Religious traditions may have differing views on handicaps and ways to treat them.
4   Previous life history and experiences — These include the fact surrounding immigration and also secondary migration, if this has occurred. Medical history and health care services, history of

psychosocial issues, previous educational experiences, and languages and cultural identities are important to the families.

5 Social and family factors — The structure of the home and the employment status of the parents is important to explore. Sometimes the older children are responsible for the younger ones because the parents are employed and out of the home.

6 History on schooling — Where and when was the student educated? What was the schooling like? What was taught? Was the schooling interrupted?

7 Educational expectations and learning styles — Parental and student expectations may differ from those of the educators because of cultural differences. Learning and communication styles may differ for the same reasons.

The issues listed above, although they may appear deceptively simple, can generate very meaningful information about refugee adolescent adaptation and functioning. This insight into the origins of psychological dysfunction can be useful in diagnosing psychological problems among Southeast Asian refugee youths (some of these issues are not discussed in this text).

Teachers face many challenges when teaching this diverse population. The collaborative inquiry based on the Vygotskian paradigm (1962, 1978), which asserted that robust knowledge and understanding are socially constructed through talk, activity and interaction around meaningful problems and tools, may be helpful. This approach is particularly useful for language-minority students, in which the students, not the teacher or the text, define the problems to be studied. Questions are asked by the students, and then they begin, through their own activity, to bridge the gap that often separates the school culture from the home culture (Heath, 1983). This approach challenges one's thoughts and beliefs. Students are encouraged to be explicit about what they mean, because they need to negotiate meanings and resolve conflicts in beliefs. Thus, they construct and reconstruct their knowledge in order to arrive at some common understanding. The collaborative inquiry process, such as collective stories, lends support to the establishment of common and shared sociocultural values (Cheng, 1989). A number of studies have shown that students participate more actively if they can set the agenda as to how and when to participate (Au, 1980; Cazden, John and Hymes, 1972; Hymes, 1971 and 1974; Philips, 1982).

Teachers should be encouraged to involve students in purposeful communicative interactions that promote the use of language. Heath (1986) presented six genres which are used in the schools and stressed the need for teachers to facilitate the multiple uses of language. The genres are defined maps and plans for stretches of discourse. Asian newcomers may not be familiar with these genres due to their diverse cultural background, social class level, different discourse patterns and turn-taking rules. The following genres need to be nurtured so that Asian and Pacific Island students will have more success in school:

1   Label quests — These are language activities in which adults either name items and their attributes or ask for their names or attributes. Labeling and knowing that attributes precede higher order knowledge such as answering why, how, and when.

2   Meaning quests — Adults infer for the young child what he or she means, interpret their own behavior or that of others, or ask for explanations of what is meant or intended. In school, students are to state what is meant, as well as how it was intended, what action will result, and how it is to be interpreted or valued.

3   Recounting — The speaker retells experiences or information known to both teller and listener. Teachers ask children to provide summaries, to recount facts known to all class members, and to display knowledge through oral and written recounts.

4   Accounting — Accounts are generated by the teller and provide information that is new to the listener or new interpretations of information that the listener already knows. Schools allow few occasions for accounts.

5   Event casting — Individuals provide a running narrative on current events of the teller and listener or forecast events to be accomplished in the future. This narrative may be simultaneous to, or may precede, the events.

6   Story-telling — These fictional accounts include animate beings who move through a series of events with goal-directed behavior.

Asian and Pacific Island students may benefit a great deal from being exposed to quality language use in productive contexts. Literacy, in the form of purposeful talk, reading and writing mediates intellectual efforts (Warren, Rosebery and Conant, 1989).

Teachers need to provide contextualized learning (Cheng and Ima, 1990; Cummins, 1980, 1981a, 1981b, 1983, 1984, 1986, 1989; Collins, Brown and Newman, 1989; Hakuta, 1986; Van Dongen and Westby, 1986). They need to be particularly careful to use items that are not culturally loaded, such as measuring words, foods, stories, money, music, geography, kitchen utensils, furniture, animals, etc. Furthermore, they need to take into consideration the students' prior knowledge by building on what they know, their native language and background of experiences.

Educators need to be challenged with the following questions (Garcia and Ochoa, 1976), and Banks (1990):

1   Am I prepared to teach cultural/linguistic/ethnically diverse Asian and Pacific Island students?

2   How do my instructional strategies reflect and accommodate the

communication and learning styles with the diversity of Asian and Pacific Island students?

3 Have I updated my knowledge and skills with regard to issues of diversity?

4 How do I evaluate my teaching effectiveness with diverse Asian and Pacific Island students?

5 How does my teaching encourage positive interaction between myself and diverse Asian and Pacific Island students?

6 Does my teaching encourage positive interaction between students?

7 What methods do I use to encourage active participation of my Asian and Pacific Island students?

8 Do my students receive positive feedback that supports improved performance?

Not all people from the same culture have the same values and beliefs; there are tremendous individual differences. For this reason, it is necessary to be extremely careful when making cultural assumptions. Nevertheless, an awareness of the general cultural and linguistic values of the diverse Asian and Pacific Island populations is an essential tool for educators. An understanding of cultural and linguistic values makes it possible to communicate more effectively with Asian and Pacific Island students, to recognize many of their difficulties, to avoid potential conflicts, and to establish an atmosphere that will facilitate learning.

Additionally, educators have the responsibility of evaluating the diverse styles of Asian and Pacific Island minority students. Teachers must examine and reexamine their own assumptions about what their students know. Teachers and students must enter into a dialogue about how to bridge the linguistic and cultural gap. Furthermore, the incongruencies between the expectations of teachers and those of Asian or Pacific Island students and their families must be considered.

There is a need to infuse Asian and Pacific Island multicultural information into the curriculum so that the students feel a sense of kinship and relevance. The opportunities for teachers to design new content is a valuable aspect of multiculturalism. Questions about transforming the curriculum may include the following:

1 Are the diverse needs of Asian and Pacific Island students met?

2 Do Asian and Pacific Island students participate at their level of competence?

3 Does the classroom create a positive and challenging environment for all students?

4 Does the lesson infuse information about cultural/ethnic/linguistic diversity?

5 Does the content reflect careful planning and organization?

6 Are topics that have social, cultural, and linguistic relevance being used?

7 How does the class capitalize on the rich diversity of Asian and Pacific Island students?

8 How do current teaching methods help the Asian and Pacific Island students develop writing and communication competencies?

9 Does the present manner of instruction help students to examine events, situations, integrations, and conflicts from diverse perspectives?

10 Is a positive attitude toward culturally/linguistically/ethnically diverse students promoted through instruction?

11 Are concerns for students' learning clearly demonstrated?

12 Are rules of writing and communication explained explicitly?

13 Are models of good writing and communication styles provided?

14 Do we provide tutorial services, support materials, and counseling when necessary?

15 Are our goals and objectives obtainable by all students?

Language serves many important functions, including that of maintaining one's own culture and acquiring a new culture and new knowledge. The effective use of a second language is essential in order to adjust successfully to a new sociocultural environment. In making the transition from the home language to a new language children make phonetic approximations of English sounds. Cantonese-speaking children tend to say *day* meaning *they*. The English of Asian American children, whose mother tongue is not English, is influenced by the language used at home. English language of Asian American children reflect the influence of Mandarin, Cantonese, Vietnamese, Chamorro, Hmong, and other languages to the point that some English utterances become unintelligible, causing teachers to comment on children's inability to communicate.

Phonological difficulties are easily observable. Substitutions of phonemes such as *sree* instead of *three*, and omissions when children say *do* instead of *dogs* are most frequent. Stress and intonations are often misplaced. They may say *te'lvision* instead of *television*. (For more information see Cheng, 1987). At the morphological and synctactic levels, however, errors differ in complexity. The most frequent grammatical (or morphemic) changes are in word-order. Children may say 'You no like it', or 'I first go, you later come'.

Additionally, semantic and pragmatic difficulties are much more subtle and prevalent, such as asking people their age without knowing that it might be offensive or misinterpreting the meaning of terms such as 'gum disease' as a disease associated with eating gums. Since all languages are rule-governed and language proficiency includes proficiency of language form, content and use, students are constantly challenged by the various contexts of languages and the embedded meanings associated with such contexts. Idiomatic usage is often misused or misunderstood.

Furthermore, even students who have good language skills may not be effective social communicators, lacking conversational competence, because they are not familiar with the social pragmatic rules that govern our inter-actions. For example, a Chinese student may have difficulty accepting praise, while an Anglo may find it rude not to praise efforts. Such inconsistencies in social communicative practices may cause communication breakdown and misunderstanding.

A recent Harvard Education Letter commented on 'Cultural Differ-ences in the Classroom,' saying that 'Most educators agree that students approach learning in many different ways and that teachers need to take these differences into account when developing their instructional strategies' (Green, 1989 p. 144). Virtually every speaker of the English language has a range of styles along a continuum of formality. The range of styles used by individual speakers and the conditions for adjustment along this continuum, however, vary considerably.

In earlier sociolinguistic studies, the critical variable defining the dimen-sion of formality and informality in language style was reduced to a single 'principle of attention' paid to speech (Labov, 1972). The more attention paid to speech, the more formal the style. Formal styles are thus defined as those used in situations in which *speech* is the primary focus, whereas infor-mal styles are those during which there is the least amount of speaker audio-monitoring (Taylor, 1986). For example, education is viewed as a formal process by most Asian and Pacific Island cultures. Reading of factual in-formation is considered valuable. It is important for Asian and Pacific Island students to be orderly and obedient. They learn by observation and by memorization. Pattern practice and rote learning are preferred over discovery learning (Cheng, 1987). Teachers are carriers of knowledge and are transmitters of information. In other words, schooling is a serious process. However, the American education system stresses critical thinking and discovery which allows for a less stressful and more open atmosphere. Furthermore, various cognitive styles may present challenges for faculty as well as students. Western culture is linear, has progressive organization and drives toward climax and catharsis (insight and relief of tension); repetition is not valued, but when it occurs, it is employed for intensifying tension. There is a very strong demand for closure (Hale-Benson, 1982). Meanwhile Asian and Pacific Island speech style tends to be more circular and coordinated and does not always require closure (Kaplan, 1966).

Nonverbal expression is an essential and integral part of the whole communication process. We use gestures, eye contact, silence, proximity, facial expression, pauses, varying intonation and vocal patterns, and spatial arrangements to convey meaning and intent. Leubitz (1973) identified four functions of nonverbal communication: to relay messages, to augment verbal communication, to contradict verbal communication and to replace verbal communication. Different cultures have different rules about nonverbal com-munication; a giggle means embarrassment in the Japanese culture, while it may indicate some humor in the American culture.

Southeast Asian people use a great deal of nonverbal communication. They often use nonverbal symbols where Americans would use verbal communication. Take, for instance, feelings of appreciation which are, most of the time, verbalized in US culture. If you hand out a book to an Southeast Asian, open the door for him/her or give a compliment, he/she will give you a broad smile instead of saying 'thank you'. The same is also true with the expression of apologies. In normal circumstances, Southeast Asian people would simply smile instead of saying 'I'm sorry'. This is sometimes misconstrued as lack of manners or rudeness. If they have not been fully acculturated, the Southeast Asians would use very sparingly the words 'thank you' and 'I'm sorry,' for, in their culture, these are usually reserved for very intense feelings of appreciation, apology or regret.

The smile for the Southeast Asian, has different meanings depending on the situation and the whole facial expression. It can be a substitute for 'thank you' or 'I'm sorry' as explained in the previous paragraph. It may also mean embarrassment, or reluctance to answer a question, or a courteous expression of disbelief. American teachers are often shocked by the smile of Southeast Asian students when the latter are scolded. The smile in this situation does not mean a challenge or disrespectful behavior, but conveys the message that they recognize their fault and that they do not bear any grudge against the teacher who has scolded them.

Youth will avoid looking into the teacher's eyes when the teacher talks to them or when they talk to the teacher. Usually, the American teacher interprets the avoidance as a sign of lack of interest, or worse, mischievous behavior or guilt. In Southeast Asian cultures, eye avoidance of someone who is senior in age or status or of the opposite sex, means respect. Keeping silent is another behavior which has different meanings in US and Southeast Asian cultures. For the Southeast Asian, it is not a sign of passivity or a lack of cooperation. It is, on the contrary, an expression of interest and respect to the teacher. Touching the child's head is generally accepted by Vietnamese people as a sign of affection, but Cambodian and Lao people consider it bad taste, or even insulting, because the head is the most sacred part of the body.

Some gestures which are friendly and innocent in US culture may take on negative meanings in Indochinese cultures. Take, for instance, the gesture of keeping the fingers crossed to express a wish for good luck. This is, for most Southeast Asians, an obscene gesture. On the contrary, the American middle finger obscene gesture does not mean anything to the Southeast Asian. Certain gestures commonly used in US culture do not have any meaning at all in Southeast Asian cultures, such as the thumb up, thumb down. For the Southeast Asian, the 'bye bye' gesture used by Americans means 'come here'. Those are only a few examples to illustrate the difference of meaning of the same gesture in two different cultures. Knapp (1972) suggested that 35 per cent of the social meaning is actually transmitted by words, whereas 65 per cent of the social meaning is conveyed through nonverbal channels. Furthermore, physical features such as body build, height, weight, skin color, and other noticeable features, may communicate messages inaccurately (Gollnick and Chinn, 1986). Teachers need to be aware of the diverse nonverbal messages that their students bring.

Educators may find it helpful to consider a number of guidelines and caveats that may be useful in developing a mode of operation that is culturally appropriate and methodologically adaptable. These include:

1   Know thyself: It is of the utmost importance for educators to critically examine their world view, values, beliefs, way of life, communication style, learning style, cognitive style, and personal life history. Through this process, one can gain insight into one's *modus operandi.*

2   Nurture an appreciation and understanding of cultural diversity: Affirm recognition of cultural differences through the development of greater knowledge of the cultural/ethnic composition of the US. (Cole and Deal, 1986).

3   Develop an understanding of the political, legal, economic and social realities of cultural pluralism: It is a social reality that the United States still struggles with the lack of equal educational opportunities for all (Taylor, 1986). While state and federal legislation may establish mandates, it is up to State Education Agencies (SEAs) and Local Education Agencies (LEAs) to implement such laws; it is the individual educator or specialist who is on the front line to carry out daily instruction for the students.

4   Increase one's ability to be eclectic: The provision of education for Asian and Pacific Island populations is in its initial stage of development. Innovative strategies are being required of language specialists because of the desperate need to develop techniques that will benefit their students. One needs to be eclectic in order to adopt new ideas and make adaptations of existing methods, thus creating new methods and approaches suitable for the Asian and Pacific Island language minority populations.

5   Identify strategies that are culturally and socially relevant: Cultural relevancy is a critical issue in the presentation of all curriculum, including instruction in language. As children go through the process of acculturation, the language of the curriculum becomes more meaningful. It is important to recognize that in the beginning there will be a lack of shared knowledge because of the differences in Asian and Pacific Island students' backgrounds (Gumperz and Hymes, 1972). For example, a child transplanted from the mountains of Laos may not know the significance of a Jack-O-Lantern, finding it culturally irrelevant, or a Hmong child may not have had the experience of eating macaroni and cheese for lunch. For the Chamorro children, typhoons are common occurrences, while snow is not a part of the everyday vocabulary. Students on

the Big Island of Hawaii can describe the details of a volcano erupting, but may fail to appreciate the meaning of a white Christmas. There is a shared 'culture of the poor' to which a large percentage of Khmer and Hmong refugees may belong, based upon their meager earnings and their possible receipt of social welfare. Children from these groups have had few opportunities for reading stories or for receiving other types of language stimulation that middle-class mainstream individuals take for granted.

6 Make no assumptions about what the children know: Not all children have experienced a birthday party. The patterns of verbal and nonverbal behavior they learn at home may be entirely different from the American norm.

7 Encourage the buddy system: Children placed in a strange new environment need to be given time to develop their social circles. Since all encounters are social encounters (Taylor, 1986), children need to feel that they are part of the group and thus can engage in peer interactions. Children who tend to make friends easily and are themselves sociable should be encouraged to take the newcomers by the hand and show them the rules of the school and class. Fellow students from the same ethnic, linguistic and cultural background need to be encouraged to work with the newcomers (Erickson, 1977, 1984, 1987).

8 Utilize the student's natural support system, all people who provide one form or another of support for the child. This may include parents, siblings, friends, neighbors, relatives, or even the community. For example, to whom does the parent go to seek advice? Who provides assistance when there is a family crisis or emergency? Who makes the decisions about education in the family? If necessary, who provides translation for the family? Who provides care for the child after school? The child's natural support system needs to be fully utilized when addressing instructional or intervention issues.

9 Obtain detailed information about the student and the family: When a student is in need of a referral, the following procedure is recommended. Once a referral is made, contact should be made immediately, involving, whenever possible, face-to-face contact with the family. If time allows, a home visit by a member of the assessment team should be made. In addition to using the background questionnaire, information should be obtained about what the family is like and how the child is functioning, as well as the parents' present childcare needs. Questions such as 'What is a typical day like?', 'What do you do during the weekends?', and 'What does your child like or dislike?' are all important questions to ask. Once the assessment is completed, recommendations for intervention are generally provided. If the professionals who are

providing the service were not members of the assessment team, they must be made fully aware of the background of the child, preferably by the team member who visited the home and collected that data.

10   Find out about the Asian and Pacific Island populations in your school district: Since the number of Asian and Pacific Island students from each language group fluctuates, it is important to find out how many Asian and Pacific Island students from different language backgrounds are attending the schools so that the parents can assist one another in serving as facilitators and informants. Sometimes, and particularly when there are only a few students from a particular language group scattered in different schools in a district, efforts should be made to locate these students and to determine how the more proficient students can be of assistance.

11   Increase one's knowledge about the home languages of the Asian and Pacific Island students that are served: (e.g. Ruhlen, 1975). Try to learn a few words from those languages. Your interest in their language will set the tone for better communication.

12   Consider peer teaching: This may be less threatening to the Asian or Pacific Island population and more appealing to their style of learning and previous pattern of participation. Difficulty in reading English may cause a public display of their incompetence (Erickson, 1987) in the classroom. Rather than asking questions which may cause embarrassment for them, you may find that peer-teaching or tutoring is a more effective way of introducing those therapy materials that require reading skills.

13   Identify and explain sociolinguistic rules: Sociolinguistic rules as turn-taking, turn-allocation interruptions, topic shift, topic maintenance, and others which underlie interaction must be explained to Asian and Pacific Island students. Although they may appear to be learning the words and sentences of English, they operate from a different socio-cultural perspective. For example, to Americans the question, 'Do you have the time?' actually means 'What time is it?' Similarly, 'Why don't we go to the park?' means 'Let's go to the park', and 'You like it, don't you?' means 'I think you like it.' To increase appropriate usage of the more ritualized sociolinguistic rules such as complimenting, greeting, and leave-taking, these rules must be explicitly taught.

14   Encourage Asian and Pacific Island students' bicultural identities: (Lambert, 1978; Lambert and Tucker, 1972): This can be done not only by acknowledging their cultural heritage but also by integrating cultural pluralism and the child's background into the therapy contexts. Themes of folk literature are excellent topics for language therapy and discussion (Van Dongen and Westby, 1986).

15   Be alert to the possible misunderstandings some Asian and Pacific

Island students exhibit: This can occur because of a lack of awareness of the social meanings of words and phrases since words derive their meanings from the social setting, context, and frame of reference. A phrase such as 'I am doing fine' can mean 'I am feeling fine' in response to the question: 'How are you doing?'; or it could mean 'I do not want any more.'

16 Recognize the need to give 'foreground' information: This may be essential for the LEP students in therapy. Gumperz (1971, 1975, 1981) discussed the notion of 'foreground' information, which is what a person needs to have in order to understand the intended meaning.

17 Maximize contextual reinforcement: There is a need to bridge cultural gaps so that the disjunctures Asian and Pacific Island children experience between school and home can be lessened. While a student at school may be told to ask questions and to challenge, the same child at home may be told to be observant and quiet and not to challenge authority. Obviously, such conflicts may lead to confusion and ambivalence.

18 Bear in mind the discourse systems by which Asians and Pacific Island children operate: Rules such as 'Do not speak when you are eating', or 'Speak only when spoken to', may be the standard mode of discourse at home.

19 Consult with other personnel: Work with school personnel, ESL teachers, and resource teachers on the topics and language arts areas they are covering in the classroom so that therapy activities will enhance the students' classroom communication skills.

20 Organize classroom activities around naturalistic interactions: This permits the child to take the lead and to build upon modeling and expansion (Cheng, 1984).

21 Take a collaborative mode: Teachers can collaborate with language professionals, teachers, ESL teachers and resource teachers. Furthermore, teachers can provide demonstrations and also participate in team teaching.

22 Use multiple cultural/language informants: When working with a culturally and linguistically diverse population, one needs to obtain information from and rely on multiple informants. Information regarding the utilization of multiple informants can be found in Cheng (1987).

23 Know your student and family. A home visit should be made if possible in order to gain insight into the way the family lives and the kind of support system the student has.

24 Learn more about your own culture through cultural capsules and cultural clusters: Cultural capsules refer to elements of American culture, such as eating cereal for breakfast, that are different from other cultures. Cultural clusters are those activities or events, such

as Thanksgiving, that are part of the general American tradition. Children from other lands may know nothing about these culture capsules and clusters. These items can become useful instructional aids to help close the cultural gaps.

25 Use mixed cultural forms: that is, a combination of mainstream classroom and non-mainstream cultural instruction practices (Au, 1980; Au and Mason, 1981; Erickson, 1984; Erickson and Mohatt, 1982). The paradigm shift then, introduces a new way to educational practices and is of utmost necessity when students of ethnic background are involved. It allows for the incorporation of Asian and Pacific Island cultural norms into the curriculum which makes way for a proper education. Perhaps we should view this program as a challenge to traditional educational ways because to challenge is to inquire, search, and question existing ways for the sole purpose of a better outcome for all involved.

Recommendations for Parents

Asian and Pacific Island students and their families have yet another mountain to climb when they enter the US school system. Their obvious lack of preparation and knowledge of the schools makes it extremely challenging for educators. It is through our consistent inquiry about their expectations, lifestyle, world view, cultural way and learning styles that we can better understand why Asian and Pacific Island children and parents behave the way they do. Most parents have no prior knowledge about the US schooling experience and often relate their own educational experiences to their children, which causes confusion for their children.

Asian and Pacific Island students face the challenges of bridging a gap between home and school cultures. Most culturally diverse students have to shift from a different style of learning, often from memorization of facts to problem solving, from dependence on teachers to self-reliance in finding information. This may require a period of adjustment for them.

The following excerpts provide a glimpse of some of the feelings the Asian and Pacific Island students experience. They are selected from student interviews, personal life history, and a book entitled *Dear Diane* (Y.M. Wong, 1983):

1 My mother doesn't speak English. She gets stuck and can't express herself, and then she starts to mix Chinese and English together. I try to talk with her about my feelings or problems, but sometimes it's too complicated. I'm embarrassed to ask my friends to come over to the house because she might say the wrong things.

2   I'm 16 years old and have a big problem. Last year, I ran away from home three times. I couldn't stand my parents' nagging: change my friends, go to school, stop talking on the phone so long, turn off the TV. When it got bad, I just split and spent a few nights at a friend's house. My third time ended with a short stay at the Juvenile Detention Center. After meeting some the other girls there, I realized I didn't want to be like them. I know that I caused my parents grief, but I'm trying to be better. They just don't know how to treat me. It's almost as if they don't quite trust me.

3   I'm 15 years old and came from Korea with my family about four years ago. I'm working hard to learn English, and I think that I'm finally "breaking even" at school. My problem is that my parents always tell me they want me to be a doctor, lawyer or engineer. They say that the only reason they came to America was so that I could go to a good school and then get a good job.

4   I'm pretty quiet in my math class. I don't want to let other students know that I'm not that smart. My teacher thinks that because I'm Asian and quiet, I'm doing all right. The farther behind I get, the more I'd just like to skip school and hang out. What can I do to let her know that I'm lost, and may need some extra help? It'd be so easy just to chuck this whole school thing.

5   Just before the end of the school year, my mom gave me a small gift to take to my teacher. It was only a box of stationary with some Korean designs created by a cousin who is a graphic artist. I was so upset! The teacher refused to accept the gift and told me that she was not taking any 'bribes' from any Koreans, or anyone else! I didn't know what to say. What's wrong with me? What can I do about this teacher?

6   I'm an American-born Korean student just beginning high school. Last weekend, some of my mom's friends and their kids from Korea came to visit. There were so many of them, they spilled out onto our front yard: I was upset when some white students from the school walked by — they looked over and saw me with all these foreigners wearing funny clothes and speaking Korean! They keep trying to make friends with me lately, although I can't speak a word of Korean. Some white students already think I'm a foreigner, even though I speak English well and wear normal clothes. If they see these Koreans hanging around, I'll be worse off than I am already. What can I do?

7　At school, teachers tell us to ask questions and to challenge what they say. At home, though, it's just the opposite. Whenever I offer an opinion that is different than what my folks think, they say I'm rude and disobedient. I suppose that I can remain silent in front of them, but isn't there a way that I can express my opinions without raising the roof?'

8　My folks came from Korea. They never hug me the way parents do on TV, even though I'm pretty sure they do love me. A friend of mine thinks that his parents don't love him because they never say so. What do you think?

9　I'm a 20-year-old college student. I'm caught between two cultures and sets of values. My parents, who are immigrants from the Philippines, are over-protective; the American culture allows much more freedom. I can't seem to find a happy medium: either I offend my folks, or I alienate my Americanized friends. Both are important to me, but how can I please them both?

10　At junior high, some of the other students, including some whom I had thought were friends, have started to call me 'Chink' and other racial names. A couple of times it's been so bad that I told my mom I was sick just so I wouldn't have to go to school that day. I'm sure she just wouldn't understand. She'd probably say I should ignore the remarks because non-Asians don't have 4000 years of culture, or something like that. I want to tell these people that their remarks are wrong and harmful, but I'm so afraid. What if they never talk to me again? How can I get them to stop?

11　Philip, is the oldest of four children from Taiwan. His Father owns a restaurant and expects him to be a lawyer. He was an outstanding student and never gave his teachers problems. His parents always make comments such as: 'You can do better.' 'You are not as industrious as Lin-Mei.' 'This is the least we expect from you.' Philip began to exhibit a great deal of anxiety during his junior year and his grades began to drop. He resented his parents' statements such as 'We sacrifice for you and later we expect you to earn good money to support your sisters, brothers, and us.' He began arriving home at late hours, often spending hours at the shopping mall. His parents reprimanded him but he did not listen. He began cutting classes and hanging around with the rough group in school.'

12 Mary, a second generation Korean, suffered from depression, a sense of worthlessness, defeat and suicidal ideation. She felt extremely hostile towards the Korean culture and Korean people. She hated the idea of being born a Korean and chose to go out only with Anglo boys. She denounced her ethnic background and denied her racial heritage. She recognized that she was Korean and not fully accepted by all segments of society. She developed a sense of alienation and isolation and was suffering from an identity crisis (Sue, 1981:134).

13 Steve was born and grew up in Oakland. His sister married a Caucasian and his parents were so upset that they stopped talking to her. Steve attempted to deny his racial identity because he felt ashamed of being Chinese. Recently, his mother passed away and he felt a great deal of guilt and began to reorient himself toward some Chinese values and cultural beliefs. His reawakening made his father very happy, especially when he began to date Asian girls (Sue, 1981, p. 135).

14 Helen, a high school junior, was born in the US. Her parents are from Japan. She met Ed in high school. They began to date, but she was afraid to tell her parents, since they wanted her to date only Japanese boys. She would go out with her girl friend and change clothes in her girl friend's home. After her date, she would change again in her girl friend's house and then go home. This went on for several years and she could not gather enough courage to tell her parents. Ed's parents were frustrated, because they wanted to meet Helen's parents, and Helen was so fearful that her parents would find out and forbid her to see Ed.

15 Jessica, a high school student in New York City had been seeing a Puerto Rican boy named Ricardo. Ricardo was very good to her, and she was extremely attracted to him. Jessica's father, a cook in a Chinese restaurant, found out about this and forbid her to go out with him. He also told her sister and brother to watch her. Out of desperation, she went to the top floor of their apartment building, jumped and killed herself.

16 Elaine, a 9-year-old Korean girl, came home from school one day and asked her mother 'Why is my hair not blonde and why isn't the color of eyes blue? I like Ashley, her hair is so pretty and her eyes are so blue. The boys in my class think she is the prettiest girl and I hate myself. Why am I so ugly and why can't my eyes be blue?

17 Jeffrey is a ten-year-old Chinese boy who hates speaking Chinese. He refuses to go to Chinese school and no matter what his parents say, he just refuses to go. He sees no point in learning the Chinese language and thinks it is ridiculous to speak the funny language. He says that he is 100 per cent American and sees absolutely no value in learning Chinese. His father, an electrical engineer, says that learning Chinese will help him choose food in a Chinese restaurant. Jeffrey says that the menu is written in English. His refusal to attend Chinese school makes his parents upset and angry. Jeffrey says, 'I'd rather commit suicide than to go to Chinese school.'

18 When they come to the United States, the parents are so busy they don't know what is happening at school. They don't really understand this society. They can't give the same comfort to the youngsters because the parents themselves are struggling. How much can they give in the way of encouragement and support to the children? Very little, although the love and caring is there. Somehow, the ones who do well are the ones who can pull themselves together and provide a peer support system for each other throughout the difficult years. The person who does not belong to this type of situation will soon seek support from gangs (Sung, 1987:164–165).

19 Mai, a 14-year-old Vietnamese girl, was walking to her classroom, and a group of boys were in her way. She murmured 'excuse me' which sounded like 'kiss me.' So the boys blocked her way and each of them began to kiss her. She tried to run away, but the boys kept on laughing and teasing her. She ended up dropping out of that school because she felt she was shamed by the boys and lost face.

20 Cheng, a 13-year-old Hmong girl, was told by her parents that soon she should be married. She didn't want to do that and she didn't know what to do.

The foregoing are just some examples of the many problems Asian and Pacific Island students encounter when trying to assimilate into the American culture. The whole ordeal is emotionally straining to all involved and many times places a burden on the Asian and Pacific Island parent/child relationship. These issues that must be addressed in order to help the relationships and to provide an easier assimilation process.

Chapter 7

Analysis and Implications of Research on Minority Student Empowerment

The debates and critical analyses of theories attempting to explain the history of minority adaptation to American democracy, in contrast with the adaptation of minorities in other countries, have led to antagonistic explanations based on the different roles attributed to social factors (stratification, institutionalized racism, equity and opportunity for all), cultural factors (the collective force of shared values, views and goals), and unique family and individual situations (home socialization for success, and personal commitment to achievement). What is emerging is a rather more cohesive perspective of the relationships between success (by any definition) and the collectively shared perspectives on the culturally-defined role of the individual in a given society.

Two very important trends seem to have emerged from recent studies. One trend recognizes the intimate relationship between the individual and the social group in the process of academic socialization; that is, the inseparability between individual learning and learning in socially-constructed settings. This trend has enlightened the nature and diversity of various types of literacies, the collective construction and interpretation of text, and the strong linkages between literacy types and sociocultural settings requiring them. This trend is illustrated by the work of sociolinguistics and psychologists who have adopted compatible theoretical frameworks based on the ethnography of communication (Gumperz and Hymes, 1964; 1972; Gumperz, 1982; Cook-Gumperz, 1986), and the work by Vygotsky (Moll and Diaz, 1987; Tharp and Gallimore, 1989). Another equally important trend represents a creative use of ethnographic approaches to the study of empowerment in a number of settings. As a response to the dialogue on differential achievement of minorities and the taxonomic advances made by cultural ecologists, other scholars have accepted the challenge of studying the process of minority disempowerment, as well as the transition from this condition to empowerment. This could be called the ethnography of empowerment.

This chapter combines both trends in an effort to explore intervention models that can assist teachers, researchers and decision-makers in schools and other institutions. Adaptive strategies are manifested not only in schools but also in other social institutions. The lessons learned from the case of Asian Americans in California can help us better conceptualize our theoretical models of minority achievement. These models must allow us to explain not only the process of disempowerment of minorities in schools (their failure to participate or to achieve), but also the process of moving out of disempowerment situations to positions in which minorities can regain control of their lives through participation in social and cultural institutions. If the cultural ecological position is too rigid to accommodate alternative responses to cultural conflict through channels permitting participation in mainstream organizations, perhaps we ought to modify it. The increasingly well documented intra-group diversity of all immigrants and refugees, especially among the most recent Asian comers, suggests that possible classifications of 'castelike' may be less applicable to entire ethnic groups than to selected segments of all groups whose characteristics must be examined.

The study of refugees and immigrants is essential to our understanding of American society, its nature and vitality, its future and its tolerance for change. If empowerment is translated as the ability to share in the American dream, to participate in the benefits bestowed upon mainstream citizens (education, status, wealth, and political power — that is, success), and disempowerment is viewed as a condition preventing individuals from sharing in American social life and its benefits, there must be an intimate relationship between the opposite social processes leading either to disempowerment or to empowerment. Additionally, because in most technological societies participation in social institutions requires literacy, or the ability to acquire knowledge through text, there is an intimate relationship between lack of literacy and disempowerment situations. Furthermore, if school, which is viewed as the institution *par excellence* responsible for teaching literacy, seems not only to fail in many instances (as reflected by dropout and illiteracy rates among young adults) but also to disenfranchise many students, we can assume that schooling (or failure to learn in schools) has an intimate relationship with maintaining certain individuals in a situation of disempowerment. Why do some people fail to learn in the schools? Why do they become ostracized and marginalized through schooling? Some of the answers are partially given by the socially-based learning and development theories of Vygotsky.

Socially-based Learning Theories and their Application

Because much of what occurs in learning environments is not only determined by the cultural values and support provided by the family and community, but also by psychosocial processes that are often unique to specific learning environments, it is necessary to draw upon learning and development theories. One of the most advanced theories in psychology today, the 'socially-based' theory of cognitive development, was originally proposed by Lev Semionovich Vygotsky in the late 1920s and later re-discovered by Western psychologists (see, for example, Vygotsky, 1962, 1978; Scribner and Cole, 1981; Wertsch, 1981, 1985; Tharp and Gallimore, 1989). Socially-based theories of cognitive development are particularly instrumental in enlightening the relationship between sociocultural and cognitive factors of learning, as well as between collective and individual factors determining higher cognitive development. The differential success of immigrant groups may depend to a great extent on the quality of the school learning environment; that is, the linguistic and sociocultural congruence between the child's home and school learning environments. What some researchers have called 'comprehensible input' is part of this congruence. However, in Vygotsky's theoretical framework, comprehensibility of what a child learns is not an attribute of the curriculum or of the instructional process controlled by the teacher; comprehensibility is determined by the 'Zone of Proximal Development' (ZPD) that a child controls with the orientation and the support of more informed peers or adults. This ZPD encompasses domains, concepts and areas of learning for which a child is ready in an appropriate learning environment. This can be described as one in which interaction is meaningful (culturally and linguistically), supportive (with opportunities for high levels of achievement motivation) and conducive to the child's active involvement in acquiring new knowledge (interactionally focused, appropriate and substantive).

While broad sociological (structural) characteristics of learning environments, both at home and in school, may explain, at least in part, the overall differences in achievement levels between ethnic groups, they do not explain intra-group differences. These differences are best approached with theories such as those developed by Vygotsky and Neo-Vygotskians (see Tharp and Gallimore, 1989). The focus of theoretical debates regarding explanations of differential achievement of ethnic and minority groups has been on this difficult transition from the collective (sociocultural) forces conditioning achievement levels, and the individual responses that may or may not follow those of the group. In predicting collective failure of some groups (often attributed to their shared cultural characteristics) we have neglected to explain the success of some of the members of that group.

Academic learning, or the ability to handle abstract concepts and to establish conceptual relationships related to subject matter, is most important, indeed indispensable for long-term successful adaptation to technological societies. But academic learning is not enough. In fact, individuals who reach high positions of political and economic power are often less competent academically than those who, having achieved well in school, fail to succeed in the marketplace. There are job ceilings and other social structural constraints that are superimposed by mainstream members of society; but there are also limiting factors in the schooling of immigrants and refugees that prevent them from acquiring cultural knowledge and skills necessary to function effectively in executive positions. Elements of disempowerment can be disguised in the form of high academic achievement. The intellectual creativity observed in some scientific fields is a by-product of intensive socialization in non-schooling activities. Yet, these activities facilitate intellectual exchanges that lead to cooperative learning experiences among peers. These exchanges are often cast in culturally-framed interactional settings, such as clubs, social activities, conferences, performances, private conversations and even in close mentoring activities. These elements of socialization necessary to achieve higher levels of cognitive development and professional performance are seldom open to minorities.

Socially-based theories of learning, as guided by the work of Vygotsky, have not remained an element of speculation. They have impacted the conceptual designs of active research in education, or 'useful' research, as others prefer to call it. Useful research is defined not only in terms of its outcomes, but also in its processes. It is the kind of research which is done cooperatively with colleagues from schools and from other higher education institutions, and which is structured primarily to help improve the quality of school instruction and the overall learning environments at home and in the schools. The need to cooperate with schools is, now more than ever, an urgent task underlined by the increasing problems associated with ethnic or economic diversification of student populations. These problems being faced by American society at large include child abuse, drug addiction, isolation and neglect of youth. Many of these youth are recipients of substandard quality of instruction, which is heightened by their confusion about cultural values or long-term goals associated with public education. Deviant, dysfunctional and even destructive behavior on the part of students is often, from their standpoint, an appropriate response to the cultural conflicts faced in school.

From the theoretical perspective of Vygotsky, all children should normally succeed in acquiring the knowledge necessary for them to function effectively in their social and cultural setting. All children can acquire this knowledge if taught within their range of ability (their zone of proximal development). When children do not learn, the assumption is not that children have failed, but that the system has failed. A systemic failure means a lack of access to socially and culturally meaningful intercourse, and as such it is a social phenomenon that must be studied in its historical and cultural roots. In other words, it is a culturally-based mechanism of exclusion; social exclusion is a symbolic way to reject an ethnic or racial group from belonging in a society. Consequently, the solution to children's learning problems is not just curriculum reform and remedial teaching of individual children, but a societal reform to remove the roots of the problem: prejudice.

Social scientists have become increasingly concerned about the social and cultural context of achievement, or the culturally-determined conditions for higher achievement beyond the narrowly conceived formal academic settings. Literacy studies in the workplace point to the number of factors related to finding and keeping a job that don't seem to be related to conceptual abilities or literacy in the strict sense of generating or interpreting text. Appropriate gestures, organizational skills, etiquette, social skills, problem-solving abilities, observational skills, and other strictly non-academic factors can often determine people's economic opportunities. Ethnographers, socio-linguists and other scholars are now studying, through discourse analysis and observations, those factors leading to the empowerment of individuals, or the ability to participate in the job market and the social life around them without prejudice.

Ethnography and Empowerment

Ethnographic approaches are increasingly being used in applied research, reform efforts, and in equity or advocacy issues. For example, in 'ethno-graphic evaluation' studies, issues have been raised about the loyalty to anthropological traditions of objectivity, validity of observations made with the primary purpose of evaluating (rather explaining) behavior, and the pitfalls of methodological laxity in short-termed efforts. A distinction must be made, however, between a research methodology and/or a theoretical approach, and its purpose or application to practical issues. Presumably, researchers can keep theoretical and methodological rigor in their design, and yet use the results for recommending appropriate action, structural reform or a change in policy. Ethnography for empowerment is precisely in this category. Studies on literacy acquisition of women and minorities, school adjustment and performance, racial segregation, teacher preparation for, and performance in ethnically diverse schools, are, among others, themes that are potentially both the focus of ethnographic research project, and extremely relevant to educational practice and policy.

While literature on the ethnography of empowerment is growing rapidly, much of the research has not been conducted with Asian Americans. The need to conceptualize, present, compare and contrast accounts of both disempowerment and empowerment of individuals and entire communities has led various scholars to use ethnographic accounts in combination with other conceptual tools. Unfortunately, the literature on the problems faced by many refugees now living in the Southwest is limited. However, the few accounts we have are extremely useful. Suárez-Orozco, for example, has been working with Central American refugees since the early 1980s. His study was conducted with young men and women between the ages of 14 and 19 coming from El Salvador, Guatemala and Nicaragua. At the time of the study, these individuals were enrolled in inner-city schools, trying to learn English, aspiring to obtain a professional career, and were characterized by their commitment to learn (1989, 1990). Their past was marked by political terror, with the killing of over 40,000 people in El Salvador by late October, 1983 (killing continued after that date), approximately 20,000 people in

Guatemala, and approximately 40,000 people in Nicaragua during the rebellion against Somoza (Suárez-Orozco, 1990:356).

The murder committed by death squards of four Maryknoll sisters and six Jesuit priests in the 1980s finally raised the level of awareness in the United States and resulted in the legal immigration of Central American refugees (34,436 for the 1971–80 period, and 32,666 for 1980–84). It is calculated that since the late 1970s when the political persecution became exacerbated, over 300,000 Salvadorians (10 per cent of the entire population) entered the US illegally (according to an estimate presented by Suárez-Orozco, 1990:359). The cases of Guatemala and Nicaragua are equally shocking. The accounts offered by Suárez-Orozco provide us with some insight about the traumas experienced by refugees. It is unfortunate that we have no equivalent studies of Indochinese refugees. The experiences of Central Americans, however, and their responses to cultural conflict in this country are comparable to those of Asian Americans. Here is an example:

> The *guerrilleros* also looked for me; they wanted to take me along.
> I remember that after they took my friend, they beat him up,
> mistreated him, and tied him up for hours. And they asked him
> about me, where I lived, what was I doing and all that. He would not
> tell them so they tied him up and mistreated him more. When
> he finally told me all this, I was terrorized. I was nervous. The
> *guerrilleros* wanted me to be a leader in one of their groups...I
> always stayed away from politics. I was also afraid of the death
> squads. They killed two of my cousins, they killed without any
> reason! I don't know why they killed them; there is no reason at all.
> I was 14 years old and saw all this (Suárez-Orozco, 1990: 365).

The analysis of numerous accounts of terror have led to a better understanding of the process victims must follow in order to regain control of their lives, to become empowered and capable of normal participation in social institutions. The 'internalization' of terror, characterized by themes of death, torture and assassinations was evident in the analyses of the Thematic Apperception Test stories obtained by Suárez-Orozco. Successful adaptation of victims of terror depends on a long process of reflective cultural analysis, or cultural therapy (Spindler and Spindler, 1982:30–31, and 1989:36–50). We believe that the process of empowerment must ultimately deal with culture shock and cultural discontinuities related to the specific backgrounds of immigrant, refugee and minority persons. Before we discuss the issues of cultural therapy, it is important to provide a broader context for the issues related to the concept of the ethnography of empowerment.

According to Barr, 'The literature on power is vast, covering hundreds of years of writing and drawing upon five primary disciplinary fields: philosophy, political science, sociology, psychology and economics' (1989:1–2). The questions addressed by these fields discusses the means to obtain power and to hold on to it, the relationship between power and morality, the corruption associated with holding power, the meaning and extent of exercising power, and the sources and instruments of power. In the sixteenth century Machiavelli offered good advice to powerholders; in the seventeenth century, Hobbes discussed the use of power to obtain personal pleasure. Both Machiavelli and Hobbes saw the use of individual power as the political arena for conflict and competition. Nietzsche in the nineteenth and twentieth centuries saw power as related to the self-worth of the individual. According to Barr's interpretation of Nietzsche 'to want power to do evil was a sign of weakness and low self-esteem' (Barr, 1989:4).

Sociological thinking on power in American society is characterized by two opposite views, the rationalist and the utopian. According to Barr the 'rationalist believes conflict and competition are essential to the nature of power in a social system', and power is intrinsically coercive in nature. Consequently, 'coercion is an essential aspect of all power relationships' (Barr, 1989:5). Within this view, power necessarily occupies a predominant place in all social systems and functions and becomes an independent social variable. Power can 'take on numerous symbolic meanings, for example, money, land, and knowledge' and the monopoly of power in the hands of an elite 'creates in the powerless a sense of alienation and frustration over their lack of power', because power elites are uncontrollable except in the face of generalized conflict created by the powerless (Barr, 1989:5–6).

In contrast, the utopians do not see power as control over other people, but as the ability to accomplish something, or 'power to do' rather than 'power over others'. Barr sees utopian power as built around trust and furthering communal interests to 'fulfill binding obligations' in a setting characterized by an 'element of accountability that keeps powerholders in check' (Barr, 1989:6). For the rationalists, there is no possible accountability of the powerful to anyone. For the utopians the powerful are accountable to the community and use power primarily to deal with new and changing situations.

Is the process of empowerment a collective process; that is, a process always related to groups of persons sharing similar characteristics, or groups sharing similar experiences, or one affecting single individuals whose personal responses to experiences lead to control or lack of it? Empowerment is often viewed as a process by which power is obtained; that is, it is the process of transition from lack of control to the acquisition of control over life, resources and the surrounding environment. Therefore, empowerment is equated with the possession of power to act, to perform effectively, and to participate in a given activity. As such, empowerment is essentially a phenomenon socially identified, whose consequences must go beyond the individual. Thus, empowerment is discussed as intimately related to the acquisition of the social status and the means required for the enjoyment of human rights. The enjoyment of human rights should be recognized cross culturally. Access to information and the ability to process information

— not necessarily only academic information — has been at the heart of empowerment discussions. For example, empowerment as applied to teachers in their professional career has been described as follows:

> Professional empowerment is a privilege of the collectivity of teachers, much less a privilege granted teachers by the power of central government offices. Professional empowerment is understood here to involve the individual teacher's possession of the conditions, means, knowledge, and skills required to teach, it is understood as a right similar to the rights of other professionals (Trueba, 1989:148).

Beyond this notion of empowerment as the fundamental right to the means required for competent professional performance, the concept of empowerment is much broader and should be viewed as linking psychological processes (internalization of knowledge through critical thinking) with the social reality in which the individuals function (the actualization of social roles). Empowerment has been applied to minority families and associated to literacy. For example, the ability of parents and their children to acquire new knowledge about the social reality of the United States, and to do this through text, is truly a significant emancipatory event. The reason is that knowledge had been inaccessible to parents previously, because of the double barrier of their illiteracy and their lack of the English language (Delgado-Gaitan, 1990; Delgado-Gaitan and Trueba, 1991).

Viewed from the perspective of an individual becoming engaged in the process of empowerment, be that as an individual teacher, a parent or a child, empowerment is constituted by a series of social and psychological events that have political consequences because they lead to the important realization that the individual can control his or her own destiny by controlling access to knowledge. This knowledge starts within the self and the place of the individual in a given society. One's own place in society cannot be surrendered. It must be defended by exercising the right to participate in the social, legal, political and economic systems which determine individual status and his/her access to knowledge or other forms of power.

The use of power, and, consequently, empowerment as the process to gain access to power, is not only a sociological or cultural reality, but also a psychological one, affecting individual self-concept and behavior. As a psychological process, empowerment can affect an individual or a group of individuals in gaining control over their own destiny, specifically by determining their degree of participation in democratic institutions. This participation in democratic institutions is gained (or regained) through the study of, and reflection on, the place historically occupied by individuals in the social and economic strata of societal institutions. Consciousness of the nature of inalienable human rights that are inherent to members of the human species regardless of sociocultural, political, economic, religious, racial or social status differences, is clearly at the heart of empowerment.

Ethnographic methods are considered methodological tools which are not only compatible but also complementary in order to follow the historical and current paths of adjustment and acculturation of immigrant, refugee and other minorities in California. This thesis argues that the use of both ethnohistory and ethnography can create a strong methodological combination for the empowerment of teachers working with culturally diverse student populations. If teachers better understand the history of minority communities, from the perspective of these communities, and if they also understand the current sociocultural environment of these communities (their values, traditions and goals), they will truly become empowered to work effectively with these communities.

It is precisely in a historical context that the ethnography of empowerment makes sense. Recent Asian and Hispanic immigrants share the American ideals of mass education, political participation and economic opportunity equally accessible to all because they feel they can belong in this country. In the case of Hispanic and Asian populations, this is particularly true for the Southwest, because both populations are historically linked in their growth and development. The question is whether or not these populations can learn how to participate in the democratic process of America, whose very foundations are linked to the recognition of the important historical role played by ethnolinguistic minority peoples (Spindler, 1977; Spindler and Spindler 1983, 1987a, 1987b).

At the heart of the effectiveness of educational ethnography to understand processes of disempowerment and empowerment is required the sharp observations of ethnographers involved in data collection. As George and Louise Spindler remark:

> There is no substitute for the alert individual observer, with all senses unstopped and sensitivities working at top efficiency. Of course this "turned on" observer is not simply collecting data impartially. There is a model of possible relationships in the mind of the ethnographer. And yet there is no substitute for this observer, for it is only the human observer that can be alert to divergences and subtleties that may prove to be more important than the data produced by any predetermined categories of observation or any instrument (Spindler and Spindler, in press).

Observations must be not only alert but also systematic and organized into a framework that permits making sense of observed phenomena. Ethnographers will not only go back to previous sites to compare behavior patterns over a period of time, but will also acquire a wider social and cultural knowledge that serves as a context for further interpretation of data collected. Furthermore, data will be compared and contrasted across cultures.

The differentiation of empowerment among Asian students forces us to revise our fundamental concepts of the relationships between schooling and power, between the possession of subject-matter information as measured by school performance and actual successful performance in the marketplace. The isolation of Asian students in careers requiring less social intercourse is creating generations of second class citizens who, having made high achievements in school, become peons in the hands of individuals who are socially and culturally more skilled, and who determine the allocation of resources. A central tenet in American democracy has been the principle of equity for all — equity of opportunity in participation across social, economic and political institutions. The potential of Asian populations is very high, yet their social and cultural isolation is preventing them from claiming a higher level of participation in the organizational structures of professional groups. The factors limiting the development of the full potential of Asian Americans are clearly linked with cultural shock and conflicting cultural values. The response to cultural shock is often one of isolation, and, consequently, of additional limitations to participate in social institutions.

The intra-group diversification of Asian Americans suggests that schooling is not the only avenue for upward mobility, not only because high achieving individuals reach a job ceiling based on criteria other than academic skills, but also because many non-schooled Asian immigrants and refugees are moving up through commerce and service careers which require less academic preparation.

Because the acquisition of academic knowledge in certain subjects, particularly towards the end of elementary school, requires a very sophisticated use of language, children's learning must be grounded in culturally-based experiences (integral to the theory of learning postulated by the sociohistorical school of psychology led by Vygotsky, 1962, 1978; Mc-Dermott, 1987a, 1987b; Goldman and McDermott, 1987; Ogbu, 1978, 1987; Trueba and Delgado-Gaitan, 1988; Trueba, 1987a, 1987b, and in 1989). Consequently, the learner must play an active role in determining the 'whats' and 'hows' of the learning process. Asian Americans find it culturally unacceptable to become aggressive, to take active roles in their own education and professional development. If they accept American values associated with aggressive professional roles, Asian Americans find it hard to keep other cultural values of their home cultures stressing just the opposite: humility, kindness, low profiles, submissiveness and obedience. The use of cultural therapy is most important in the empowerment of many minority groups, but especially of Asian Americans. The theoretical position adopted in the discussion of cultural therapy requires an understanding of the relationship between disempowerment and empowerment. Naturally, the application of cultural therapy to daily practice also requires a great deal of creativity and self-confidence on the part of disempowered persons, but the desired outcomes will occur. Empowerment is not a process that one can force on someone else. It must come from within.

Both empowerment and disempowerment are linked to the social construction of reality in an stratified society with differential access to power.

The psychological phenomena accompanying disempowerment processes, for example, in the form of asymmetrical power relationships which include systematic exposure to degradation incidents and prejudicial treatment — such as the one received by victims of war and terrorism — affect profoundly the self-concept and personality structure of the individuals being disempowered. Victims of prejudicial treatment (see, for example, DeVos, 1973, 1980, 1982, 1983; Suárez-Orozco, 1989, 1990) experience a gradual internalization of the negative attributes ascribed to them by the power-holders. Thus, individuals of low status develop a low self-esteem, a feeling of incompetence, and a sense of helplessness.

One can assume that the process of empowerment is the mirror image and must follow steps that reverse the previous trends. Disempowered individuals must become aware of their condition, and redefine their experiences of prejudicial treatment in ways that do not reflect personal fault or limitations of the victim. Because disempowered persons are often traumatized or disabled, those disabling experiences must be counteracted by positive experiences, which are successful and produce high public status and recognition. For example, in the case of abused women who engage in physical training to defend themselves, they must experience their physical power of rejecting assaults. As victims of previous attacks, they have the need to regain self-confidence and esteem, and must begin by acting out their new self-confidence in socially and culturally defined interactional settings. It is not enough to engage in solitary psychological exercises. It is a social process extended through a series of events. Disempowerment is the result of a socialization which leads to lack of self-confidence, psychological and sociocultural conflicts, and ultimately to failure in meaningful participation. By the same token, empowerment is the opposite socialization process, in which individuals internalize high self-esteem, ability to function effectively, confidence to work well, and access to opportunities for the identification of information and resources enhancing individual or collective goals. The social construction of failure mirrors the social construction of success within the same social structural settings and cultural units in which individuals learn to function and behave appropriately, such as in the family, schools, and other public settings (Trueba, 1988a:210–211; and in Trueba and Delgado-Gaitan, 1988:208–214; Delgado-Gaitan and Trueba, 1991).

The literature on empowerment has extended from family studies and intervention models in the health sciences to psychological and anthropological research, studies on learning environments and literacy, and on instructional effectiveness (see comprehensive reviews in Delgado-Gaitan, 1990; Delgado-Gaitan and Trueba, 1991).

More clearly, the recent work has advanced the specific nature of the relationship between literacy acquisition processes in children with their parents' process of empowerment to function effectively in public institutions other than school (Delgado-Gaitan, 1990). What has not been defined clearly is the theoretical perspectives on the social and cultural contexts of empowerment or disempowerment processes. Specifically, in anthropology we have yet to define how the overall umbrella of studies conducted via ethnographic methods deals with the socialization for empowerment in education. Educational anthropology in general, and cultural therapy in particular, has come of age, and as such has impacted the discourse on the nature of mankind and the processes whereby humans learn to behave as humans and transfer knowledge and values from one generation to another. Ethnographic research in education has been rooted in contributions by psychological anthropologists, who studied adaptive mechanisms and the cultural factors of achievement motivation. Yet, ethnographic research continues to be an elusive and increasingly more controversial instrument used by scholars from a number of disciplines and with diverse theoretical frameworks. It is recognized as being a unique instrument to study the process of successful adaptations of minorities to technological societies, which leads to their empowerment in these societies.

The interface between social and cognitive isolation of minority students, both at home and in the schools, does not occur only in the case of low achievers. This isolation of language minority children entails cognitive neglect, limited opportunities at home to acquire the social skills that open opportunities for learning and acquiring critical thinking abilities, as well as the ability to internalize cultural values of the host society. Many of the language minority children, including those classified as 'most successful', compare their life at home with that of their mainstream friends, and experience feelings of low self-esteem. Some of the refugees experience a continuing inability to keep up with their school work. They find no help in school, because 'Asians are smart and will succeed anyhow, why bother.' Fortunately, many Asian children are breaking their isolation by becoming more vocal. They want to be involved in mainstream cultural activities and to become cultural brokers in their homes, with their peers, in their ethnic community, and as translators and volunteer workers in their communities.

Cultural therapy was originally described by George and Louise Spindler as an encounter with cultural evidence showing individual biases associated with interethnic interaction. In their original study of Roger Harker, an exemplary teacher who was unconscious of his preferential treatment to children who shared his cultural background, the Spindlers showed him:

> ...where and how his perceptions and understanding were skewed, and quite out of line with both reality as I [George] perceived it and the realities of classroom life as the children perceived them. At first he was disbelieving and hostile. Eventually he assimilated what was being presented (Spindler and Spindler, 1982:30).

The Spindlers recognize that there are different ways of coping with cultural conflict, such as the one Roger Harker was facing in his ethnically diverse classroom. Cultural therapy is viewed as a possible instrument to resolve such conflicts. Problems in self-esteem and self-competencies are difficult to resolve, yet cultural therapy as a process may help:

> This process involves a kind of consciousness raising similar to Paulo Freire's 'conscientizacion' (Freire, 1973). The cultural reasons for one's failure to achieve instrumental competence [demonstrated in high school achievement and high self-esteem] and for reasons one's loss of self-esteem, as self-efficacy is damaged, are explored with the personnel involved. We have done some cultural therapy with individual teachers. In a sense, all our teaching in introductory anthropology, cultural transmission, and particularly in our ethnographic methods seminar, intended as it is to increase cultural awareness or consciousness, can be thought of as a kind of cultural "therapy"....
> In our case study of Roger Harker, the ethnographic data collected in his classroom and from interviewing was discussed with him in a series of sessions. He had volunteered for our "case study" research in order to "improve his professional competence". He gained insight into his classroom behavior from this experience. He discovered that he was defeating his own stated goals and how he was defeating them. He wanted to treat all children fairly and was committed to equity, but actually interacted with, literally taught, only those who were culturally like himself....Further observation suggested that this "therapy" influenced his classroom behavior in the desired direction (Spindler and Spindler, 1989:41–42).

Is cultural therapy a technique that can be applied to students as well? If so, what is the appropriate way to use it? How could Asian Americans benefit from such ethnographic methods? The role of anthropologists as therapists is not far removed from some of the practices of early psychological anthropologists alluded to in Chapter 1, such as Dorothy Lee, George Spindler, Margaret Mead and Solon Kimball. There are a number of questions that need to be answered if cultural therapy is to be used with language minority students: Should we use their mother tongue? Should we train individuals familiar with their culture? Should we identify ethnographers who, knowing the language and culture of students, can observe student behavior in class and conduct sessions with language minority students in order to help them understand their own behavior in class and in school?

In the tradition of P. Freire and George Spindler, the ability to function as a full member of society, to understand the social and cultural significance of the moment in history in which we are living, is to become empowered. Becoming empowered means knowing 'the world and knowing the word', that is, understanding the relationship between history, culture and literacy. This is precisely what the ethnography of empowerment is intended to do. First, the ethnography of empowerment incorporates ethnohistory in order to bring an adequate interpretation of past events from the cultural perspective of the ethnic or minority community, that is, it brings an 'emic' or 'within group' perspective. Ethnography recognizes that the interpretation of the past is both the definition of the present and the projection of the future. As we saw it earlier, in his analysis of responses to terror in Argentina, Suárez-Orozco (1990:353–383) has recently reminded us that the pattern of collective denials of atrocities committed affects not only the victims but also the victimizers. For example, the construction of the death camps by the Nazis was so unbearable that many Germans continue to deny their historical documentation and repress all memories associated with the camps. Paradoxically, this denial caused them to become unable to feel compassion and to grieve for the dead. The disappearance of many intellectuals in Argentina led to similar patterns. Hysterical denials were associated with the inability of certain individuals to get out of their disempowerment and regain control of their lives.

The pre-arrival traumas, as well as the cultural insensitivity of Americans dealing with Asian refugees, can result in cultural conflicts which contribute to the creation of an artificial ceiling in their intellectual development and a barrier to their participation in the social, cultural, economic and political institutions of America. The use of ethnographic research methods in conjunction with ethnohistorical accounts, psychological research and cultural therapy can not only help school personnel in dealing with the problems of Asian Americans who have recently arrived in the United States, but can also use these methods as part of cultural therapy. Cultural therapy can reveal specific cultural conflicts associated with demanding opposite patterns of behavior, for example, competitive or aggressive behavior in academic and professional training, and kindness, low profile, humility and tolerance in the home and personal life.

The studies of the present reality of minority students in their social and cultural environment (also as an 'emic' perspective), are instruments that have been used by anthropologists as methodological tools which are mutually compatible, mutually supportive and functionally complementary. By documenting the past and making it understandable within the cultural present, ethnohistory provides broad and longitudinal guidelines to build the future. Ethnographic research is indeed an integral part of empowerment by making sense of past inequities in their historical and cultural contexts. Beyond this first step of making sense of inequities, ethnography can help study processes of proactive empowerment, especially in the analysis of interethnic or intercultural value conflicts. Ethnography makes ethnohistory relevant to the present, and part of the future. Empowerment is contingent upon a historical understanding of conflict, abuse, and misunderstandings. In this sense, empowerment is a process that, through ethnographic methods (observations, documentation and reflection) creates a bridge between the past, the present and the desired future. Both ethnohistory and ethnography can empower teachers and students of all minority groups to understand the home and school cultures better, the potential value conflicts and the need for effective communications and increased participation in social institutions. Empowerment is also intimately related to minority children's communicative ability during their transition from their home culture and language to the mainstream culture and language of the United States. It is not enough for Asian and Pacific Island children to do well in mathematics and the natural sciences. They need to acquire a full command of the English language and all the necessary social skills, in order to participate at all levels of academic activities, as well as in the labor market. The power of English literacy for all minority students, especially for Asian and Pacific Island children, is crucial. Literacy in its broadest sense, that is, the ability to function in the mainstream linguistic and cultural context beyond academic performance and school activities, is essential to fully develop talents associated with creative activities, higher order reasoning, appropriate social behavior in academic circles with colleagues, problem-solving in research settings, and, ultimately, in order to participate in all the possible realms of social, artistic, literacy and economic life in America.

To disregard the needs of Asian and Pacific Island children on the grounds that they will survive (even if most of them do) violates the democratic principles of equity and educational opportunity for all. Asian children should have the opportunity to develop their full potential, and should not be penalized because they excel in certain aspects of their development.

Instructors of Asian and Pacific Island children who notice that these children are facing cultural conflicts and language difficulties in the early stages of their transition to American schools, should make it possible for children to continue to use their home languages, without isolating them from English-speaking circles. Linguistic minority children in cultural transition should resort to mother tongues or home languages as needed, without excluding exposure to English. Teachers of Asian-American children should make an effort to tailor the curriculum to children's knowledge and experiences, in order to facilitate the development of linguistic and social skills outside academic subjects. These teachers would need latitude and flexibility in organizing their teaching activities, as well as in creating rewards and support systems to encourage children in their efforts to understand American values.

In the process of becoming empowered, learning to succeed in social interactional contexts has important implications for success in other settings, including strictly academic and psychological activities. The opposite can also be true. The acquisition of cognitive and social skills in school can open doors in the workplace. While academic success can help minority children integrate cultural values and develop a strong self-concept, failure on social situations can produce a low self-concept and psychological isolation. Part of the explanation of these facts is presented by George and Louise Spindler in their discussion of the Instrumental Model:

The instrumental activities model is based on the notion that cultures consist, in part, of the organization of activities that one engages and that result in one's acquiring possessions, recognition, power, status, and satisfaction. These activities are *linked* to these results. The articulation and prioritizing of these linkages are learned as the culture is acquired. In stable traditional societies, the arrangements of linkages is understood and used as appropriate to one's sex, age, and prescribed stations in life. In changing and, particularly, modernizing societies, some linkages are learned early that later become outmoded. Some are learned inadequately. Some are dimly perceived but not mastered. Some are neither perceived nor learned by some individuals. Instrumental linkages range from explicit to implicit and the latter are usually acquired through long and early socialization (Spindler and Spindler, 1989:36).

These notions are essential to understand both the nature of cultural conflict and cultural therapy. Conflict is the result of the discontinuities suffered by children who do not understand the instrumental linkages between American cultural values and the types of behaviors reflecting the understanding between organization of activities, and expected outcomes (acquisition of possessions, recognition, power, status, etc.) or the linkage between activities and desired outcomes. In some instances, Asian American children may not perceive as desirable certain outcomes that contradict their home cultural values, or if they perceive as desirable those outcomes (recognition, power, etc.), they do not see the link, the relationship between an activity and the expected outcome. For example, public performance is a means of receiving recognition. The nature and range of these discontinuities, whether brought in with the home culture or acquired in the context of attempting to adjust to American society, is in a genuine sense, at the heart of cultural conflicts. Consequently, cultural therapy must explore, document and explain such discontinuities in order to help individuals resolve problems in inter-ethnic and inter-cultural interaction.

If we use cultural therapy, as part of the ethnography of empowerment, we should take into consideration the following issues:

1 Students learn best in learning environments in which their cultural discontinuities do not render them handicapped, that is, environments in which the purpose of learning activities is clearly understood, and the values of such activities promote are accepted. This is particularly true of literacy. By placing students in 'culturally congruent' environments (as described above) failure is minimized, and success becomes an additional instrument of empowerment. Hopefully, culturally different children will be given specific academic activities, will discover their potential to reduce cultural discontinuities, and thus use these activities to convert potential

failure into opportunities for healing, intellectual growth and positive self-concept.

2   Most children have a repertoire of learning experiences and strengths (domains they know well because such domains are associated with survival and other important activities in the home culture). The challenge faced by educators is to identify learning strengths, skill level and domain-specific knowledge of language minority students in order motivate them to learn. This is part of creating a 'culturally congruent learning environment'.

3   Not all techniques and teaching strategies are culturally meaning-ful to language minority students. Teachers can explore diverse in-structional strategies, observe children and periodically record their sustained involvement and achievement outcomes. What worked with Kamehameha children (the talk story) does not work with Native American or Alaskan children. The amount of verbal pro-duction expected as a result of a teacher's teaching is entirely differ-ent across cultures.

4   Children are also flexible and want to adjust. After careful reflection, the choice of particular instructional strategies may not have the desired effect immediately. Some children are culturally pro-grammed to take their time before they commit to participate in any social activity, especially if performing in public is part of the activity. Upon identifying a successful approach, teachers could retain such approach for a length of time, until additional obser-vations and findings suggest the need for change. What is important, however, is that children see the consistency of instructional goals even when the approaches are changed. In this manner children can internalize the link between activities and desired cultural outcomes (recognition, power, etc.), as well as the expected norms of behavior.

5   All children need rewards, but the nature of the rewards is cultural-ly determined. Public praise is not necessarily a cross-culturally accepted way of rewarding successful academic performance. Teachers need to know what is the culturally appropriate way of providing children with positive strokes. However, because some children acquire American values very quickly, teachers need to observe the various responses of children to traditional verbal and other rewards given to mainstream children.

6   One of the most difficult tests of endurance is working with culturally different children, especially those who belong to non-Western cultures. To acquire the knowledge and develop the skills necessary to work effectively with these children one needs the help of more experienced teachers. Teachers learn (as children do) in socially-based settings. Experiences of failure to communicate with children, or continued lack of expected responses in language minority children (in contrast with the responses of mainstream

ones), can be deeply discouraging. When the events in class become potentially demoralizing, a group of teachers, or a support group can be extremely helpful.

These recommendations are common sense suggestions based on the experience of other teachers. They are not a substitute for intensive, long-term pre-service and in-service training. The goal of teacher support groups is not only their personal survival in the face of difficulties, but also their professional development designed to help children break the vicious cycle of stress, poor performance, embarrassment, depression and dropout. Teachers can be highly instrumental in the full development of children's talents and in the reduction of the cultural conflicts associated with discontinuities and lack of instrumental competencies resulting thereof.

Cultural therapy focuses on cultural conflict and the right choice of adaptive strategies to overcome such conflict. Resolution of cultural conflicts is a necessary condition for the academic achievement of minority students. Illiterate minority students have been socialized to fail by an insensitive educational system that views them as handicapped and as academically unsuccessful students, who never acquired the social skills to move on the ladder of executive positions commensurate with their academic success. We can learn a great deal from the successful academic socialization of Asian American students, but can also learn from their failure to reach the levels of social and cultural competence required for the full development of their talents.

References

ASHBY, A. (1983) *Micronesian Customs and Beliefs*, Eugene, OR: Rainy Day Press.

AU, K.H. (1980) 'Participation structures in a reading lesson with Hawaiian children: Analysis of a culturally appropriate instructional event', *Anthropology and Education Quarterly*, **11**(2), pp. 91–115.

AU, K.H. (1981) 'The comprehension-oriented reading lesson: Relationships to proximal indices of achievement', *Educational Perspectives*, **20**, pp. 13–15.

BANKS, J.A. (1990) *Transforming the Curriculum*, Conference on Diversity, Oakland, CA: California Teacher Credentialing Commission.

BANKS, J.A., CORTEZ, C.E., GAY, G., GARCIA, R. and OCHOA, A.S. (1976) *Curriculum Guidelines for Multiethnic Education*, Washington, DC: National Council for the Social Studies.

BARATZ-SNODEN, J.C. and DURAN, R. (1987) *The Educational Progress of Language Minority Students: Findings from the 1983–84 NAEP Reading Survey*, Princeton, NJ: National Assessment of Educational Progress/Educational Testing Service.

BARR, D.J. (1989) *Critical Reflections on Power*, Cornell University Project, Department of Human Services Studies, College of Human Ecology. Ithaca, NY.

BEACH, W.G. (1932) *Oriental Crime in California*, Palo Alto, CA: Stanford University Press.

BILINGUAL EDUCATION OFFICE, CALIFORNIA STATE DEPARTMENT OF EDUCATION (1983a) *Handbook for Teaching Korean-speaking Students*, Los Angeles, CA: Evaluation, Dissemination and Assessment Center, California State University.

BILINGUAL EDUCATION OFFICE, CALIFORNIA STATE DEPARTMENT OF EDUCATION (1983b) *Handbook for Teaching Vietnamese-speaking Students*, Sacramento, CA: Author.

BILINGUAL EDUCATION OFFICE, CALIFORNIA STATE DEPARTMENT OF EDUCATION (1984) *Handbook for Teaching Cantonese-speaking Students*, Sacramento, CA: Author.

BILINGUAL EDUCATION OFFICE, CALIFORNIA STATE DEPARTMENT OF EDUCATION (1986) *Handbook for Teaching Filipino-Speaking Students*, Sacramento, CA: Author.

BILINGUAL EDUCATION OFFICE, CALIFORNIA STATE DEPARTMENT OF EDUCATION (1987) *Handbook for Japanese-speaking Students*, Sacramento, CA: Author.

BIT S. (1981) 'A study of the effects of reward structures on Academic achievement and sociometric status of Cambodian students', Unpublished doctoral dissertation, San Francisco, CA University of San Francisco.

BOARDMAN, A.E. and ALOYD, A. (1978) 'Process of education for twelfth grade Asian and Puerto Rican American children', *Integrated Education*, **16**, pp. 44–6.

BOGGS, S.T. (1985) *Speaking, Relating, and Learning: A Study of Hawaiian Children at Home and at School*, Norwood, NJ: Ablex Publishing Corp.

BOUVIER, L.F. and MARTIN, P.L. (1987) *Population Change and California's Education System*, Washington, DC: Population Reference Bureau, Inc.

References

BROADMAN, A. and WOOD, D. (1978) 'The process of education for twelfth grade Asian American students', *Cross Reference*, **7**, pp. 338–530.

CALIFORNIA STATE DEPARTMENT OF EDUCATION (1981) *Schooling and Language Minority Students: A Theoretical Framework*, Los Angeles, CA: California State University, Evaluation, Dissemination and Assessment Center.

CALIFORNIA STATE DEPARTMENT OF EDUCATION (1986) *Beyond Language: Social and Cultural Factors in Schooling Language Minority Students*, Los Angeles, CA: California State University, Evaluation, Dissemination and Assessment Center.

CAPLAN, N., WHITEMORE, J., BUI, Q. and TRAUTMANN, M. (1985) *Scholastic Achievement Among the Children of Southeast Asian Refugees*, Ann Arbor, MI: The Institute for Social Research.

CARTER, T.P. and SEGURA, R.D. (1979) *Mexican Americans in School: A decade of change*, New York, NY: College Entrance Examination Board.

CAZDEN, C. and MEHAN, H. (1989) 'Principles from sociology and anthropology: Context, code, classroom, and culture', in REYNOLDS, M.C. (Ed.) *Knowledge Base for the Beginning Teacher*, Oxford, England: Pergamon Press.

CAZDEN, C., JOHN, V. and HYMES, D. (Eds) (1972) *Functions of Language in the Classroom*, New York, NY: Teachers College Press.

CHAN, K.S. (1983) 'Limited English speaking, handicapped, and poor: Triple threat in childhood', in MAE, C.C. (Ed.) *Asian- and Pacific American Perspectives in Bilingual Education: Comparative Research*, New York, NY: Teachers College, Columbia University.

CHENG, L. (1984) 'The assessment of communicative competence using a naturalistic instrument', *Clairmont Reading Conference Yearbook*, Clairemont, CA: Clairemont Graduate School.

CHENG, L. (1987) 'English communicative competence of language minority children: Assessment and treatment of language "impaired" preschoolers', in TRUEBA, H. (Ed.) *Success or failure? Learning and the language minority student*, New York: Newbury/Harper & Row, pp. 49–68.

CHENG, L. (1989) 'Service delivery to Asian/Pacific LEP children: A cross-cultural framework'. *Topics in Language Disorders*, **9**(3), pp. 1–14.

CHENG, L. (1991) *Assessing Asian Language Performance*, Oceanside, CA: Academic Communication Associates.

CHENG, L. and IMA, K. (1989) *Southeast Asians in California*, San Diego, CA: Los Amigos Research Associates.

CHENG, L. and IMA, K. (1990) *Understanding the Refugee Hmong*, San Diego, CA: Los Amigos Research Associates.

CHUA-EOAN, H.G. (1990) 'Strangers in paradise', *Time*, **135**(15), pp. 32–5.

COLE, L. and DEAL, V. (1986) *Communication Disorders in Multicultural Populations*, Rockville, MD: American Speech-Hearing Association.

COOK-GUMPERZ, J. (Ed.) (1986) *The Social Construction of Literacy*, Cambridge, MA: Cambridge University Press.

CUMMINS, J. (1980) 'The cross-lingual dimensions of language proficiency: Implications for bilingual education and the optimal age issue', *TESOL Quarterly*, **14**, pp. 175–87.

CUMMINS, J. (1981a) 'The entry and exit fallacy in bilingual education', *National Association for Bilingual Education Journal*, **4**(3), pp. 26–60.

CUMMINS, J. (1981b) 'The role of primary language development in promoting educational success for language minority students', in *Schooling and Language Minority Students: A Theoretical Framework*, Los Angeles: California State University at Los Angeles Evaluation Dissertation and Assessment Center, pp. 3–49.

CUMMINS, J. (1983) *Heritage Language Education: A Literature Review*, Toronto, Canada: Ministry of Education, Ontario.

CUMMINS, J. (1984) *Bilingual Special Education: Issues in Assessment and Pedagogy*, San Diego, CA: College Hill Press.

CUMMINS, J. (1986) Empowering Minority Students: A framework for intervention. *Harvard Educational Review*, **56**(1), pp. 18–35.

CUMMINS, J. (1989) *The Empowerment of Minority Students*, Los Angeles, CA: California Association for Bilingual Education.

DEAVILA, E. and DUNCAN, S.E. (1980) 'Definition and measurement of bilingual students', in *Bilingual Program, Policy, and Assessment Issues*, Sacramento, CA: California State Department of Education.

DEAVILA, E. and HAVASSY, B.E. (1974) 'Testing of minority children: A Neo-Piagetian approach', *Today's Education*, **63**, pp. 72–5.

DELGADO-GAITAN, C. (1986a) 'Mexican adult literacy: New directions for immigrants', in GOLDMAN, S. and TRUEBA, H.T. (Eds) *Becoming Literate in English as a Second Language*, Norwood, NJ: Ablex, pp. 9–32.

DELGADO-GAITAN, C. (1986b) 'Teacher attitudes on diversity affecting student socio-academic responses: An ethnographic view, *Journal of Adolescent Research*, **1**, pp. 103–114.

DELGADO-GAITAN, C. (1990) *Literacy for Empowerment*, London, England: Falmer Press.

DELGADO-GAITAN, C. and TRUEBA, H. (1991) *Crossing Cultural Borders: Education for Immigrant Families in America*, London, England: Falmer Press.

DEVOS, G. (1967) 'Essential elements of caste: psychological determinants in structural theory', in DEVOS, A. and WAGATSUMA, H. (Eds) *Japan's Invisible Race: Caste in Culture and Personality*, Berkeley CA: University of California Press, pp. 332–84.

DEVOS, G. (1973) 'Japan's outcastes: The problem of the Burakumin', in WHITAKER, B. (Ed.) *The Fourth World: Victims of group oppression*, NY: Schocken Books, pp. 307–27.

DEVOS, G. (1980) 'Ethnic adaptation and minority status', *Journal of Cross-Cultural Psychology*, **11**, pp. 101–24.

DEVOS, G. (1983) 'Ethnic identity and minority status: Some psycho-cultural considerations', in JACOBSON-WIDDING, A. (Ed.) *Identity: Personal and socio-cultural*, Upsala, NY: Almquist & Wiksell Tryckeri AB, pp. 90–113.

DEVOS, G. (1984) 'Ethnic persistence and role degradation: An illustration from Japan', Paper read April, 1984 at the American-Soviet Symposium on Contemporary Ethnic Processes in the USSR. New Orleans, LA.

DEVOS, G. and WAGATSUMA, H. (1966) *Japan's Invisible Race: Caste in Culture and Personality*, and Berkeley, CA: University of California Press.

DULAY, H.C. and BURT, M.K. (1975) 'New approach to discovering universals strategies of child second language acquisition', in DATO, D. (Ed.) *Developmental Psycholinguistics: Theory and Applications*, Washington, DC: Georgetown University Press.

DUNCAN, S.E. and DE AVILA, E.A. (1979) 'Bilingualism and cognition: Some recent findings', *NABE Journal*, **IV**, pp. 15–50.

DUONG, N.D. (1981) *A Collection of Papers in Vietnamese Culture*, Houston, TX: Indochinese Culture Center and Harris County Employment and Training Administration Youth Program.

ERICKSON, F. (1977) 'Some approaches to inquiry in school/community ethnography', *Anthropology and Education Quarterly*, **8**(3), pp. 58–69.

ERICKSON, F. (1984) 'School literacy, reasoning, and civility: An anthropologist's perspective, *Review of Educational Research*, **54**(4), pp. 525–44.

ERICKSON, F. (1987) 'Transformation and school success: The politics and culture of educational achievement', *Anthropology and Education Quarterly*, **18**(4), pp. 335–56.

ERICKSON, F. and MOHATT, G. (1982) 'Cultural organization of participation structures in two classrooms in Indian students', in SPINDLER, G. (Ed.) *Doing the*

Ethnography of Schooling: Educational Anthropology in Action, New York, NY: Holt, Rinehart and Winston, pp. 132–75.

ESPINOSA, R. and OCHOA, A. (1992) *The Educational Attainment of California Youth: A Public Equity Crisis*, San Diego, CA: San Diego State University, Department of Policy Studies and Cross Cultural Education.

FIRST, J. and WILSHIRE-CARRERA, J. (1988) *New Voices: Immigrant Students in US Public Schools*, Boston, MA: National Coalition of Advocates for Students.

FOLEY, D. (1991) 'Reconsidering anthropological explanations of ethnic school failure', *Anthropology and Education Quarterly*, **22**(1), pp. 60–86.

FONG, E., HOM, G., IMA, K. and YUNG, K. (1989) 'Academic achievement patterns of Asian/Pacific Islander students on the eighth grade CAP (California Assessment Program)', Paper presented at the annual conference of the American Educational Research Association, San Francisco, April, 1989.

FOOTE, T., ESPINOSA, R. and GARCIA, J. (1978) *Ethnic Groups and Public Education in California*, San Diego, CA: San Diego State University, College of Education.

GARCIA, J. and ESPINOSA, R. (1976) *Major Student Ethnic Minority Group Concentration in the California Public School*, San Diego, CA: San Diego State University, College of Education.

GARDNER, R.W., ROBEY, B. and SMITH, P. (1985) 'Asian American: Growth, change and diversity', *Population Bulletin*, **40**(4), pp. 1–44.

GIBSON, M. (1987) 'Playing by the rules', in SPINDLER, G. (Ed.) *Education and Cultural Process: Anthropolotical Approaches*, (2nd ed.) Prospect Heights, IL: Waveland Press, Inc., pp. 274–83.

GIBSON, M. (1988) *Accommodation Without Assimilation: Sikh Immigrants in an American High School*, Ithaca, NY: Cornell University Press.

GIFFORD, B.R. and GILLETT, P. (1986) 'Teaching in a great age of immigration', *Social Education*, **5**(3), pp. 184–88.

GIROUX, H. and McLAREN, P. (1986) 'Teacher education and the politics of engagement: The case for democratic schooling', *Harvard Educational Review* **26**(3), pp. 213–38.

GOLDMAN, S. and TRUEBA, H. (Eds) (1987) *Becoming Literate in English as a Second Language: Advances in Research and Theory*, Norwood, NJ: Ablex Corporation.

GOLDSTEIN, B. (1985) 'Schooling for Cultural Transitions: Hmong Girls and Boys in American high schools', unpublished doctoral dissertation, University of Wisconsin, Madison.

GOLLNICK, D.M. and CHINN, P.C. (1986) *Multicultural Education in a Pluralistic Society*, (2nd ed.). Columbus, OH: Charles E. Merrill.

GOMEZ, C.T. (1981) 'Cultural identity and academic achievement: The development of a cultural identity index for Filipino-American students', Unpublished doctoral dissertation, San Francisco, CA: University of San Francisco.

GREEN, M.F. (1989) *Minorities on Campus: A Handbook for Enhancing diversity*, Washington, DC: American Council on Education Publications Department.

GROSJEAN, F. (1982) *Life with Two Languages*, Cambridge, MA: Harvard University Press.

GUIANY, E.P. (1980) 'The relationship between home environment and reading achievement among Filipino-American third-grade and fifth-grade pupils', Unpublished doctoral dissertation, University of the Pacific, Stockton, CA.

GUMPERZ, J. (1971) *Language in Social Groups*. Palo Alto, CA: Stanford University Press.

GUMPERZ, J. (1975) 'Sociocultural knowledge in conversational inference', in SAVILLE-TROIKE, M. (Ed.) *Twenty-eighth Annual Round Table-monograph Series on Language and Linguistics*. Washington, DC: Georgetown University Press.

GUMPERZ, J. (1981) 'Conversational inference and classroom learning', in GREEN, J. and MALLAT, C. (Eds) *Ethnography and Language in Educational Settings*, Norwood, NJ: Ablex.

GUMPERZ, J. (Ed.) (1982) *Language and Social Identity*, Cambridge, MA: Cambridge University Press.

GUMPERZ, J. and HYMES, D. (Eds) (1964) 'The ethnography of communication', *American Anthropologists*, **66**(6).

GUMPERZ, J. and HYMES, D. (1972) *Directions in Sociolinguistics: The Ethnography of Communication*. New York, NY: Holt, Rinehart & Winston.

GUTHRIE, G.P. (1985) *A School Divided: An Ethnography of Bilingual Education in a Chinese Community*, Hillsdale, NJ: Lawrence Erlbaum and Associates.

HAKUTA, K. (1986) *Mirror of Language: The Debate on Bilingualism*, New York, NY: Basic Books.

HALE-BENSON, J. (1982) *Black Children: Their Roots, Culture, and Learning Styles* (rev. ed.). Baltimore, MD: The Johns Hopkins University Press.

HEATH, S.B. (1983) *Ways with Words: Language, Life and Work in Communities and Classrooms*, New York, NY: Cambridge University Press.

HEATH, S.B. (1986) 'Sociocultural contexts of language development', in *Beyond Language: Social and Cultural Factors in Schooling Language Minority Students*, California State University, Los Angeles, CA: Evaluation, Dissemination and Assessment Center.

HIRSCHMAN, C. and WONG, M.G. (1981) 'Trends in socioeconomic achievement among immigrant and native-born Asian-Americans, 1960–1976', *The Sociological Quarterly*, **XXII**, pp. 495–513.

HSIA, J. (1983) 'Cognitive assessment of Asian-Americans', in MAE, C.C. (Ed.) *Asian- and Pacific-American perspectives in Bilingual Education: Comparative Research*, New York, NY: Teachers College, Columbia University.

HSAI, J. (1988) *Asian-Americans in Higher Education and at Work*, Hillsdale, NJ: Lawrence Erlbaum.

HSU, F.L.K. (1971) *The Challenge of the American Dream: The Chinese in the United States*, Belmont, CA: Wadsworth Publishing Co.

HYMES, D. (1971) *On Communicative Competence*, Philadelphia, PA: University of Pennsylvania Press.

HYMES, D. (1974) *Foundations in Sociolinguistics*, Philadelphia, PA: University of Pennsylvania Press.

IMA, K. and CHENG, L. (1990) *Climbing New Mountains: The Hmong*, San Diego, CA: Los Amigos Research Associates.

IMA, K. and RUMBAUT, R. (1989) 'Southeast Asian refugees in American schools: A comparison between limited English proficient (LEP) and fluent English proficient (FEP) students', *Topics in Language Disorders*, 9, pp. 54–75.

IMA, K., VELASCO, OU K., and YIP, B. (1983) *Adjustment Strategies of Khmer Refugees in San Diego: Six Ethnographic Case Histories*, Final report to the Office of Refugee Resettlement, Department of Health and Human Services, San Diego, CA: Union of Pan Asian Communities.

JORDAN, C. and THARP, R.G. (1979) 'Culture and education', in MARSELLA, A., THARP, R.G. and CIBROWSKI, I. (Eds) *Perspectives in Crosscultural Psychology*, New York, NY: Academic Press.

JORDAN, C., AU, K.H. and JOSETING, A.K. (1983) 'Patterns of classroom interaction with Pacific Islands children: The importance of cultural differences', in MAE, C.C. (Ed.) *Asian- and Pacific American Perspectives in Bilingual Education: Comparative Research*, New York, NY: Teachers College, Columbia University.

KAN, S.H. and LIU, W.T. (1986) 'The educational status of Asian Americans: An update from the 1980 census', in TSUCHIDA, N. (Ed.) *Issues in Asian and Pacific American Education*, Minneapolis, MN: Asian/Pacific Learning Resource Center, University of Minnesota.

KANAHELE, G. (1980) *Stand Tall: A Search for Hawaiian Values*, Honolulu, HI: Hawaii University Press.

KAPLAN, R. (1966) 'Cultural thought patterns in intercultural education', *Language Learning*, **16**, pp. 1–20.

KINZIE, J.D., SACK, W.H., ANGELL, R., MANSON, S. and RATH, B. (1986) 'The psychiatric effects of massive trauma on Cambodian children, I: The children', *Journal of the American Academy of Child Psychiatry*, **25**, pp. 370–376.

KITANO, H. (1985) *Race Relations*, Englewood Cliffs, NJ: Prentice-Hall.

KITANO, H. (1989) 'A model for counseling Asian Americans', in PEDERSEN, P.B., DRAGUNS, J.G., LONNER, W.J. and TRIMBLE, J.E. (Eds) *Counseling Across Cultures*, Honolulu, HI: Hawaii University Press, pp. 139–51.

KITANO, H. and DANIELS, R. (1988) *Asian Americans: Emerging Minorities*, Englewood Cliffs, NJ: Prentice-Hall.

KNAPP, L. (1972) *Nonverbal Communication in Human Interaction*, New York, NY: Holt, Rinehart & Wilson.

KRASHEN, S. and BIBER, D. (1988) *On Course: Bilingual Education's Success in California*, Sacramento, CA: California Association for Bilingual Education.

LABOV, W. (1972) 'Some principles of linguistic methodology', *Language in Society*, **1**, pp. 97–120.

LAMBERT, W. (1978) 'Some cognitive and sociocultural consequences of being bilingual', in ALATIS, J.E. (Ed.) *International Dimensions of Bilingual Education*, Washington, DC: Georgetown University Press.

LAMBERT, W.E. and TUCKER, G.R. (1972) *Bilingual Education of Children: The St. Lamert Experiment. Rowley, MA: Newbury House.*

LEE, E.W. (1988) 'A descriptive analysis of CTBS achievement of reclassified students in the Alhambra elementary school district', Report to the Alhambra Elementary School District, Elementary Assessment/Orientation Center, Alhambra, CA.

LEE, E. and LEE, M. (1980) 'A study of classroom behaviors of Chinese American children and immigrant Chinese children in contrast to those of Black American children and white American children in an Urban Head Start program'. Unpublished doctoral dissertation, University of San Francisco.

LEE, Y. (1984) 'A comparative study of academic achievement among East Asian Americans (Chinese, Japanese, and Korean Americans) and Anglo Americans: An ethnographic study', Paper presented at the annual meeting of the American Educational Research Association, New Orleans, LA.

LEUBITZ, L. (1973) *Nonverbal Communication: A Guide for Teachers* Skokie, IL: National Textbook.

LEWIS, O. (1968) *La Vida: A Puerto Rican Family in the Culture of Poverty*, New York, NY: Vintage.

LIEM, N. (1980) 'Vietnamese-American crosscultural communication', *Bilingual Resources*, **3**, pp. 9–15.

LOPEZ, D. (1982) 'Language maintenance and shift in the United States today: The basic patterns and their social implications', *Asian Languages*, **4**, pp. 1–28. Los Alamitos, CA: National Center for Bilingual Research.

LUANGPRASEUT, K. (1987) *Laos Culturally Speaking: Introduction to the Lao culture*, San Diego, CA: San Diego State University, Multifunctional Resource Center.

LUM, J.B. (1971) 'An effectiveness study of English as a second language (ESL) and Chinese bilingual methods', unpublished doctoral dissertation, University of California, Berkeley.

LUND, N.J. and DUCHAN, J.F. (1988) *Assessing Children's Language in Naturalistic Contexts*, Englewood Cliffs, NJ: Prentice-Hall.

LYMAN, S.L. (1974) *Chinese Americans*, New York: Random House.

MACIAS, J. (1987) 'The hidden curriculum of Papago Teachers: American Indian strategies for mitigating cultural discontinuity in early schooling', in SPINDLER, G.

and L. (Eds) *Interpretive Ethnography of Education: At Home and Abroad*, New Jersey: Lawrence Erlbaum Associates, Publishers, pp. 363–80.

Masuda, M., Lin, K. and Tazuma, L. (1979) 'Adaptational problems of Vietnamese refugees, I: Health and mental health status', *Archives of General Psychiatry* **36**, pp. 955–61.

Masuda, M., Lin, K. and Tazuma, L. (1980) 'Adaptational problems of Vietnamese refugees, II: Life changes and perceptions of life events' *Archives of General Psychiatry*, **37**, pp. 447–50.

McDermott, R. (1987) 'Achieving school failure: An anthropological approach to illiteracy and social stratification', in Spindler, G. (Ed.) *Education and Cultural Process: Anthropological approaches* (2nd Ed.). Prospects Heights, IL: Waveland Press, Inc., pp. 173–209.

McLaughlin, B. (1984) *Second-language Acquisition in Childhood: Preschool Children* (Volume I, 2nd Ed.), Hillsdale, NJ: Lawrence Erlbaum Associates.

Misaki, H.K. (1933) *Delinquency of Japanese in California*, Stanford University Series in Education-Psychology, Stanford, CA: Stanford University Press.

Miyamoto, S.F. (1939) *Social Solidarity Among the Japanese of Seattle*, Seattle, WA: University of Washington Press.

Mohatt, G. and Erickson, F. (1981) 'Cultural differences in teaching styles in an Odawa school: A sociolinguistic approach', in Trueba, H.T., Guthrie, G. and Au, K. (Eds) *Culture and the Bilingual Classroom: Studies in Classroom Ethnography*, Rowley, MA: Newbury House, pp. 105–119.

Moll, L. and Diaz, E. (1987) 'Change as the goal of educational research', *Anthropology and Education Quarterly*, **18**(4), pp. 300–11.

Monzon, R.I. (1984) 'The effects of the family environment on the academic performance of Filipino-American college students', Unpublished M.A. thesis. San Diego, CA: San Diego State University.

The New Encyclopaedia Britannica (1984) 'Hong Kong', **8**, Chicago, IL: Benton, pp. 1060–65.

The New Encyclopaedia Britannica (1984) 'Korea, History of', 'Korea, North'; 'Korea, South', **10**, Chicago, IL: Benton, pp. 507–34.

Ng, W.C. (1977) 'An evaluation of the labor market status of Chinese Americans', *Amerasia*, **4**(2), pp. 101–22.

Nidorf, J.F. (1985) 'Mental health and refugee youths: A model for diagnostic training', in Owan, T., *et al.* (Eds) *Southeast Asian Mental Health: Treatment, Prevention, Services, Training, and Research*, Washington, DC: US Department of Health and Human Services.

Ogbu, J. (1974) *The Next Generation: An Ethnography of Education in an Urban Neighborhood*, New York, NY: Academic Press.

Ogbu, J. (1978) *Minority Education and Caste: The American System in Cross-cultural Perspective*, New York, NY: Academic Press.

Ogbu, J. (1981) 'Origins of human competence: A cultural-ecological perspective', *Child Development*, **52**, pp. 413–29.

Ogbu, J. (1982) 'Cultural discontinuities and schooling', *Anthropology and Education Quarterly*, **13**(4), pp. 290–307.

Ogbu, J. (1983) 'Minority status and schooling in plural societies', *Comparative Education Review*, **27**(2), pp. 168–90.

Ogbu, J. (1987) 'Variability in minority responses to schooling: Nonimmigrants vs. immigrants', in Spindler, G. and Spindler, L. (Eds) *Interpretive Ethnography of Education: At Home and Abroad*, Hillsdale, NJ: Lawrence Erlbaum Associates, pp. 255–78.

Ogbu, J. (1989) 'The individual in collective adaptation: A framework for focusing on academic underperformance and dropping out among involuntary minorities', in WEIS, L., FARRAR, E. and PETRIE, H. (Eds) *Dropouts from School: Issues, Dilemmas, and Solutions*, Albany, NY: State University of New York Press, pp. 181–204.

OGBU, J. and MATUTE-BIANCHI, M.E. (1986) 'Understanding sociocultural factors: Knowledge, identity and school adjustment', in *Beyond Language: Social and Cultural Factors in Schooling Language Minority Students*. Sacramento, CA: Bilingual Education Office, California State Department of Education, pp. 73–142.

OLSEN, L. (1988) *Crossing the Schoolhouse Border*, (California Tomorrow Policy Research Report), San Francisco, CA: California Tomorrow.

OSBORNE-WILSON, C., SINATRA, R. and BARATTA, A.N. (1989) 'Helping Chinese students in the literacy transfer process', *Journal of Reading*, pp. 330–36.

OUK, M., HUFFMAN, F. and LEWIS, J. (1988) *Handbook for Teaching Khmer Students*, Folsom, CA: Folsom Cordova United School District and the Southeast Asian Community Resource Center.

PHILIPS, S. (1982) *The Invisible Culture: Communication in classroom and community on the Warm Springs Indian Reservation*, New York, NY: Longman Press.

REBECCA, S.M. (1981) 'A study of the relationship between the value orientations and academic achievement of Filipino-American students', Unpublished doctoral dissertation, University of San Francisco.

ROBSON, B. (1985) 'Hmong literacy, formal education, and their effects on performance in an ESL class', in DOWNING, BRUCE et al. (Eds) *Hmong in the West*, Minneapolis, MN: University of Minnesota Press.

RODRIGUEZ, R. (1982) *Hunger of Memory: The Education of Richard Rodriguez, An Autobiography*, Boston, MA: David R. Godine.

ROGOFF, B. (1990) *Apprenticeship in Thinking: Cognitive Development in Social Context*, New York, NY: Oxford University Press.

RUEDA, R. (1987) 'Social and communicative aspects of language proficiency in low-achieving language minority students', in TRUEBA, H. (Ed.) *Success or Failure: Linguistic Minority Children at Home and in School*, NY: Harper & Row, pp. 185–97.

RUHLEN, J. (1975) *A Guide to the Languages of the World*, Stanford, CA: Language Universals Project, Stanford University.

RUMBAUT, R.G. and WEEKS, J. (1986) 'Fertility and Adaptation: Indochinese refugees in the United States', *International Migration Review*, **20**(2), pp. 428–466.

RUMBAUT, R.G. (1985) 'Mental health and the refugee experience: A comparative study of Southeast Asian refugees', in OWAN, T.C. (Ed.) *Southeast Asian Mental Health: Treatment, Prevention, Services, Training, and Research*, Rockville, MD: National Institute of Health, pp. 433–86.

RUMBAUT, R.G. and IMA, K. (1988) *The Adaptation of Southwest Asian Refugee Youth: A Comparative Study*. Washington, DC: US Office of Refugee Resettlement.

SAN MIGUEL JR., G. (1987) '*Let all of them take heed': Mexican Americans and the Campaign for Educational Equality in Texas, 1910–1981*, Austin, TX: University of Texas Press.

SATO, C.J. (1982) 'Ethnic styles in classroom discourse', in HINES, M. and RUTHERFORD, W. (Eds) *On TESOL '81*, Washington, DC: TESOL Press, pp. 11–24.

SCHWARTZ, A.J. (1971) 'The culturally advantaged: A study of Japanese-American pupils', *Sociology and Social Reseach*, **55**(3), pp. 341–53.

SCRIBNER, S. and COLE, M. (1981) *The Psychology of Literacy*, Cambridge, MA: Harvard University Press.

SHU, R.L. (1985–1986) 'Kinship system and adaptation: Samoans of the United States' *Amerasia*, **12**(1), pp. 23–47.

SHULMAN, L. (1987a) 'Knowledge and teaching: Foundations of the new reform', *Harvard Educational Review*, **57**(1), pp. 1–24.

SHULMAN, L. (1987b) 'Sounding an alarm: A reply to Sockett', *Harvard Educational Review*, **57**(4), pp. 473–82.

SIEGEL, V. and HALOG, L. (1986) 'Assessment of limited English proficient children with special needs', in TSUCHIDA, N. (Ed.) *Issues in Asian and Pacific American Education*, Minneapolis, MN: Asian Pacific American Learning Resource Center, pp. 13–20.

SKUTNABB-KANGA, T. and TOUKOMAA, P. (1976) 'Teaching migrant children's mother tongue and learning the language of the host country in the context of the sociocultural situation of the migrant family', Helsinki, Finland: The Finnish National Commission for UNESCO.

SOCKETT, H. (1987) 'Has Shulman got the strategy right?' *Harvard Educational Review*, **57**(2), pp. 208–19.

SPINDLER, G. (Ed.) (1955a) *Anthropology and Education*, Stanford, CA: Stanford University Press.

SPINDLER, G. (1955b) 'Sociocultural and psychological processes in Menomini acculturation', **5**, *University of California Publications in Culture and Society*, Berkeley, CA: University of California Press.

SPINDLER, G. (1968) *Culture in Process: An Inductive Approach to Cultural Anthropology* (with BEALS, A. and SPINDLER, L., New York, NY: Holt, Rinehart and Winston, (revised 1973).

SPINDLER, G. (1977) 'Change and continuity in American core cultural values: An anthropological perspective' in DeRENZO, G.D. (Eds) *We the People: American character and social change* Westport, CT: Greenwood Press, pp. 20–40.

SPINDLER, G. (1982) *Doing the Ethnography of Schooling: Educational anthropology in action*, New York, NY: Holt, Rinehart & Winston.

SPINDLER, G. (1987a) 'Beth Ann — A case study of culturally defined adjustment and teacher perceptions', in SPINDLER, G. (Ed.) *Education and Cultural Process: Anthropological Approaches*, (2nd. Ed.) Prospect Heights, IL: Waveland Press, Inc., pp. 230–44.

SPINDLER, G. (1987b) 'The transmission of culture', in SPINDLER, G. (Ed.) *Education and Cultural Process: Anthropological Approaches, Second edition*, Prospect Heights, IL: Waveland Press, Inc., pp. 303–34.

SPINDLER, G. (1987c) 'Why have minority groups in North America been disadvantaged by their schools?', in SPINDLER, G. (Ed.) *Education and Cultural Process: Anthropological Approaches*, Second Edition, Prospect Heights, IL: Waveland Press, Inc., pp. 160–72.

SPINDLER, G. and SPINDLER, L. (1971) *Dreamers without Power: The Menomini Indians*, New York, NY: Holt, Rinehart and Winston, (republished by Waveland Press, 1984).

SPINDLER, G. and SPINDLER, L. (1982) 'Roger Harker and Schonhausen: From the familiar to the strange and back again', in SPINDLER, G. (Ed.) *Doing the Ethnography of Schooling*, New York, NY: Holt, Rinehart & Winston, pp. 20–47.

SPINDLER, G. and SPINDLER, L. (1983) 'Anthropologists' view of American culture', *Annual Review of Anthropology*, **12**, pp. 49–78.

SPINDLER, G. and SPINDLER, L. (Eds) (1987a) *The Interpretive Ethnography of Education: At Home and Abroad*, Hillsdale, NJ: Lawrence Erlbaum Associates.

SPINDLER, G. and SPINDLER, L. (1987b) 'Cultural dialogue and schooling in Schoenhausen and Roseville: A comparative analysis', *Anthropology and Education Quarterly*, **18**(1), pp. 3–16.

SPINDLER, G. and SPINDLER, L. (1987c) 'Teaching and learning how to do the ethnography of education', in SPINDLER, G. and SPINDLER, L. (Eds) *Interpretive*

Ethnography of Education at Home and Abroad, NJ: Lawrence Erlbaum Associates, Inc., pp. 17–33.

SPINDLER, G. and SPINDLER, L. (1987d) 'In prospect for a controlled cross-cultural comparison of schooling in Schoenhausen and Roseville', in *Education and Cultural Process: Anthropological Approaches*, Second Edition, Prospect Heights, IL: Waveland Press, Inc., pp. 389–400.

SPINDLER, G. and SPINDLER, L. (1987e) 'Transcultural sensitization', in *Education and Cultural Process: Anthropological Approaches*, Second Edition, Prospect Heights, IL: Waveland Press, Inc., pp. 467–80.

SPINDLER, G. and SPINDLER, L. (1989) 'Instrumental competence, self-efficacy, linguistic minorities, and cultural thereby: A preliminary attempt at integration', *Anthropology and Education Quarterly*, **10**(1), pp. 36–50.

SPINDLER, G. and SPINDLER, L. (1990) *The American Cultural Dialogue and its Transmission*, London, England: Falmer Press.

SPINDLER, G. and SPINDLER, L. (in press) 'Cultural process and ethnography: An anthropological perspective', in LeCOMPTE, M. and GOETZ, J. (Eds) *Handbook of Qualitative Research in Education*, New York, NY: Academic Press.

STEPHANY, G.V. (1984) 'The relationship between achievement in second language acquisition of southeast Asian students and influencing variables', Unpublished doctoral dissertation, Des Moines, IA: Drake University.

STRONG, E.K. (1934) *The Second-generation Japanese Problem*, Palo Alto, CA: Stanford University Press.

SUÁREZ-OROZCO, M.M. (1987) 'Towards a psychosocial understanding of Hispanic adaptation to American schooling', in TRUEBA, H. (Ed.) *Success or Failure: Linguistic Minority Children at Home and in School*, New York, NY: Harper & Row, pp. 156–68.

SUÁREZ-OROZCO, M.M. (1989) *Central American Refugees and US High Schools: A psychosocial study of motivation and achievement*, Stanford, CA: Stanford University Press.

SUÁREZ-OROZCO, M.M. (1990) 'Speaking of the unspeakable: Toward a psychosocial understanding of responses to terror', *Ethos*, **18**(3), pp. 353–83.

SUÁREZ-OROZCO, M.M. and SUÁREZ-OROZCO, C. (1991) 'The cultural psychology of Hispanic Immigrants: Implications for education research', paper presented at the Cultural Diversity Working Conference, Teacher Context Center, Stanford, CA: Stanford University October 4–6, 1991.

SUE, D.W. (1981) *Counseling the Culturally Different: Theory and practice.* New York, NY: John Wiley & Sons.

SUNG, B.L. (1987) *The Adjustment Experience of Chinese immigrant Children in New York City*, New York, NY: Center for Migration Studies.

TAKAKI, R. (1989) *Strangers from a Different Shore: A History of Asian Americans*, Boston, MA: Little, Brown & Co.

TAYLOR, O.L. (1986) *Treatment of Communicative Disorders in Culturally and Linguistically Diverse Populations*, San Diego, CA: College-Hill Press.

TE, H.D. (1987a) *Introduction to Vietnamese Culture*, San Diego, CA: San Diego State University, Multifunctional Resource Center.

TE, H.D. (1987b) 'Linguistic and cultural considerations in assessing Vietnamese LEP students', Presentation at the California Speech-Language-Hearing Association State Conference, April, 1987, San Diego, CA.

THARP, R. and GALLIMORE, R. (1989) *Rousing Minds to Life: Teaching, Learning and Schooling in Social Context*, New York, NY: Cambridge University Press.

TO, C. (1979) 'The educational and psychological adjustment problem of Asian immigrant youth and how bilingual-bicultural education help', paper presented at the National Association of Asian American and Pacific Education Conference, Los Angeles CA.

TRUEBA, H. (1983) 'Adjustment problems of Mexican American children: An anthropological study', *Learning Disabilities Quarterly*, **6**(4), pp. 8–15.

TRUEBA, H. (1987a) *Success or Failure?: Learning and the language minority student.* New York, NY: Newbury/Harper & Row.

TRUEBA, H. (1987b) 'Organizing classroom instruction in specific sociocultural contexts: Teaching Mexican youth to write in English', in GOLDMAN, S. and TRUEBA, H. (Eds) *Becoming Literate in English as a Second Language: Advances in Research and Theory*, Norwood, NJ: Ablex Corporation.

TRUEBA, H. (1988a) 'Peer socialization among minority students: A high school dropout prevention program', in TRUEBA, H. and DELGADO-GAITAN, C. (Eds) *School and Society: Learning Content Through Culture*, New York: Praeger Publishers, pp. 201–17.

TRUEBA, H. (1988b) 'Culturally-based Explanations of Minority Students' Academic Achievement', *Anthropology and Education Quarterly*, **19**(3), pp. 270–287.

TRUEBA, H. (1988c) 'English literacy acquisition: From cultural trauma to learning disabilities in minority students', *Linguistics and Education 1*, pp. 125–52.

TRUEBA, H. (1989) *Raising Silent Voices: Educating Linguistic Minorities for the 21st Century*, New York, NY: Harper & Row.

TRUEBA, H. (1990) 'The role of culture in literacy acquisition', *International Journal of Qualitative Studies in Education*, **3**(1), pp. 1–13.

TRUEBA, H. and DELGADO-GAITAN, G. (Eds) (1988) *School and Society: Learning Content Through Culture*, New York, NY: Praeger Publishers.

TRUEBA, H., JACOBS, L. and KIRTON, E. (1990) *Cultural Conflict and Adaptation: The Case of Hmong Children in American Society*, London, England: Falmer Press.

TRUEBA, H., SPINDLER, G. and SPINDLER, L. (Eds) (1989) *What Do Anthropologists have to Say about Dropouts?*, London, England: Falmer Press.

TSANG, S. (1983) *Mathematics Learning Styles of Chinese Immigrant Students*, Oakland, CA: ARC Associates.

TSANG, S. (1988) 'The mathematics achievement characteristics of Asian-American students', in COCKING, R.R. and MESTRE, J.P. (Eds) *Linguistic and Cultural Influences on Learning Mathematics*, Hillsdale, NJ: Lawrence Erlbaum Associates, pp. 123–36.

US BUREAU OF THE CENSUS (1981) *Census of Population: Asian and Pacific Island by State, 1980*, Supplementary Report PC80-S1-12, Washington, DC: US Government Printing Office.

US BUREAU OF THE CENSUS (1984) *1980 US Census*, Current Populations Report, Washington, DC: US Government Printing Office.

US BUREAU OF THE CENSUS (1990) *Census of Population: Asian and Pacific Islander by State, 1990*, Washington, DC: US Government Printing Office.

US DEPARTMENT OF COMMERCE (1987) 'The Hispanic Population in the United States: March 1986 and 1987' (Advance Report), Washington, DC: US Government Printing Office.

VAN DONGEN, R. and WESTBY, C. (1986) 'Building the narrative mode of thought through children's literature' *Topics in Language Disorders*, **7**(1), pp. 70–83.

VYGOTSKY, L.S. (1962) *Thought and Language.* Cambridge, MA: MIT Press.

VYGOTSKY, L.S. (1978) *Mind in Society: The development of higher psychological processes*, in COLE, M.V., JOHN-TEINER, V., SCRIBNER, S. and SOUBERMAN, E. (Eds) Cambridge, MA: Harvard University Press.

WAGGONER, D. (1988) 'Language minorities in the United States in the 1980s: The evidence from the 1980 Census', in MCKAY, S.L. and WONG, S.C. (Eds) *Language Diversity, Problem or Resource: A Social and Educational Perspective on Language Minorities in the United States*, New York, NY: Newbury House Publishers, (pp. 69–108).

References

WARREN, B., ROSEBERY, A.S. and CONANT, F.R. (1989) *Check Konnen: Learning Science by Doing Science in Language Minority Classrooms*, New York, NY: Bolt, Beranek & Newman.

WERTSCH, J. (1981) *The Concept of Activity in Soviet Psychology*, New York, NY: M. E. Sharpe, Inc.

WERTSCH, J. (1985) *Vygotsky and the Social Formation of the Mind*, Cambridge: Harvard University Press.

WONG, M.G. (1980) 'Model students? Teachers' perceptions and expectations of their Asian and white students', *Sociology of Education*, **53**, pp. 236–46.

WONG, S.C. (1987) 'The language learning situation of Asian immigrant students in the US: A socio- and psycholinguistic perspective. *Journal of the National Association for Bilingual Education*, **11**, pp. 203–34.

WONG, S.C. (1988) 'The language situation of Chinese Americans', in MCKAY, S. and WONG, S.C. (Eds) *Language Diversity: Problem or resource?* (pp. 193–228). Rowley, MA: Newbury House.

WONG, Y.M. (1983) *Dear Diane: Letters from our Daughters*, Oakland, CA: Asian Women United of California.

WONG-FILLMORE, L. (1985) 'Learning a second language: Chinese children in the American classroom', in ALATIS, J. and STACZEK, J. (Eds) *Perspectives on Bilingusalism and Bilingual Education*, Washington, DC: Georgetown University Press, pp. 436–452.

WONG-FILLMORE, L. (in press) 'Language and cultural issues in early education', in KAGAN, S.L. (Ed.) *The Care and Education of America's Young Children: Obstacles and Opportunities*, The 90th Yearbook of the National Society for the Study of Education.

WONG-FILLMORE, L. and BRITSCH, S. (1988) 'Early education for children from linguistic and cultural minority families', paper prepared for the Early Education Task Force of the National Association of State Boards of Education.

YEE, L.Y. and LA FORGE, R. (1974) 'Relationship between mental abilities, social class, and exposure to English in Chinese fourth graders', *Journal of Educational Psychology*, **66**(6), pp. 826–34.

YUAN TIEN, H. (1989) 'China: Population', in *The Encyclopedia Americana: International Edition*, **6**, Danbury, CT: Grolier Incorporated, pp. 501–3.

Index